THE FIVE NATIONS CHAMPIONSHIP 1947-1993

THE FIVE NATIONS CHAMPIONSHIP 1947-1993

JOHN GRIFFITHS

METHUEN

First published in Great Britain in 1994 by Methuen London,
an imprint of Reed Consumer Books Ltd, Michelin House,
81 Fulham Road, London SW3 6RB, and Auckland, Melbourne,
Singapore and Toronto.

A product of Forster Books.

Designed by Bob Bickerton.

A CIP catalogue record for this book is available from the British Library.

Typeset by GDC Ltd.

Printed by Mackays of Chatham PLC, Chatham, Kent

ISBN 0 413 359 611

CONTENTS

ACKNOWLEDGEMENTS

I have been fortunate to have received excellent guidance and support in producing this book. My thanks go first to the countless journalists past and present whose reports of matches have been essential background reading to the project. Although it is impossible to acknowledge all correspondents, I should particularly like to thank Vivian Jenkins, Stephen Jones, John Mason and David Hands for their accurate and lively reports in the *Sunday Times*, *Daily Telegraph* and *The Times*. And the various Playfair and Rothmans annuals have also been useful for checking facts and details of matches.

I am indebted to two friends, Tim Auty and John Jenkins, for unwavering help with archive material and players' statistics. Tim supplied numerous team groups from his impressive photograph collection and John laboured patiently to provide details of all players who have appeared in Five Nations matches since 1947, correcting several mistakes concerning dates of births published in previous works. I should also like to thank the Scottish and Irish Rugby Unions and Bill Treadwell, the secretary of the England Rugby Internationals Club, for their help in researching some birth dates, and Agence A.B.C., Allsport, Colorsport, The Dominion, Phillip Griffiths, Lafayette, Presse Sports, Sport and General, Western Mail and the Rugby Football Union for kindly allowing me to reproduce the great majority of the photographs in this book.

Finally, my grateful thanks go to Tony Pocock for commissioning this book and to Bob Bickerton for his original design. Chris and Jo Forster oversaw the technical operation with their customary mix of skill and patience. Moreover, without their good humour and forbearance the exercise would have collapsed months ago.

John Griffiths
October 1993

Bill Beaumont - the high flying captain of England.

PREFACE

The Five Nations championship, focal point of the northern hemisphere's rugby season, is under threat. The introduction of the Rugby World Cup, it has been argued, will demote the Five Nations to the status of a side-show. Moreover, the increasing emphasis placed on domestic league and cup programmes in Britain and Ireland is leading to such a congestion of fixtures that suggestions have recently been made to push the Five Nations tournament back to the end of the season.

Both arguments were rehearsed not so long ago with regard to the home nations international soccer tournament. That competition is now defunct; and there is a possibility that rugby's foremost international contest could go the same way. I sincerely hope that will not happen. The Five Nations championship began in 1910 and (except for interruptions caused by the two World Wars, the temporary exclusion of France in the 1930s, and for political reasons in 1972) has become the showpiece of the game in Europe, enjoying massive media interest and drawing countless numbers of people to Rugby Union football through excellent television coverage. Long may it continue.

This book is a celebration of Five Nations rugby since the Second World War - of milestones that mark the passing of the years, of special matches to remember, and of one hundred of the leading players who have taken part in Five Nations tournaments during this time. However, the players I have chosen to include are not necessarily the best performers of the past forty-six years. The criterion for inclusion is that the player must have made a significant contribution to an international side which has won a share of championship honours or carried off the title outright. The reader will search in vain for some of the greatest of the game's post-war exponents. Bleddyn Williams, prince of Welsh centres, for instance, was unable to participate fully in Wales's Grand Slams of 1950 and 1952; Jim Renwick of Scotland and David Duckham and John Pullin, two of England's stalwarts in the 1960s and 1970s, were regularly deprived of championship honours (apart from the quintuple tie of 1973), despite making wonderful contributions to British rugby as Lions. Similarly, Tom Kiernan of Ireland, Hughie McLeod, David Rollo and Arthur Smith of Scotland, and Guy Basquet of France were all outstanding performers who missed out on championship honours.

My favourite side of the era covered in this book would be the Wales XV of 1971 which won the Grand Slam. It was a team of all the talents - a superb pack serving a back division which exuded confidence and was blessed with extraordinary natural footballing skills. I make no apology for including six of that side in the player portraits' section. And what a fifteen a Five Nations selector could pick from those hundred players. I would back the following side to beat all comers :

JPR Williams; Gerald Davies, Philippe Sella, Mike Gibson, Serge Blanco; Barry John, Gareth Edwards; Ray McLoughlin, Peter Wheeler, Graham Price, Willie-John McBride, Delme Thomas, Jean-Pierre Rives, Mervyn Davies, John Jeffrey.

Gareth Edwards - probably the finest post-war scrum-half.

1947

Relying mainly on their pack, England resumed Five Nations rugby after the war by winning three matches to share the championship title with Wales. England had beaten Wales 9-6 at Cardiff with the help of 'Nim' Hall's second-half drop-goal, the last 4-pointer in a Five Nations match. It was at the end of that season that the drop-goal was reduced to 3 points.

When England beat Scotland at Twickenham Jack Heaton kicked four conversions, the record for an England player against Scotland.

In the same year Ireland beat England 22-0, a memorable victory which included five tries, still their highest return from a post-war Five Nations match against England. This extraordinary win, in which Ireland proved that they had the nucleus of a powerful pack supported by shrewd half-backs, was a portent of Irish triumphs to come.

Many of the players blooded in the 1945-46 series of 'Victory' internationals formed the backbone of France's Five Nations teams, the first to take part in the championship since 1931. (France had been suspended from the tournament because the Home Unions were dissatisfied with the control and conduct of the game in France.) France won their opening matches against Scotland and Ireland but lost 0-3 and 3-6 respectively to Wales and England.

1948

Ireland gained their first Triple Crown since 1899 and their only Grand Slam to date when they beat Wales 6-3 at Ravenhill, Belfast, in a match described on page 18.

Against England in Paris, a match which France won 15-0, Yves Bergougnan's drop-goal for France was the first 3-pointer to be registered in the Five Nations tournament. In the same year, France's defeat of Wales by 11-3 in Swansea marked France's first Five Nations win on Welsh soil.

1949

Playing percentage rugby, cutting errors to a minimum, Ireland took the Triple Crown and the Five Nations title for the second season running, beating Wales again, this time by 5-0 at Swansea, in a match described on page 19.

1950

A team which included six new caps, led by a makeshift captain, John Gwilliam, who stepped up to skipper the side when Rees Stephens and Bleddyn Williams withdrew from the team, beat England 11-5 - only the second win for Wales at Twickenham since 1910. Wales then went on to collect the Triple Crown for the first time for thirty-nine years in a match against Ireland described on page 20.

In the same year Ireland beat Scotland 21-0, their biggest winning points margin in their series of matches against Scotland in the Five Nations championship.

1951

After four seasons of disappointing results, Scotland pulled off the most unexpected win of the season, thrashing Wales (the Grand Slam holders) by 19 points. That famous victory at Murrayfield is described on page 21.

Ireland's golden era ended with their third championship title in four years but a 3-3 draw in Cardiff robbed them of the Triple Crown and Grand Slam.

France finished as runners-up for the first time. Defeat in Ireland by a single point was the only hitch in a season in which France, at their eleventh attempt since 1911, won at Twickenham for the first time (see page 21).

1952

'Nim' Hall's safety-first tactics behind an improving pack brought England their first away win in the championship since 1947.

In Wales, under John Gwilliam's strong leadership, Wales won the Grand Slam for the second time in three seasons. Their front five dominated the set scrummages, their jumpers had aerial control at the line-outs, and Cliff Morgan and Rex Willis shrewdly dictated the tactics from half-back.

When France beat Scotland 13-11 it was their first Five Nations victory at Murrayfield.

1953

For England, the promise of the previous season when they finished runners-up to Wales was converted into championship-winning form. An exciting new midfield triangle, comprising Jeff Butterfield, Martin Regan and Phil Davies, added an effective attacking dimension to complement England's well-established

Karl Mullen captained Ireland to their third post-war ti
JS McCarthy, JE Nelson, DJ O'Brien, GW Norton,
NJ Henderson, JH Smith, Sir W Tyrrell, KD Mullen,

pack. A draw in Dublin was the only blemish on England's copy-book.

In beating Scotland 26-8 at Twickenham, England scored no less than six tries, which remains a record for England-Scotland encounters, and 'Nim' Hall equalled Jack Heaton's record by kicking four conversions in the game.

In Dublin, Ireland beat Scotland 26-8, Ireland's highest score in matches against Scotland. Seamus Byrne scored a hat-trick of tries and Robin Gregg converted four tries to equal Irish records for the series set between the wars.

1954

Although England won the Triple Crown comfortably enough, their forward looked jaded in Paris at the end of the season. Defeat by France left England sharing the championship title with Wales and France.

France were at the top of the table for the first time and only a 13-19 defeat by Wales in Cardiff blighted their hopes of winning the Grand Slam.

In Ireland and Wales, 1954 saw the last Five Nations matches to be staged respectively at Ravenhill, Belfast and St Helen's, Swansea.

land v England 1951. Standing: RR Chambers, Kibbin, WHJ Millar, Mr T Jones (referee). Seated: Kay, T Clifford, CS Griffin. Front: JW Kyle, JA O'Meara.

1955

A long, grim sequence of seventeen defeats for Scotland - fifteen in the Five Nations championship - ended with a morale-boosting 14-8 win against Wales in a match in which Arthur Smith marked his international debut with a brilliant try. Scotland were deprived of the Triple Crown at Twickenham, losing narrowly by 6-9 to England.

Wales, for the second year running, stopped France's bid for the Grand Slam. Jean Prat, the French captain whose expertise and strong personality were significant factors in the rise of French rugby, retired from international matches after leading his side to another shared championship with Wales.

In his last international season, Prat set an Anglo-French record, becoming the only forward to date to have dropped two goals in a Five Nations match between England and France.

1956

Wales won the title outright though a surprise defeat in Dublin against Ireland deprived Cliff Morgan's team of the Triple Crown.

1957

A young England side, rallying round their captain and driving force, Eric Evans, carried off the Grand Slam, England's first such success for twenty-nine years. That great match is described on page 22.

1958

At the age of thirty-seven Eric Evans hung up his boots for England but not before leading another unbeaten England side, with an outstanding pack, to win the Five Nations title.

France beat Wales in Cardiff for the first time and Michel Vannier became the first Frenchman to drop two goals in a match against Wales.

1959

France won the championship title outright for the first time. Their success, under Lucien Mias's shrewd captaincy, was the culmination of an impressive unbeaten run of ten Tests dating back to March 1958. Their defeat of Wales, by 11-3, at Stade Colombes in April, is one of France's post-war matches to remember (see page 22).

In Paris, against Scotland, a year after Michel Vannier's achievement against Wales, Pierre Lacaze became the first Frenchman to drop two goals in a match against Scotland.

1960

A new-look side, with seven new caps, remained unchanged throughout the season - a first for any country in the Five Nations championship - and enabled England to win the Triple Crown. A draw in Paris left them sharing the honours with France.

The England v Wales match at Twickenham (see page 23) provided a wonderful shot in the arm for rugby football. It was Richard Sharp's debut match and from the start he played with a gusto rarely seen in an England fly-half.

France enjoyed a golden period between 1960 and 1962, losing only once in the Five Nations tournament. The arrival of an exceptional fly-half, Pierre Albaladejo, put the vintage label on the exciting 'champagne rugby' played by France. A draw with England, with whom they shared the championship title, deprived France of the Grand Slam in 1960 but they were outright champions in 1961 (despite drawing with England at Twickenham), and retained the title in 1962 though beaten 0-3 by Wales in Cardiff.

In Paris, Pierre Albaladejo became the first player to drop three goals in a Five Nations match when France beat Ireland 23-6.

1961

England, Scotland and Wales, following the lead given by France and Ireland, conformed to the now universal system of numbering players: 15 for the full-back; 14-11 for the threequarters; 10-9 for the half-backs; and 8-1 for the forwards from back row to front row. The International Board followed the Five Nations notation in 1966-67.

1962

This was Scotland's best season in the championship since 1938. A success rate of two wins and a draw included Scotland's first victory at Cardiff for thirty-five years.

In Paris, when France beat England 13-0, Michel Crauste scored a hat-trick of tries, a record for a forward in a Five Nations match.

The Ireland v Wales match had to be postponed from the spring to November because of an outbreak of smallpox in South Wales. When the match eventually was played, ending in a 3-3 draw, it was the last Five Nations match between Ireland and Wales to finish devoid of tries.

In Paris, when France beat Ireland 11-0, Claude Lacaze became the first full-back to score a try in the Five Nations tournament.

1963

In Dublin, the Ireland v England encounter saw the last scoreless draw to date in the Five Nations championship.

In Dublin also, Christian Darrouy set a French record for Five Nations matches against Ireland when he ran in a hat-trick of tries.

 Barry John, with Gerald Davies at his shoulder, breaks through the Irish defence to set up a try for Wales again

Fielding an inexperienced team, England became champions after winning at Cardiff for what was destined to be the last time for twenty-eight years.

1964

Scotland finished top of the Five Nations table, bracketed with Wales. It was a memorable win against England, described on page 23 - the first Calcutta Cup victory for Scotland since 1950 which gave Brian Neill's team a share of the championship.

The year marked Wales's first unbeaten season for a dozen years. They were led to the top of the table (sharing honours with Scotland) by Clive Rowlands, a wily tactician. Draws are rare in Five Nations matches but Wales managed two during the season - against England and France.

At Twickenham, Ireland beat England 18-5, Tom Kiernan converting three tries - a record for an Irish player in a Five Nations match against England.

1965

New laws designed to make the game more open and attractive enabled a Wales back division, spearheaded by David Watkins, to display its attacking talents. Clive Rowlands's team brought Triple Crown honours to Wales for the first time since 1952 after beating Ireland 14-8 at Cardiff Arms Park (see page 24).

At Murrayfield, when Wales beat Scotland 14-12, Brian Simmers became the first Scot to drop two goals in a match against Wales.

land in Cardiff in 1969.

1966

Although deprived of the Triple Crown by a spirited Irish team in Dublin, Wales retained the championship title, thanks to a thrilling match-winning try by Stuart Watkins against France.

1967

This was the year in which Keith Jarrett, the teenage Newport full-back, first blazed across the Five Nations sky. Against England, in a match which Wales won 34-21, Jarrett set two individual Welsh records for Wales-England matches: 19 points and five conversions. Wales registered their highest score in the series and the match also recorded the highest aggregate number of points in the series.

In Paris, where Guy Camberabero equalled the French record for most drop-goals against Wales, scoring two, he also created another unusual record, scoring with four different actions: try, conversions, penalty and drop-kick.

1968

After losing to France, the eventual champions, in 1968, Ireland enjoyed a record unbeaten run, stretching into 1969, which included victories against Australia, France (in 1969) and all the other Home Unions. However, the championship prize eluded them in 1969 in a rough match against Wales at Cardiff, leaving Ireland runners-up to Wales.

Four hard-earned wins gave France the Grand Slam for the first time. However, French critics lamented their country's reliance on ten-man rugby, longing instead for a return to the total rugby which had thrilled crowds all over the world in the early 1960s. Nonetheless, there were huge celebrations in Cardiff when France completed *le Grand Chelem,* a match described on page 24.

1969

Clive Rowlands, now installed as Wales's coach, arranged frequent meetings for the team and its reserves during the season. This first-ever 'squad system' paid dividends immediately: Wales won the championship title outright as well as the Triple Crown. And their new full-back, J.P.R. Williams, imaginatively exploited the new law which restricted direct kicking to touch.

In the match between Wales and England at Cardiff, won by Wales 30-9, Maurice Richards equalled the record for Wales v England Five Nations encounters for most tries in a match, scoring four for Wales.

1970

The championship was shared between Wales and Christian Carrère's France.

Bob Hiller became the only Englishman to date to drop two goals in a match against Ireland.

In the Ireland v Scotland game in Dublin and between France and Ireland in Paris, no penalty-goals were scored, the last occasion on which this has happened in those two series of matches.

1971

Probably the best Wales team of modern times set off in search of the Grand Slam, beating England 22-6 at the Arms Park, a match described on page 25. John Dawes of London Welsh proved to be the most effective national captain since John Gwilliam.

When Wales beat England at Cardiff, Barry John equalled the record for most drop-goals in a Five Nations match between England and Wales by kicking two.

1972

This was the most frustrating season in Irish rugby history. A side captained by Tom Kiernan beat France and England away in consecutive matches but Ireland's political problems forced both the Scottish and Welsh Unions to cancel visits to Dublin, leaving the Five Nations tournament uncompleted.

In Paris, France beat England by 37-12. It was France's highest score and biggest winning points margin in Anglo-French encounters in the Five Nations. Pierre Villepreux created a record for a match in the series, kicking five conversions in what proved to be the last Five Nations game to be staged at Stade Colombes.

In Cardiff, another big score was registered when Wales beat Scotland by 35-12, Wales's highest score and biggest points winning margin of the series. Barry John set a series record, scoring 15 points, and equalling the record for most conversions by a Welshman against Scotland, kicking three.

When Colin Telfer scored the first try in Scotland's match against France, which Scotland won by 20-9, it was the first 4-pointer to be registered in a Five Nations match.

The year also marked Ireland's last victory against France in Paris.

1973

Andy Irvine and Ian McGeechan, both in their first seasons in the Five Nations tournament, helped Scotland (under the thoughtful leadership of Ian McLauchlan) to claim their share of the championship's unique quintuplet tie.

When Scotland beat Ireland by 19-14 at Murrayfield, Dougie Morgan dropped two goals to equal the Scottish record for a match against Ireland.

Scotland's match against France in Paris was the first Five Nations game to be staged at the redeveloped Parc des Princes ground.

1974

Ireland became popular outright champions in their hundredth year of international rugby and for the first time since 1951. This was the inaugural season of the now familiar rotation of 'double-headers' and Ireland, who were the first nation to finish their four fixtures, had to wait two weeks for both France and Wales to lose in their final round of matches before they could celebrate their title. The critical match in their bid for the championship was their victory over England by 26-21 at Twickenham in mid-February (see page 26).

In that match at Twickenham, Ireland registered their highest score of the series of Five Nations matches against England. Again, in that same match, England's Alan Old set an individual record for the series, landing five penalties.

1975

John Dawes succeeded Clive Rowlands as the coach of a Wales side which introduced six new caps. This new-look XV stamped its authority immediately, winning convincingly in Paris and going on to achieve the championship title outright.

In fact, their victory against France proved to be their last win to date in Paris.

1976

It was in 1976 and in the following three years that Wales enjoyed their greatest glory. Four consecutive Triple Crown seasons were theirs, a unique achievement in the history of the competition among the Home Unions. There were Grand Slams in 1976 and 1978, and the decade of the dragon ended with a rousing win against England in 1979 (see page 26) when Wales became outright winners of the championship for the last time to date.

In Dublin, in the same year, Andy Irvine created a record for a Scotsman against Ireland, kicking four penalty-goals in the last match between the sides in which no try was scored.

Also in Dublin, the year marked the highest score by Wales against Ireland, in a match which Wales won by 34-9 and Phil Bennett created an individual record for most points in a match in this series, scoring 19.

1977

France achieved a second Grand Slam, and the key to the prize was the France v Wales match in Paris. Ably led by Jacques Fouroux, the scrum-half, France dominated the game and their loose forwards bottled up the threat posed by the dangerous Wales backs.

In Paris also, France achieved their biggest winning points margin against Scotland when they won by 23-3.

England achieved their biggest winning points margin of the series when they beat Scotland by 26-6 at Twickenham.

In the Wales v Ireland match at Cardiff, Geoff Wheel (Wales) and Willie Duggan (Ireland) were the first players to be

Scotland v England 1980. Bill Beaumont is borne from the field after leading England to their first Grand Slam for twenty-three years.

sent off in a Five Nations match when they took their marching orders from Norman Sanson of Scotland for punching.

1978

In Paris, Alan Old dropped two goals for England against France, an England record for a match between the two countries.

When France beat Scotland by 19-16, they recorded their last win against Scotland at Murrayfield.

Steve Fenwick, playing for Wales against Ireland, became the first player to kick four penalty-goals in matches between Wales and Ireland.

1979

During the Wales v Ireland encounter in Cardiff, when Wales won by 24-21, Steve Fenwick repeated his 1978 performance and Tony Ward of Ireland equalled the Irish record for most points in a match against Wales, scoring 13.

1980

Bill Beaumont led England into the light at the end of a long, dark tunnel. Seventeen years of failure and disappointment for England ended when a popular team captained by a popular hero overcame the challenge of a mighty Wales side before proceeding to win the Grand Slam at Murrayfield (see page 27).

There was praise, too, that season for the perceptive coaching of England's Mike Davis while Tony Neary's distinguished service ended on a high note. Neary, a faithful and forceful flanker, whose career had spanned the decade of England's Five Nations disasters, retired as his country's leading cap-winner.

At Twickenham, Paul Ringer of Wales became the only player to date to be sent off in England v Wales matches.

Against France, in Paris, in a match won by England by 17-13, John Horton equalled Alan Old's record, dropping two goals in the match.

In the Ireland v Wales match, won 21-7 by Ireland in Dublin, Ollie Campbell became the only Irish player to date to convert three tries in a match against Wales.

1981

With powerful scrummagers and imaginative backs, France won the Grand Slam under Jean-Pierre Rives, a captain who championed open, running rugby. The crucial match was at Twickenham in March. If France beat England, they would achieve a third post-war Grand Slam. If England won, they would share the championship with France. The match is described on page 28.

When Scotland beat Wales 15-6 at Murrayfield, Scotland's winning total included a penalty try, the first ever awarded in a Five Nations match. David Burnett of Ireland gave the try when Andy Irvine was impeded by Gareth Davies.

1982

Ireland won the Triple Crown for the fifth time, the key match of their successful season being their defeat of England at Twickenham by a single point, a match described on page 28.

In Paris, Dusty Hare kicked five penalty-goals, the record for an England player against France. England won the match by 27-15.

In Dublin, when Ireland beat Scotland by 21-12, Ollie Campbell of Ireland set two individual records for a match in the series: 21 points which included no less than six penalty-goals.

The year also marked Scotland's first post-war win in Cardiff. Andy Irvine converted four of Scotland's tries, equalling the Scottish record for the series.

In the same year, when Wales beat France 22-12 in Cardiff, Gwyn Evans created a series record, kicking six penalty-goals in a match destined to be Wales's last win against France.

1983

Dusty Hare and Ollie Campbell equalled the Ireland v England series record, each kicking five penalties. Campbell established an Irish record by scoring a total of 21 points in the match.

Bryan Gossman became the first Scot to drop two goals in a match against France. France won the game by 19-15.

The year also marked the last Welsh home win against Ireland; and also the last Irish win against France.

1984

When Scotland beat France by 21-12 at Murrayfield, a match described on page 29, they completed their first Grand Slam since 1925 and in doing so brought the Triple Crown north for the first time for forty-six years.

In the same year, when Wales beat England 24-15, Malcolm Dacey became the only player in the series to drop two goals in a match at Twickenham.

When Scotland beat Ireland 32-9 in Dublin, they achieved their biggest winning points margin for Scotland v Ireland matches.

During the France v Ireland game in Paris (won by France 25-12) Jean-Pierre Garuet became the first Frenchman to be sent off in a Five Nations match, receiving his marching orders from Clive Norling of Wales.

In Cardiff, when France beat Wales 21-16, Jean-Patrick Lescarboura collected two French records for the series: four penalties and a total of 17 points.

1985

Coach Mick Doyle resuscitated Ireland, who had been whitewashed in the 1984 championship. Ireland ended the season as champions and Triple Crown winners, only a draw with France blocking their bid for the Grand Slam. Since then they have enjoyed no similar success.

At Twickenham, during England's 9-9 draw with France, Jean-Patrick Lescarboura dropped three goals in the match to equal the record for a Five Nations international.

At Murrayfield, when Scotland were on the losing side to Wales, John Rutherford equalled the record for the most drop-goals by a Scotsman in a match against Wales, kicking two.

At Cardiff, Michael Kiernan equalled the Irish record for most points in a match against Wales - 13 - and Ireland won the game by 21-9.

In Dublin, Michael Kiernan was again on target, this time during Ireland's 15-15 draw with France, kicking five penalty-goals, the record for an Irish player against France.

1986

Six new caps, including the Hastings brothers, Finlay Calder and David Sole, presented the new Scotland coach, Derrick Grant, with a share, with France, of the Five Nations championship.

At Murrayfield, when Scotland beat France 18-17, Gavin Hastings, on his international debut, set the record for the most points by a Scot in a match against France, scoring 18 including six penalty-goals, in itself an additional record.

When Scotland overwhelmed England at Murrayfield by 33-6, they achieved their highest score and their biggest winning points margin. Gavin Hastings set a record for the series, collecting 21 points with five penalties.

When England defeated Wales 21-18 at Twickenham, Rob Andrew created a record for a player in the series, scoring 21 points.

In Paris, Guy Laporte set two scoring records for a French player against England - 17 points and three penalty-goals - as France beat England by 29-10.

When Wales beat Scotland by 22-15 at Cardiff Paul Thorburn equalled the record for most points by a player in the series, scoring 15 points from five penalties. One of his successful place kicks was from inside his own half.

1987

An outstanding pack with an athletic back-row initiating countless ploys was the cornerstone of France's fourth and most recent Grand Slam.

At Twickenham, Marcus Rose established the record for most points by an England player against Scotland, scoring 17 points. England won the match by 21-12.

At Cardiff, Mark Wyatt set a record for a Welsh player in Wales v England matches, scoring five penalty-goals. Wales won the match by 19-12.

At Murrayfield, John Rutherford equalled Dougie Morgan's record for most drop-goals in a match, kicking two. Scotland beat Ireland in the match by 16-12.

When France beat Scotland by 28-22 in Paris, they achieved their highest score of the series. It included three tries by Eric Bonneval - also a record for a French player against Scotland. And a third record was established by Philippe Bérot, whose 13 points were the most scored by a French player in a match against Scotland.

1988

Wales won the Triple Crown, their only success of the decade. A narrow defeat by France in Cardiff robbed them of the Grand Slam and forced them to share the championship with France.

England's victory over Ireland by 35-3 was their biggest winning points margin in the series. There were three tries by Chris Oti for England - the only post-war hat-trick of tries by a player in the series.

In Cardiff, Jonathan Davies equalled the Welsh record for most drop-goals by a player in a match against Scotland, kicking two. Wales won the match by 25-20.

1989

Despite being beaten by England at Twickenham, France emerged as champions. This was their last Five Nations success during Jacques Fouroux's long term as national coach. Often criticised for his forward-orientated methods, the record Fouroux achieved in charge of France's team between 1981-90 speaks for itself. Of the forty Five Nations teams he prepared during that time, no less than twenty-eight won their matches and two matches were drawn.

At Murrayfield, when Scotland beat Ireland 37-21, the sides achieved a new record aggregate score for a match in the series

Pierre Berbizier sets up an attack against Wales in Paris in 1989. France enjoyed an emphatic win by 31-12.

and Scotland reached their highest total against Ireland. Peter Dods set a new Scottish record: 17 points and a record four conversions in the match.

In Dublin, Michael Kiernan scored 17 points including five penalties to set a record for an Irish player in matches against France.

In Paris, Jean-Baptiste Lafond created a French record for the series, converting three tries in the match against Wales, won by France 31-12.

1990

Scotland fielded what was arguably their best post-war side, coached by Ian McGeechan. They won the Grand Slam with an unforgettable performance against an hitherto unbeaten and much vaunted England side, in a match described on page 29.

When England beat Wales 34-6 at Twickenham they recorded their highest score and biggest winning points margin in Five Nations matches against Wales.

At Murrayfield, Alain Carminati of France became the only player to date to be sent off in a Scotland v France Five Nations match.

In Paris, when France beat Ireland 31-12, Didier Camberabero became the only Frenchman to date to land five penalty-goals in a match against Ireland.

In Cardiff, the Wales lock, Kevin Moseley, became the first player to be sent off in a match between the two sides. In the same game (won 29-19 by France), Didier Camberabero with three conversions equalled the record for most conversions by a French player against Wales.

1991

One of England's best all-round sides of the century realised its full potential under the shrewd coaching of Roger Uttley and the wise management of Geoff Cooke. They regained the Grand Slam in arguably England's most memorable match of the century, the decider with France at Twickenham (see page 30).

Against Scotland, at Twickenham, Simon Hodgkinson equalled England's record for most points by a player against Scotland. In kicking 17 points, he also became the first England player to land five penalties in a Calcutta Cup match.

Simon Hodgkinson was also on target against Wales in Cardiff, setting an individual record for a Five Nations match, when he kicked seven penalty-goals. He also equalled the series record for most points in a match by a player, scoring 21.

Craig Chalmers, for Scotland against Wales at Murrayfield, became the first player in the series to score with every action: try, conversion, penalty-goal and drop-goal.

In Paris against Scotland, Didier Camberabero equalled the series record, dropping two goals in the match.

Also in Paris, against Wales, France marked up their highest score and biggest winning points margin of the series, 36-3. Their total included six tries - a record for France against Wales.

In Cardiff, when Wales drew 21-21 with Ireland, the match marked the highest ever aggregate score draw in the Five Nations championship.

1992

With standards of play falling in the other nations, Will Carling's England team broke numerous scoring records as they romped to a second Grand Slam. The team collected an unprecedented 118 points in the championship while Jonathan Webb, set an individual Five Nations record, scoring 67 points in England's four matches.

When England beat Ireland by 38-9 at Twickenham they registered their highest score in England v Ireland matches. Jonathan Webb, with 22 points, set the record for most points by a player in a match in the series.

In Paris, when France beat Ireland 44-12, they registered their highest score in a Five Nations match and their biggest winning points margin against Ireland. Sebastien Viars created a new Five Nations record, scoring 24 points. His five conversions also set a record for a French kicker in matches against Ireland.

Again in Paris, for the first time in a Five Nations match, two players from the same team were sent off when Mr Hilditch of Ireland gave marching orders to Gregoire Lascubé and Vincent Moscato when France were overwhelmed by 13-31 by England.

1993

France opened the Five Nations season with their fifth successive

Relief after a famous win. Scottish players savour t
Gary Armstrong. Tony Stanger, the try-scorer, is at

championship loss against England. However, England's subsequent decline opened the way for a settled French team to become outright champions for the tenth time.

When England beat Scotland 26-12 at Twickenham, Rory and Tony Underwood became the first pair of brothers to score tries for England in the same Calcutta Cup match.

In Dublin, Eric Elwood became the first Irishman to drop two goals in a match against England.

Derek Stark's first-half try against Ireland at Murrayfield was the first 5-pointer scored in a Five Nations match.

And in Cardiff, Ieuan Evans's winning try against England marked the first Five Nations match in which the 5-point try affected the outcome of a game.

Also at Murrayfield, against Wales, Gavin Hastings set Scottish records for the series, scoring 15 points from five penalty-goals.

nd Slam win against England. Left to right: Ian McGeechan, John Jeffrey, Craig Chalmers, Iwan Tukalo and t.

Ireland v Wales Ravenhill : 13 March 1948

IRELAND 6 WALES 3

There were 32, 000 spectators crammed like sardines into the Ravenhill ground in Belfast to witness a match billed as the biggest Irish sporting event of the century. The Irish rugby authorities could have sold sufficient tickets to fill the ground three times over for a match which promised to reward Ireland with their first Grand Slam. Those who endured the tension of probably the most exciting eighty minutes of rugby ever played on Irish soil, went away rejoicing at their team's narrow victory by two tries to one.

In an even first half, it was the tactical insight of Jack Kyle and the efficient play of their forwards which combined to give Ireland the lead after twenty minutes. Chris Daly wrenched the ball from a maul, fed Ernie Strathdee, and a transfer to Kyle sent the fly-half scampering away to his left. A perfectly weighted cut-out pass floated across the paths of his centres towards the ample frame of the left-wing, Barney Mullan, who bulldozed his way through Ken Jones's tackle for a try.

Wales equalised before half-time. Les Williams burst along the left wing but the ball was bundled into touch near the Irish goal-line. From the line-out, Bleddyn Williams made a dazzling side-step and weaved a path through would-be tacklers for a try.

Karl Mullen's side established a stranglehold on the game early in the second half which they never relaxed. Determined tackling and shrewd kicking were the orders of the day, strictly adhered to by the Irish team. As a result, Wales were confined to their own 25-yard line for most of the half. The winning score came ten minutes after the interval. Kyle regularly caused consternation in the Welsh defences and Frank Trott, the Wales full-back, had any number of problems as he defended against an Irish back-row which constantly harried him by following up kicks.

It was a fumble by Trott, in fact, which led directly to Ireland's crucial score. The Welshman failed to deal with a kick ahead, Des O'Brien hacked the ball over the Welsh line and Daly dived on it before it rolled over the dead-ball line.

The crowd went berserk with joy and Daly is said to have remarked to a colleague, 'If there's no more scoring, I'll be canonized.' A half-hour of nail-biting for the Irish followed, though, in reality, they had little to fear in the closing stages. Indeed, the wonder of it all was that their dominant forwards failed to force another Irish score.

Nonetheless, it was a tremendous relief for the Irish supporters when the end came. Thousands of Irishmen streamed on to the pitch to mob their heroes. Daly wasn't exactly canonized that afternoon, but his shirt was torn to shreds by enthusiastic trophy-hunters keen to steal a memento of an historic Irish rugby occasion.

Ireland: J A D Higgins; B O'Hanlon, W D McKee, P J Reid, B J Mullan; J W Kyle, E Strathdee; A A McConnell, K D Mullen (captain), J C Daly, C P Callan, J E Nelson, J W McKay, D J O'Brien, J S McCarthy.
Scorers: tries - Mullan, Daly.

Wales: R F Trott; K J Jones, W B Cleaver, B L Williams, W L T Williams; G Davies, H Tanner (captain);
C Davies, D M James, E P Davies, J R G Stephens, J A Gwilliam, O Williams, L Manfield, G W Evans.
Scorer: try - B L Williams.

Referee: Mr M A Allan (Scotland)

The 1948 Ireland team.

Wales v Ireland St Helen's, Swansea : 12 March 1949

WALES 0 IRELAND 5

In anticipation of playing what had become known as 'Triple Crown' rugby, the principal characteristic of which was concentration on effective scrummaging, Wales brought in Billy Cleaver, a reliable kicker at fly-half, who was well able to nurse his forwards.

Although the Welsh forwards were often prominent in the loose in the first-half, it was noticeable that the possession given to Haydn Tanner and the Welsh backs was of poor quality. The spoiling tactics of the Irish back-row were ruthlessly efficient and the only glimmer of a scoring chance for Wales - a typically forceful burst by Jack Matthews just before half-time - was snuffed out by careful Irish covering.

Ireland clinched the match, and with it the Triple Crown, when Jack Kyle slipped away on the narrow side of a scrum in the second half. He drew the defence before sending a high cross-kick to the Welsh goal. His kick was inch perfect and Jim McCarthy jumped above a couple of bewildered Welsh defenders, gathered the ball and landed for the decisive try. George Norton converted.

At the close of the match McCarthy was hoisted shoulder high and chaired from the field at Swansea while souvenir hunters tore the jersey from his back.

Forward superiority had, once again, been Ireland's passport to success. Karl Mullen's hooking was infallible and gave Kyle, the most complete footballer of the day, the means to spin an intricate tactical web which opponents could not destroy. Whereas Ireland's triumph was essentially the result of good team work, it was entirely fitting that Kyle's genius should pave the way for the solitary try of the match.

Scotland's failure to defeat England at Twickenham one week later entitled Ireland to carry off the Five Nations championship outright for the second successive year.

Wales: R F Trott; K J Jones, J Matthews, B L Williams, T Cook; W B Cleaver, H Tanner (captain); E Coleman, W H Travers, D C J Jones, J A Gwilliam, A Meredith, W R Cale, J R G Stephens, G Evans.

Ireland: G W Norton; M F Lane, W D McKee, N J Henderson, B O'Hanlon; J W Kyle, E Strathdee; L Griffin, K D Mullen (captain), T Clifford, J E Nelson, R D Agar, J S McCarthy, D J O'Brien, J W McKay.
Scorers: try - McCarthy; conversion - Norton

Referee: Mr T N Pearce (England)

The Ireland XV who retained the Triple Crown and championship title in 1949. Standing: WD McKee, MF Lane, B O'Hanlon, JW McKay, CP Callan, TJ Gavin. Seated: GW Norton, JE Nelson, DJ O'Brien, KD Mullen, A McConnell, T Clifford, JS McCarthy. Front: E Strathdee, JW Kyle.

Ireland v Wales Ravenhill : 11 March 1950

IRELAND 3 WALES 6

Wales's stiffest challenge of the season came in the final leg of their Triple Crown trail, against Ireland, the reigning champions, in Belfast. Wales had relied on the powerful scrummaging and line-out dominance of a talented octet of forwards in their earlier wins of the season, against England and Scotland. They now met an Irish pack with similar virtues to their own, and in an absorbing power struggle between the forwards, it soon became obvious that the winning team would be the one which made fewer mistakes.

The game was essentially a gruelling battle between the forwards, with little open play. In the first half, Lewis Jones went close to scoring with two huge penalty-kicks at goal and, to the amazement of the substantial Welsh contingent in the packed ground, their lock Don Hayward tried to drop a goal. Few tight forwards have ever dropped a goal in a club match, let alone attempted one in an international.

The scoring opened seven minutes after half-time. The Welsh back row, putting pressure on the Irish halves, induced an error upon which Jack Matthews capitalised. He ran diagonally, committed the Irish left-wing to the tackle and, with a perfectly timed pass, sent Ken Jones on a twenty-yard race for the corner.

Minutes later Ireland were level. A mistake by a Welsh forward at a maul presented George Norton with a penalty, and the Irishman, backed by the breeze, kicked the goal. Both packs went hammer and tongs at each other as the minutes passed in the second half and it looked as if the battle for supremacy would end in stalemate.

Then, three minutes from time, the Welsh back row caught Jack Kyle in possession after a scrum. Ray Cale and Billy Cleaver worked the ball loose, Matthews gathered it and fed Lewis Jones, who transferred it to Malcolm Thomas on the left wing. Thomas had little space in which to operate but somehow managed to squeeze himself over in the corner despite the attentions of a horde of corner-flagging Irish forwards. In the mayhem the corner-flag was knocked over, but after discussion with the Irish touch judge, the referee awarded Wales the try which sealed their first Triple Crown triumph since 1911.

Ireland: G W Norton; M F Lane, R J H Uprichard, G C Phipps, L Crowe; J W Kyle, R Carroll; T Clifford, K D Mullen (captain), D R McKibbin, J E Nelson, R D Agar, J S McCarthy, D J O'Brien, J W McKay.
Scorer: penalty - Norton.

Wales: G Williams; K J Jones, B L Jones, J Matthews, M C Thomas; W B Cleaver, W R Willis; J D Robins, D M Davies, C Davies, D J Hayward, E R John, W R Cale, J A Gwilliam (captain), R T Evans.
Scorers: tries - K J Jones, Thomas.

Referee: Mr R A Beattie (Scotland)

The first Wales Triple Crown side for thirty-nine years: Wales v Scotland 1950. Standing: WR Willis, JD Robins, DJ Hayward, ER John, RT Evans, MC Thomas, MJ Dowling (referee). Seated: WR Cale, DM Davies, C Davies, JA Gwilliam, J Matthews, KJ Jones, WB Cleaver. Front: WC Major, BL Jones.

Scotland v Wales Murrayfield : 3 February 1951

SCOTLAND 19 WALES 0

Scotland won a rare but famous victory which will be discussed for as long as men gather to talk about the Five Nations championship. Wales, the reigning champions, began at tremendous speed in front of 80,000 spectators, tearing into the Scots and forcing them to defend with courage. Twelve of the Welshmen had toured Australasia with the Lions seven months earlier, but Scotland showed that they were no great respecters of reputations and safely survived the initial assault by the visitors.

The Scottish back-row effectively disrupted the Welsh halves, and Glyn Davies, the fly-half, was harassed out of the game. (Towards the end of the match John Gwilliam, the Welsh captain, in desperation rearranged his midfield and switched Lewis Jones to fly-half.) As the game progressed, Scotland gained the upper hand at forward and it hardly surprised the experts when the Scots went into the second half sitting on a slender lead, Ian Thomson having landed 3 penalty points.

The third quarter of the match was uneventful until Peter Kininmonth, the Scottish captain, inspired his side with an unexpected score. Gerwyn Williams, the Welsh full-back, missed touch with a kick from inside his own 25. Kininmonth caught the ball, lined the goal up in his sights and sent a lovely drop-kick straight between the posts.

Thereafter, the Scottish backs played sound rugby football to score three tries against a Welsh defence which totally surrendered. The new cap, Robert Gordon, crossed twice, supporting a break by Donald Scott for the first try and diving on a loose ball after a rush led by Doug Elliot for the second. Jim Dawson completed the scoring seconds from the end of the match when he picked up in the loose and charged over.

Scotland's massacre of Wales was the most extraordinary 'David versus Goliath' match of post-war Five Nations rugby. Many explanations were offered for the incredible change in Welsh form : the more plausible were that too many of the players were stale after the long Lions tour and the team was too complacent after the 23-5 rout of England a fortnight earlier. Yet in truth, on the day, Scotland were the more enthusiastic and spirited side, and thoroughly deserved their great triumph.

Scotland: I H M Thomson; R A Gordon, D A Sloan, D M Scott, D M Rose; A Cameron, I A Ross; J C Dawson, N G R Mair, R L Wilson, R Gemmill, H M Inglis, W I D Elliot, P W Kininmonth (captain), R C Taylor.
Scorers: tries - Gordon (2), Dawson; conversions - Thomson, Inglis; penalty - Thomson; drop-goal - Kininmonth.

Wales: G Williams; K J Jones, J Matthews, B L Jones, M C Thomas; G Davies, W R Willis; J D Robins, D M Davies, C Davies, E R John, D J Hayward, A Forward, J A Gwilliam (captain), R T Evans.

Referee: Capt M J Dowling (Ireland)

England v France Twickenham: 24 February 1951

ENGLAND 3 FRANCE 11

In forty years of visits to Twickenham, French rugby had been the dandelion compared to England's rose. But on this occasion, on a wet, muddy pitch, a talented French side conquered its Twickenham inferiority complex with a convincing win. Fittingly, Jean Prat and Guy Basquet, two back-row forwards whose long service to the French national team had made them household names in the game in Europe, scored all France's points.

There had been so much rainfall in the week prior to the match that the RFU groundstaff had sanded large areas of the pitch on the eve of the game. Their move gave the players the confidence to run with the ball and it was a breakaway by George Rittson-Thomas, an Oxford swimming Blue, that carved out the space for Brian Boobbyer to open the scoring in the twenty-seventh minute.

France went ahead before half time when a burst by their left wing, Michel Pomathios, set up a maul from which Guy Basquet emerged to score, lunging himself between Bruce Neale and John Kendall-Carpenter's attempted tackles. Jean Prat, with a superb kick from near the touchline, converted.

There were problems for England early in the second half when Edwin Hewitt was off the field with an eye injury. The England forwards, however, acquitted themselves intelligently in the heavy conditions, creating any number of chances for their backs. Lack of understanding among the threequarters frustrated England's hopes of regaining the lead.

With the game moving into its final quarter, the home pack visibly began to wilt, the sticky going taking its toll of the England pack. Basquet and Prat, sensing their opponents' decline, drew on their experience to inspire the French pack to perform with tremendous enthusiasm. The French effort waxed as England's waned and the lead, never in jeopardy, was stretched to 8 points through Prat. The Lourdes flanker completed an outstanding individual performance with a try in the sixty-sixth minute from a blind-side burst by Gerard Dufau and a splendid drop-goal in the seventy-fourth minute.

England: E N Hewitt; C G Woodruff, I Preece, B Boobbyer, V R Tindall; E M P Hardy, G Rimmer; W A Holmes, E Evans, R V Stirling, B A Neale, D T Wilkins, G C Rittson-Thomas, J M Kendall-Carpenter (captain), V G Roberts.
Scorer: try - Boobbyer.

France: R Arcalis; A Porthault, G Brun, G Belletante, M Pomathios; A Alvarez, G Dufau; P Bertrand, P Pascalin, R Bernard, L Mias, H Foures, J Prat, G Basquet (captain), R Bienes.
Scorers : tries - Basquet, Prat; conversion - Prat; drop-goal - Prat.

Referee: Mr V S Llewellyn (Wales)

England v Scotland Twickenham : 16 March 1957

ENGLAND 16 SCOTLAND 3

England made a tentative start to their most important international since the war. In front of an expectant, capacity crowd, and with the Grand Slam, Triple Crown and Calcutta Cup on offer, England's backs reacted nervously to the few opportunities they had for attack in the opening twenty minutes. Pessimists in the crowd began to wonder if the enormity of the occasion would prove too burdensome for the young England team, though many took solace from the fact that Eric Evans, the inspiring captain, was coping calmly with the frantic play of the Scottish forwards in the loose.

English hearts were in their mouths once in the first half when a high kick by Ken Scotland forced Bob Challis to err and Arthur Smith followed up at speed, only to be beaten by a cruel bounce. But before the break, and with the England forwards establishing firm control in the tight, England slipped into the lead.

Jeff Butterfield, a creative genius in the centre, carved out an opening for Phil Davies to score in the right corner after thirty-five minutes. It was a dainty dish to set before the Queen, Prince Philip and Prince Charles, who were in attendance, and whetted appetites for the feast that promised to follow.

The second half began with the Scottish forwards finding their backs against the wall. Only desperate cover-tackling by their threequarters held the English at bay and it seemed certain that the lively home backs would eventually cut loose and sink Scotland's hopes.

Even so, with only ten minutes remaining Scotland were still in touch, 3-6 behind, when England, sensing that a Scottish breakaway was highly unlikely, threw everything bar the kitchen sink into attack. The Scottish backs at last crumbled under immense pressure and Reg Higgins, whose play in the second half verged on brilliance, burst clear to send Peter Thompson flying in for the score which broke the game. Challis converted from the touchline.

England maintained their flowing attacks and the Scottish forwards, worn down by the steady forward pressure of the strong, uncompromising English pack, conceded another try when the admirable Higgins crossed in the corner for Challis to add the touchline conversion with the last kick of the match.

England: R Challis; P B Jackson, J Butterfield, W P C Davies, P H Thompson; R M Bartlett, R E G Jeeps; C R Jacobs, E Evans (captain), G W D Hastings, J D Currie, R W D Marques, P G D Robbins, A Ashcroft, R Higgins.
Scorers: tries - Davies, Thompson, Higgins; conversions - Challis (2); penalty - Challis.

Scotland: K J F Scotland; A R Smith, T McClung, K R Macdonald, J L F Allan; G H Waddell, A F Dorward; H F McLeod, R K G MacEwen, T Elliot, E J S Michie, J W Y Kemp, G K Smith, J T Greenwood (captain), A Robson.
Scorer: penalty - Scotland.

Referee: Mr R Mitchell (Ireland)

France v Wales Stade Colombes : 4 April 1959

FRANCE 11 WALES 3

The ebullient French forwards introduced a refreshing attacking dimension to international rugby. Fast interpassing among forwards, who perfected the technique of peeling off the line-out in a formidable wedge-shaped pattern, launched many dangerous attacks which were tricky to defend against.

Victory in this match, played in spring sunshine with the temperature touching 70°F, ensured that France became outright winners of the Five Nations tournament for the first time. Wales took the lead when Terry Davies landed a penalty in the fifteenth minute but Antoine Labazuy equalised soon afterwards with a penalty from the touchline when a Welshman strayed offside at a scrummage.

France's forwards were clearly on top in all departments of the game. Amazing fitness and agility, accurate handling, frequent switches of direction, perpetual support and the ability to keep moving forward were the features of their play. With the sun on French backs and 55,000 partisan supporters cheering them on, the confidence of the home pack was sky-high. The Welsh forwards, by contrast, resembled eight tired Sisyphuses desperately condemned to push their weights, inch by inch, towards an unassailable summit .

The mountain facing the Welsh grew taller in the twenty-second minute when a breathtaking French attack from a line-out, initiated by Lucien Mias, enabled Francois Moncla to break through for a try which Labazuy effortlessly transformed into a 5-point lead.

It was one-way traffic in the second half. Indeed, the wonder of it all was that Wales conceded only one score - a tribute to their defence in the uncomfortable heat. Alfred Roques, Arnaud Marquesuzaa and Jacky Bouquet narrowly missed scoring opportunities before Moncla scored his second try, four minutes from the end.

Pierre Danos dispossessed the Wales scrum-half and Michel Crauste and Mias paved the way for the score. Moments later Mias, whose inspiring leadership had been a key element in France winning the championship outright for the first time, was borne from the scene of his greatest triumph by jubilant supporters.

France: P Lacaze; H Rancoule, J Bouquet, A Marquesuzaa, J Dupuy; A Labazuy, P Danos; A Quaglio, R Vigier, A Roques, B Mommejat, L Mias (captain), M Crauste, J Barthe, F Moncla.
Scorers: tries - Moncla (2); conversion - Labazuy; penalty - Lazabuy.

Wales: T J Davies; J Collins, R J Hurrell, M J Price, D I E Bebb; M C Thomas, W R Watkins; T R Prosser, B V Meredith, D R Main, R H Williams, D J E Harris, R C C Thomas (captain), G D Davidge, H J Morgan.
Scorer: penalty - Davies.

Referee: Dr N M Parkes (England)

England v Wales Twickenham : 16 January 1960

ENGLAND 14 WALES 6

Rugby football received a wonderful shot in the arm when England, throwing caution to the wind in their opening match of the 1960 championship, gave a marvellous exhibition of open play to stun Wales.

Wales fielded seven members of the 1959 British Lions touring team, and the thousands of supporters who had made the pilgrimage from the valleys were confident that Wales would see off the challenge of an experimental England side. There were six new caps in the side originally selected for the game, but a seventh, the Oxford undergraduate, Richard Sharp, was drafted into the team when Bev Risman withdrew through injury at the eleventh hour.

Sharp demolished Wales. From the start he played with a gusto rarely seen in an England fly-half. He danced around the highly-rated Welsh flanker, Haydn Morgan, and constantly had an ordinary Welsh back division at sixes-and-sevens.

Don Rutherford kicked England into the lead with an early penalty and soon afterwards Mike Weston, another brilliant debutant, showed off a classical style in centre-threequarter play when he broke through, drew the Welsh defence and sent Jim Roberts haring over on the left. Rutherford converted and kicked his second penalty before Sharp initiated the move which put the last nail in the Welsh coffin.

The England fly-half made a majestic break near half-way, tearing a huge hole in the Welsh defence. Weston continued the move before feeding Roberts, one of several Englishmen queueing up to score . Roberts duly touched down before the referee blew his whistle to staunch the fast and furious flow of points - 14 in all and the most scored by England in the first-half of an international since 1947.

After half-time, the out-of-touch visitors fared slightly better, Terry Davies reducing the Welsh deficit with two long-distance penalty-goals. Wales were too far behind, however, to threaten England's lead and it was a very happy crowd of Englishmen who sought refreshment when Mr Taylor finally whistled for no-side . The toast of all England, until deep into a night of celebration, was one Richard Adrian William Sharp.

England: D Rutherford; J R C Young, M S Phillips, M P Weston, J Roberts; R A W Sharp, R E G Jeeps (captain); C R Jacobs, S A M Hodgson, T P Wright, R W D Marques, J D Currie, P G D Robbins, W G D Morgan, R E Syrett.
Scorers: tries - Roberts (2); conversion - Rutherford; penalties - Rutherford (2).

Wales: T J Davies; J R Collins, M J Price, G Windsor-Lewis, D I E Bebb; C Ashton, C Evans; T R Prosser, B V Meredith, L J Cunningham, G W Payne, R H Williams (captain), B Cresswell, J Faull, H J Morgan.
Scorer: penalties - Davies (2).

Referee: Mr J A S Taylor (Scotland)

Scotland v England Murrayfield : 21 March 1964

SCOTLAND 15 ENGLAND 6

Scotland's forwards stood firm at the scrummages, their jumpers dominated the line-outs, and a talented back-row successfully pinned down the English halves.

There was no scoring until, on the half-hour mark, Ron Glasgow completed a move from the base of a scrum and swooped for a try which Stewart Wilson converted with a fine kick. Two of Scotland's new forwards were prominent in the next score. Peter Brown went on the rampage from a line-out and linked with Jim Telfer, whose sustained commitment in the Scottish back-row was a big bonus in Scotland's championship challenge. Telfer, as any good No. 8 should do, provided the crucial link to give Norman Bruce a try. The Scots were cock-a-hoop when Wilson converted the try into a 10-0 lead at the break.

Although Roger Hosen kicked a penalty for England to open the second-half scoring, England never threatened Scotland's forward superiority. The tireless Telfer capped a masterly individual performance with Scotland's third try and all England could muster in reply was a push-over try in the dying moments of the match.

Scotland had thoroughly deserved the success which brought the Calcutta Cup back to the strong-room at the Scottish Rugby Union's offices at Murrayfield for the first time for fourteen years. But more significant was the news that, on the same afternoon in Cardiff, Wales's failure to overcome a lively French side had allowed Scotland to sneak into a bracket with the Welsh at the top of the Five Nations championship.

Scotland: S Wilson; C Elliot, B C Henderson, I H P Laughland, G D Stevenson; D H Chisholm, A J Hastie; D M D Rollo, N S Bruce, J B Neill (captain), P C Brown, M J Campbell-Lamerton, J P Fisher, J W Telfer, R J C Glasgow.
Scorers: tries - Bruce, Glasgow, Telfer; conversions - Wilson (3).

England: J G Willcox; R W Hosen, M S Phillips, M P Weston, J M Ranson; T J Brophy, S R Smith; C R Jacobs (captain), H O Godwin, D F B Wrench, C M Payne, A M Davis, P J Ford, T G A H Peart, D P Rogers.
Scorers: try - Rogers; penalty - Hosen.

Referee: Mr R C Williams (Ireland)

Wales v Ireland Cardiff Arms Park : 13 March 1965

WALES 14 IRELAND 8

For the first time since 1911, both Wales and Ireland were fighting to win the Triple Crown . Arguably, no Five Nations match at the ground since the Second World War had generated so much excitement and interest, and tickets for the showdown were traded at big premiums in pre-match dealings. The only dampener on the proceedings was the weather. The ground was wet and muddy, as it always seemed to be at Cardiff for the big matches in the late 1950s and early 1960s. Yet the conditions did not deter the teams in their attempts to play exciting rugby.

The 58,500 fans saw Wales with their backs very much against the wall in the first half. Tom Kiernan missed a penalty in the first minute, both he and David Hewitt failed with relatively easy kicks a little later, and for twenty minutes Wales were under intense pressure when John Dawes was off the field receiving treatment for an injury. During Dawes's absence Alun Pask, the Welsh No. 8, withdrew from the scrum to cover as emergency full-back, with Terry Price moving into Dawes's vacant centre position. Pask played like an expert in his unpractised role. He was steadiness personified and his kicking and catching under the high ball were exemplary.

Wales scarcely ventured into Irish territory during the first half and Welsh supporters, who would quite happily have settled for a 0-0 scoreline at half-time, had a pleasant surprise just before the interval when a long, diagonal kick by David Watkins, from inside his own half, led to a try.

Stuart Watkins put Kiernan under pressure, a Welshman tapped the ball over the Irish line and David Watkins touched down. Terry Price, the boy-wonder with the perfect big-match temperament, converted with a splendid kick into the breeze, ten yards from the right touchline. Wales stretched their lead fourteen minutes after the break when Dewi Bebb, a great snapper up of unconsidered trifles, pounced on a tap-down by Brian Price from a line-out near the Irish corner-flags.

Then Kiernan kicked a penalty, improving Ireland's score from 0-8 to 3-8 but Wales's captain, Clive Rowlands, with tantalising taps up the touchline, gave heart to his forwards by forcing a series of line-outs in the Irish 25. From one throw-in on the Irish line an Irish back was relieved to kick the ball towards half-way. The relief, however, was short-lived. Terry Price gathered the ball in the lee of the old north stand, near the Irish ten-yard line, and, to the delight of the Welsh crowd, sent the ball dead straight beteen the Irish posts. 'A good one, a very good one, and it's over', G V Wynne-Jones told listeners tuned in to the big match.

Five minutes from the end, Kevin Flynn worked a scissors with Roger Young, who ran wide from a scrum, and Kiernan converted the try to take Ireland to within three points of Wales. But it was Terry Price, the Five Nations player of the season, who rounded off the scoring with a penalty after the Irish were lured offside at a scrum, two minutes from time.

Wales: T G Price; S J Watkins, J R Uzzell, S J Dawes, D I E Bebb; D Watkins, D C T Rowlands (captain); D Williams, N R Gale, R G Waldron, B Price, K A Rowlands, G J Prothero, A E I Pask, H J Morgan
Scorers: tries -D Watkins, Bebb; conversion - T G Price; penalty - T G Price; drop-goal - T G Price.

Ireland: T J Kiernan; D Hewitt, M K Flynn, J C Walsh, P J McGrath; C M H Gibson, R M Young; S MacHale, K W Kennedy, R J McLoughlin (captain), W J McBride, W A Mulcahy, M G Doyle, C H Wall, N A A Murphy.
Scorers: try - Flynn; conversion - Kiernan; penalty - Kiernan.

Referee: Mr P G Brook (England)

Wales v France Cardiff Arms Park : 23 March 1968

WALES 9 FRANCE 14

For French rugby enthusiasts, winning the Grand Slam had become a mission; a quest for rugby's Holy Grail. They finally saw their countrymen carry off the prize in Cardiff on a wet, muddy ground after an epic struggle against not only a spirited Wales team but also the elements.

This was not the best team France had ever fielded in the Five Nations tournament. Man for man, the players of the championship-winning teams from 1959 to 1962 were more adventurous runners with the ball than the class of 1968. But for strength, spirit and teamwork, Christian Carrère's men could not be faulted. They won few marks for style, but their ability to concentrate effectively for fully eighty minutes was a trait which hitherto had been dormant in French sides.

Wales, backed by the healthy breeze, sailed into a 9-3 lead before half-time. Doug Rees opened Wales's account with a penalty and Barry John placed a kick ahead perfectly after a Welsh strike against the head for Keri Jones to cross at the south-east corner of the ground. Guy Camberabero pulled back 3 points with a drop-goal but a transgression by a French forward at a line-out presented Doug Rees with his second penalty-goal.

The French forwards gave nothing away in the second half. Wales, admittedly, had their problems: John O'Shea, the prop, was struggling with a painful rib injury sustained in the first minute of the match, and Barry John tended to overdo the tactical kicking when Wales faced the wind and steady drizzle.

The turning point of the game came when Lilian Camberabero, Guy's brother, made a hash of a drop at goal from near Wales's posts. The ball was deflected in flight but Carrère was on it in a flash for a try which was converted. Lilian Camberabero was involved in the decisive score of the match minutes later. Michel Greffe broke from the back of a scrum and made a blind-side opening for the scrum-half to touch down for a try. Brother Guy completed the scoring when Jeff Young was penalised for mindlessly tackling Elie Cester without the ball.

Wales: D Rees; W K Jones, S J Dawes, W H Raybould, M C R Richards; B John, G O Edwards (captain); D J Lloyd, J Young, J P O'Shea, W D Thomas, M L Wiltshire, R E Jones, W D Morris, J Taylor.
Scorers: try - W K Jones; penalties - Rees (2).

France: C Lacaze; J-M Bonal, C Dourthe, J Maso, A Campaes; G Camberabero, L Camberabero; M Lasserre, M Yachvili, J-C Noble, A Plantefol, E Cester, W Spanghero, M Greffe, C Carrère (captain).
Scorers : tries - Carrère, L Camberabero; conversion - G Camberabero; penalty - G Camberabero; drop-goal - G Camberabero.

Referee: Mr H B Laidlaw (Scotland)

Wales v England Cardiff Arms Park : 16 January 1971

WALES 22 ENGLAND 6

What has become known as the decade of the dragon began on this wet, miserable day in Cardiff. Welsh rugby was reaching its prime, an efficient system of coaching and squad training bringing together a team of all the talents. Wales had shared the title with France in 1970 but it was not until 1971 that a settled team emerged to win the Grand Slam.

The match with England showed all the components of Wales's dream team working effectively. The pack overwhelmed an inexperienced England team and Barry John and Gareth Edwards, the fulcrum of the side, exercised tight tactical control. The threequarters, who revelled in the gilt-edged possession provided by their forwards and halves, had a productive afternoon, despite poor conditions, scoring three tries. Moreover, J P R Williams organised the defence so tightly that the England backs had little opportunity to realise their attacking potential.

Barry John, inevitably, stamped his name on the scorecard with a drop-goal in the eighth minute, but Charlie Hannaford dived on a loose ball from a wayward Wales line-out tap to equalise two minutes later. Wales never looked back after that. By half-time they were firmly in the saddle. Two spectacular tries by Gerald Davies, playing on the wing for the first time in the Five Nations championship, were converted from the left touchline by John Taylor. In between, John Bevan, who was making his international debut, scored on the other flank, and Wales were 16-3 clear at the changeover.

Wales settled for a more subdued approach in the second half. J P R Williams, the place-kicker nominated to take the longer shots at goal, exchanged penalties with Peter Rossborough before Barry John, the man-of-the-match, completed the scoring with another drop-goal.

In the opinion of Viv Jenkins, who as teenager, player and critic had regularly watched, played in and reported on Welsh international rugby since 1926, this was the most outstanding side that Wales had ever fielded.

Wales: J P R Williams; T G R Davies, S J Dawes (captain), A J L Lewis, J C Bevan; B John, G O Edwards; D B Llewelyn, J Young, D Williams, W D Thomas, M G Roberts, W D Morris, T M Davies, J Taylor.
Scorers: tries - T G R Davies (2), Bevan; conversions - Taylor (2); penalty - J P R Williams; drop-goals - John (2).

England: P A Rossborough; J P A G Janion, C S Wardlow, J S Spencer, D J Duckham; I D Wright, J J Page; D L Powell, J V Pullin, K E Fairbrother, P J Larter, B F Ninnes, A L Bucknall (captain), R C Hannaford, A Neary.
Scorers: try - Hannaford; penalty - Rossborough.

Referee: Mr D P d'Arcy (Ireland)

Gerald Davies, in splendid isolation, sprints for a corner try in his first championship match as a wing threequarter.

England v Ireland Twickenham : 16 February 1974

ENGLAND 21 IRELAND 26

Willie-John McBride, winning his fifty-sixth cap for Ireland and breaking the world record for international appearances set by Colin Meads of New Zealand, led Ireland to a victory which opened up their chances of winning the championship.

The forwards were well matched but one man stood out above all others behind the scrum : Mike Gibson. Almost ten years to the day since he made his international debut - also against England at Twickenham - Gibson showed that he had lost none of his magic powers as a maker and scorer of tries. Twice in the second half he scored tries which pushed Ireland to the safety of a 26-9 lead. England were 10-6 behind at the break, two penalties by Alan Old answering a penalty by Tony Ensor, a try by Terry Moore from a shortened line-out and a drop-goal by Mick Quinn.

Ireland's purple patch came in the first twenty minutes of the second half, when the crowd were entertained by an attractive display of running rugby. Gibson's handling and running off the ball drew praise from everyone, from doyens of the press-box who had seen the Irishman perform with grace countless times before to youngsters on the terraces making their first visit to Twickenham.

Johnny Moloney took advantage of a fumble by Old and ran to the line for one try before Gibson delivered his two knockout scores - the first with a dummy and the second on the overlap after a diagonal run out of defence by Ensor - to put paid to England's chances.

The best England could muster in reply was a late try by Peter Squires from a charge by Andy Ripley. Old converted to add to his three second-half penalties.

England: P A Rossborough; P J Squires, G W Evans, D Roughley, D J Duckham; A G B Old, S J Smith; C B Stevens, J V Pullin (captain), F E Cotton, R M Uttley, C W Ralston, P J Dixon, A G Ripley, A Neary.
Scorers: try - Squires; conversion - Old; penalties - Old (5).

Ireland: A H Ensor; T O Grace, R A Milliken, C M H Gibson, A W McMaster; M A M Quinn, J J Moloney; R J McLoughlin, K W Kennedy, J F Lynch, W J McBride (captain), M I Keane, J F Slattery, T A P Moore, S A McKinney.
Scorers: tries - Gibson (2), Moloney, Moore; conversions - Gibson (2); penalty - Ensor; drop-goal - Quinn.

Referee: Mr M Joseph (Wales)

Wales v England Cardiff Arms Park 17 March 1979

WALES 27 ENGLAND 3

The decade of the dragon ended as it had begun, with Wales thumping England in Cardiff. A clutch of retirements in 1978 had forced the Welsh selectors to replace the almost irreplaceable. Gone were the glitterati, Gareth Edwards, Gerald Davies and Phil Bennett, who had regularly performed miracles with hands and feet. In their place, in an experimental Wales side, were new hopes - Elgan Rees, David Richards and another pair of devilish halves, Gareth Davies and Terry Holmes. But still there to oversee a new side take Wales to an unprecedented fourth successive Triple Crown was J P R Williams, one of the only two survivors of the corresponding match in 1971. (The veteran lock, Mike Roberts, unexpectedly recalled for this match, was the other.)

England were on a roll after beating a strong French side at Twickenham and a win at Cardiff would have entitled them to a share of the Five Nations championship with France. Some hope: the old Welsh qualities, composure at half-back, implacable defence and rugged dominance up front, were the strengths which benefited Wales most as they coasted to their most conclusive win against England since 1905.

Wales were usually slow starters during their years of Five Nations domination in the 1970s, and this match was no exception to that rule. Gareth Davies dropped a goal in the thirteenth minute - shades of Barry John in the 1971 match - but twenty minutes passed before Wales stretched their lead with a lovely try.

Derek Quinnell, a player who never won as many caps as his whole-hearted commitment deserved, made a spirited drive which brought play to the England 22. The Welsh forwards moved the ball back from the maul and David Richards pierced the disorganised England cover for a try.

Neil Bennett pulled back 3 penalty points for England before the pause and England enjoyed their best moments of the match in the first twenty minutes of the second half. Then J P R Williams had to retire with a calf injury and, curiously, England surrendered just when their chances of success seemed to be rising. A counter-attack by Alastair Hignell was the last attacking gesture England managed before Roberts barged over from a line-out. His popular try was the first of 20 points scored in the final twenty minutes.

At the end, all Wales celebrated what was perceived as a new beginning for Welsh rugby. Alas, the success of a fresh-faced team was, in fact, the final spluttering of a once-sumptuous machine which, as subsequent events were to confirm, was one stop from the scrapyard.

Wales: J P R Williams (captain) (rep, C Griffiths); H E Rees, D S Richards, S P Fenwick, J J Williams; W G Davies, T D Holmes; S J Richardson, A J Phillips, G Price, A J Martin, M G Roberts, P Ringer, D L Quinnell, J Squire.
Scorers: tries - Rees, Richards, Ringer, Roberts, J J Williams; conversions - Martin, Fenwick; drop-goal - Davies.

England: A J Hignell; P J Squires, R M Cardus, P W Dodge, M A C Slemen; W N Bennett, P Kingston; C E Smart, P J Wheeler, G S Pearce, W B Beaumont (captain), N E Horton, A Neary, J P Scott, M Rafter.
Scorer: penalty - Bennett.

Referee: M J-P Bonnet (France)

Scotland v England Murrayfield : 15 March 1980

SCOTLAND 18 ENGLAND 30

England laid the foundation for a famous victory by running up an unassailable lead of 16 points in the first half-hour. Bill Beaumont's pack overwhelmed the Scots with the sheer power of their scrummaging, and the purposeful running of Leicester's Clive Woodward time and again exposed the weaknesses of a brittle Scottish defence.

Woodward's free-ranging runs in the centre paved the way for England's first tries. In the fifteenth minute Maurice Colclough, who had a productive afternoon in the line-out, won clean possession which was quickly shipped out to Woodward. With a clever piece of footwork the centre left David Johnston, his marker, clutching Scotch mist before John Carleton, on the overlap, accepted Woodward's pass to score. Ten minutes later, Woodward ducked and weaved an almost impossible track through territory policed by the Scottish back-row and presented Mike Slemen with an easy run-in at the left corner.

Steve Smith created the next score. Throughout the match he played with confident authority, distributing the ball to his backs when attacking opportunities arose and nursing his forwards with delicate tactical kicks when England were under pressure. It was his sortie in tandem with John Scott on the short side of a scrum-five which led to Carleton's second try, in the thirtieth minute.

Scotland replied with a penalty by Andy Irvine - a fine kick which cannoned off the upright - but Dusty Hare, whose kicking earlier in the season had carried England to victory against Wales, restored the 16-point lead with a penalty just before half-time.

The 75,000 spectators were treated to forty minutes of sustained high-class entertainment in the second half. Casting off their inhibitions, Scotland turned every scrap of possession which came their way into attacking ball, often bringing the excited crowd to its feet. Irvine landed a penalty, more than a dozen Englishmen handled the ball to set up a wonderful try by Smith after Roger Uttley had won a line-out, and a thrust by Jim Renwick, which led to a splendid try by Alan Tomes, had the clans massed on the terraces rejoicing long after Irvine had added the goal.

Yet the strength of Beaumont's team was its ability to respond quickly to scores by opponents. Hare calmly slotted over another penalty and when Irvine misjudged the flight of a speculative punt by Paul Dodge, Carleton gathered the ball on the bounce and sprinted forty metres to complete the first hat-trick by an Englishman in an international for fifty-six years.

Scotland gamely continued to play entertaining football. John Rutherford made a classic fly-half break to dot the ball down for a try under the England posts, and Johnston and Irvine made gallant efforts to augment Scotland's score. But it was all to no avail and, on the day, England deserved to walk off with all the silverware the Five Nations championship has to offer : Grand Slam, Triple Crown, Championship and Calcutta Cup.

Scotland: A R Irvine (captain); K W Robertson, J M Renwick, D I Johnston, B H Hay (rep J S Gossman); J Y Rutherford, R J Laidlaw; J N Burnett, K G Lawrie, N A Rowan, A J Tomes, D Gray, D G Leslie, J R Beattie, M A Biggar.
Scorers: tries - Rutherford, Tomes; conversions - Irvine (2); penalties - Irvine (2).

England: W H Hare; J Carleton, C R Woodward, P W Dodge, M A C Slemen; J P Horton, S J Smith; F E Cotton, P J Wheeler, P J Blakeway, W B Beaumont (captain), M J Colclough, R M Uttley, J P Scott, A Neary.
Scorers: tries - Carleton (3), Slemen, Smith; conversions - Hare (2); penalties - Hare (2).

Referee: M. J-P Bonnet (France)

Leading by example. Bill Beaumont, the England captain, takes on Jim Renwick in the Grand Slam match. Roger Uttley and Mike Biggar are the players to the right.

England v France Twickenham : 21 March 1981

ENGLAND 12 FRANCE 16

In a match conducted in a thoroughly sporting manner, the importance of its outcome notwithstanding, the efficient French eight disrupted the English at the scrummage but found no antidote to the Englishman who played for Angoulème, Maurice Colclough, at the line-out. The massive lock cleaned out allcomers in the air, winning two-thirds of the throws.

France, who were lucky to make use of a gale-force wind in the first-half, opened a 16-point gap by half-time. Guy Laporte started the scoring with a long drop-goal: how often have drop-goals been vital scores in famous championship wins for France? And shortly afterwards Jean-Pierre Rives put Pierre Lacans over on the left at the north end of the ground after a quick throw-in near the England 22. This try, in fact, was awarded in error. The ball Pierre Berbizier used to throw in had been supplied by a bystander. Law 23 B(10), then in force, prescribed that only 'the ball that went into touch is used,' and that it had 'been handled only by the players and thrown in correctly.'

Nevertheless, France deserved their points and Laporte converted with a fine kick. Three minutes before the pause, France increased their lead with an impressive try. Rives was the active agent in a flowing move which saw the ball transferred to the left wing for Laurent Pardo to score. Although Laporte fluffed the conversion, he delivered a demoralising blow to English hopes seconds before the interval when he dropped his second goal.

The second half was an exciting affair with England slowly clawing their way back into contention through four penalty-goals kicked by Marcus Rose. In the end, though, no one could cavil at France's win by two tries to nil. Fair stood the wind for France!

England: W M H Rose; J Carleton, C R Woodward, P W Dodge, M A C Slemen; G H Davies, S J Smith; C E Smart, P J Wheeler, P J Blakeway, W B Beaumont (captain), M J Colclough, N C Jeavons, J P Scott, D H Cooke.
Scorers: penalties - Rose (4).

France: S Gabernet; S Blanco, R Bertranne, D Codorniou, L Pardo; G Laporte, P Berbizier; P Dospital, P Dintrans, R Paparemborde, D Revailler, J-F Imbernon, J-P Rives (captain), J-L Joinel, P Lacans.
Scorers: tries - Lacans, Pardo; conversion - Laporte; drop-goals - Laporte (2).

Referee: Mr A M Hosie (Scotland)

England v Ireland Twickenham : 6 February 1982

ENGLAND 15 IRELAND 16

Ireland were comfortable winners, despite the narrow margin between the sides, and stayed on course for their first Triple Crown since 1949 . The Irish forwards were the architects of victory: the back row disrupted the England pack and bustled the backs off the ball in open play, while Ciaran Fitzgerald was an inspiring captain who led by example, from the middle of the front row, like his distinguished predecessor Karl Mullen.

Ireland took the lead in the twelfth minute when Ollie Campbell kicked a penalty-goal downwind for off-side. Ten minutes later, poor defence by the England backs at a scrum-five enabled Hugo MacNeill to slice through for a try in the corner. Campbell's conversion attempt from touch hit the post, but he made amends before the changeover, adding a penalty to one by Marcus Rose for England.

Soon after the restart, Donal Lenihan was caught receiving a hoist at a line-out and Rose duly kicked the penalty, but hopes of an English victory were dashed fifteen minutes later when Ginger McLoughlin, the strongman from Shannon, carried half the English pack over with him for a rousing try in the south-west corner of the ground. Robust mauling by Ciaran Fitzgerald and accurate handling on the blind-side led to the score. Campbell converted from the right touchline - the most difficult kick for the right-footed round-the-corner expert.

England staged a spirited fightback in the final quarter of the match. Rose punished an indiscretion by Willie Duggan and Peter Winterbottom, charging forward from the tail of a lineout, initiated the best move of the match in the closing minutes. Held up five metres from the Irish line, he managed to set up the maul, his colleagues worked the ball clear to Huw Davies and the fly-half sent Mike Slemen round the Irish defence for a try which Rose converted.

England: W M H Rose; J Carleton, C R Woodward, A M Bond, M A C Slemen; G H Davies, S J Smith (captain); C E Smart, P J Wheeler, P J Blakeway, J P Syddall, M J Colclough, N C Jeavons, J P Scott, P J Winterbottom.
Scorers: try - Slemen; conversion - Rose; penalties - Rose (3).

Ireland: H P MacNeill; T M Ringland, M J Kiernan, P M Dean, M C Finn; S O Campbell, R J M McGrath; P A Orr, C F Fitzgerald (captain), G A J McLoughlin, M I Keane, D G Lenihan, J F Slattery, W P Duggan, J B O'Driscoll
Scorers: tries - MacNeill, McLoughlin; conversion - Campbell; penalties - Campbell (2).

Referee: Mr A M Hosie (Scotland)

Scotland v France Murrayfield : 17 March 1984

SCOTLAND 21 FRANCE 12

The noise that exploded over Murrayfield at the end of this Grand Slam triumph was the sound of Scotland releasing years of pent-up frustration - in fact, since their only previous Grand Slam fifty-nine years before.

This particular triumph, though, had been four years in the making. During the early 1980s, sensible coaching by Jim and Colin Telfer had lifted the skill levels of the Scottish squad members and infused the players with confidence.

With years of experience of New Zealand methods, both as player and coach, Jim Telfer had systematically set out to stamp an All Black style on the Scottish national side. The 1984 Grand Slam triumph was the pinnacle of Telfer's coaching achievements.

These qualities, particularly aggressive, first-time tackling, were much in evidence against France in a match which began with both sides seeking the Grand Slam. Relentless French pressure, especially the attacking attitudes of their brilliant backs, threatened to submerge the Scots in the first half. Yet through secure defence and a French propensity for giving away promising positions by committing infringements, Scotland were still very much in contention at half-time when France led 6-3 : a great try by the self-assured scrum-half, Jerome Gallion, and a conversion by Jean-Patrick Lescarboura set against the first of Peter Dods's five penalties.

In the second half the French became more and more jittery about their failure to establish a clear lead. Jean-Pierre Rives, their captain, often took it upon himself to remonstrate with the decisions of Mr Jones, the Welsh referee. True, some of the referee's rulings made little sense, but there was no prejudice in his judgements. Rives's irresponsible behaviour, in the last international of his long career, did no favours for France's cause.

The game really began to turn Scotland's way as it entered the final quarter. The most dangerous French player up to this point was Gallion, the try-scorer. He had been the chief French play-maker but a collision with David Leslie removed him to hospital with concussion. Somehow, one sensed, French hopes of victory went down the road in the ambulance carrying Gallion.

With ten minutes to go, the scores were delicately poised at 12-12 when Scotland's forwards lined out for a throw near the French line. Jean-Luc Joinel deflected the ball from Colin Deans's throw-in but it was Jim Calder who pounced for the try when Pierre Berbizier failed to tidy up the tap. Dods converted and kicked his last penalty, for a late tackle, in the eightieth minute to seal the Grand Slam.

Scotland: P W Dods; J A Pollock, K W Robertson, D I Johnston, G R T Baird; J Y Rutherford, R J Laidlaw; J Aitken (captain), C T Deans, I G Milne, A J Campbell, A J Tomes, J H Calder, I A M Paxton, D G Leslie.
Scorers: try - Calder; conversion - Dods; penalties - Dods (5).

France: S Blanco; J Bégu, P Sella, D Codorniou, P Estève; J-P Lescarboura, J Gallion (rep, P Berbizier); P Dospital, P Dintrans, D Dubroca, F Haget, J Condom, J-P Rives (captain), J-C Orso, J-L Joinel.
Scorers: try - Gallion; conversion - Lescarboura; penalty - Lescarboura; drop-goal - Lescarboura.

Referee: Mr W Jones (Wales)

Scotland v England Murrayfield : 17 March 1990

SCOTLAND 13 ENGLAND 7

From the moment that David Sole led his team out to take on brash, unbeaten England, there was a feeling that Will Carling's invaders would have their work cut out to win this Grand Slam decider at fortress Murrayfield. Sole's dignified bearing as he walked his men on to the pitch epitomised the defiant spirit with which Scotland promised to overcome England.

England, having demolished Ireland (23-0), France (26-7) and Wales (34-6) with sumptuous displays of attacking rugby, were favourites to win their first Grand Slam for ten years. But Ian McGeechan, the most astute coach in the Five Nations championship, had prepared his troops for the battle with his usual attention to detail. The hours spent in his study plotting his team's defence, and the practices with his forwards, perfecting their rucking techniques, paid off handsomely on the day.

No one had given Scotland much chance of breaking down the England forwards' tight mauling in the loose. Yet this was precisely the area of England's game that the Scottish back-row targeted for destruction. John Jeffrey and Finlay Calder concentrated on disrupting England's mauls by insinuating themselves into positions which prevented the ball's passage back to the England halves. Denied the main plank of their game policy, England revealed a surprising lack of tactical flexibility. As a tight match progressed, so the initiative gradually passed to the Scots.

Scotland led, in fact, from the fifth minute of the first half. Craig Chalmers kicked two early penalties before Jeremy Guscott was unleashed for a fine try which gave the Scottish crowd a glimpse of the exquisite skills that had captivated the spectators at England's earlier Five Nations matches. Chalmers's third penalty, after thirty-five minutes, gave Scotland a lead of 9-4 at half-time.

Then, early in the second half, the Scots delivered their killer blow. Gary Armstrong made a break from a scrum at half-way and gave a pass to Gavin Hastings, who chipped the ball into England's 22. The ball bounced kindly into the path of Tony Stanger, Scotland's right wing, who made no mistake, grounding it for the decisive score of the match.

Simon Hodgkinson, who missed two penalties at crucial times in the match, managed to put one over in the fifty-fifth minute. Scotland's fervent rejection of England's desperate bids for victory in the final quarter of an hour, however, sent Carling's side home 'tae think again' as their adopted anthem, *Flower of Scotland,* intones.

Scotland: A G Hastings; A G Stanger, S Hastings, S R P Lineen, I Tukalo; C M Chalmers, G Armstrong; D M B Sole (captain), K S Milne, A P Burnell, C A Gray, D F Cronin, J Jeffrey, D B White (rep, D J Turnbull), F Calder.
Scorers: try - Stanger; penalties - Chalmers (3).

England: S D Hodgkinson; S J Halliday, W D C Carling (captain), J C Guscott (rep, M D Bailey), R Underwood; C R Andrew, R J Hill; P A G Rendall, B C Moore, J A Probyn, P J Ackford, W A Dooley, M G Skinner, M C Teague, P J Winterbottom.
Scorers: try - Guscott; penalty - Hodgkinson.

Referee: Mr D J Bishop (New Zealand)

England v France Twickenham : 16 March 1991

ENGLAND 21 FRANCE 19

For only the fourth time in Five Nations history, two teams met with the Grand Slam the prize. But never has such a Grand Slam showdown produced such a marvellous spectacle. In a match of continuous excitement, for players and spectators alike, England and France fought an epic battle to bring down the curtain on the 1991 championship.

Simon Hodgkinson nudged England into the lead with a penalty-goal for a ruck offence when the match was barely two minutes old, but it was Serge Blanco, the incomparable French captain making his final appearance in a Five Nations match, who provided the abiding memory of the game ten minutes later. Hodgkinson missed a penalty shot at goal. As the English retreated to await the expected drop-out, Blanco sensed an opening and launched a hopeful sally from his deadball-line instead of opting for the security of a touchdown.

Some sally! A miraculous counter-attack along the east touchline involving Jean-Baptiste Lafond, Philippe Sella and Didier Camberabero reached its climax seconds later when Philippe Saint-André gathered Camberabero's cross-kick and scored beneath the England goal.

Will Carling's team, denied the Grand Slam by Scotland almost a year to the day previously, responded by showing the depth of its character. The England forwards were immense in the scrum, lineout and loose, and the composure of the entire team in the face of breathtaking French attacks was the vital quality which underpinned England's confidence.

That confidence helped carry England to a comfortable 18-9 lead at half-time, a score which included England's best moment of the match when Rory Underwood finished off a slick move from second-phase ball, set-up by Mike Teague. Underwood arced past Lafond - no slouch - for a try wide out in the thirtieth minute.

The drizzle which had failed to dampen spirits in the first half fell more heavily after the interval and England resorted to the tactics of ten-man rugby in an attempt to sit on their lead. All the thrills were now provided by the French. Camberabero scored when he dived on a loose ball after following his own chip ahead, and Blanco's sublime skills were the catalyst for another touchline try, this time by Franck Mesnel, in the dying minutes. How England survived the frantic final passages of play as France threatened to snatch victory with an unpredictable move owed much to luck. But survive they did, and when no-side came the heavy sigh of relief from spectators, officials and players was soon superseded by cries of celebration.

If, as they say, the outstanding events of a man's life flash before him on his deathbed, then those who were privileged to watch this match will have a treasure of memories to relive before passing into the next life.

England: S D Hodgkinson; N J Heslop, W D C Carling (captain), J C Guscott, R Underwood; C R Andrew, R J Hill; J Leonard, B C Moore, J A Probyn, P J Ackford, W A Dooley, M C Teague, D Richards, P J Winterbottom.
Scorers: try - Underwood; conversion - Hodgkinson; penalties - Hodgkinson (4); drop-goal - Andrew.

France: S Blanco (captain); J-B Lafond, P Sella, F Mesnel, P Saint-André; D Camberabero, P Berbizier; G Lascubé, P Marocco, P Ondarts, M Tachdjian (rep, M Cecillon), O Roumat, X Blond, A Benazzi, L Cabannes.
Scorers: tries - Saint-André, Camberabero, Mesnel; conversions - Camberabero (2); penalty - Camberabero.

Referee: Mr L J Peard (Wales)

Rory Underwood races in for England's try.

ENGLAND PLAYER PROFILES

Rob Andrew and Will Carling.

Bill BEAUMONT
(Fylde)

One man more than any other was responsible for the revival in England's rugby fortunes in the late 1970s. He was Bill Beaumont,the Fylde and Lancashire lock who typified the English bulldog breed and who took over as national captain in 1978.

Bill went on to skipper his country on twenty-one occasions and collected eleven wins during his service as leader. Moreover, he raised the status of the England captaincy to a level of respectability and importance which it had last commanded under Eric Evans and Dickie Jeeps in the 1950s and 1960s. During the early 1970s the position had been handed around like a hot potato. Skippers came and went, chosen for their ability to act out the coach's plans on the field. Good old-fashioned qualities of leadership were ignored, or probably not even recognised by a procession of myopic selection committees.

Yet Bill had no track record to suggest that his stewardship would be successful. Indeed, his early experiences of rugby football (as a full-back in the Ellesmere College 3rd XV) hardly suggested that he would even make the transition to a decent club player. It was John Burgess, Bill's coach when he first entered the Lancashire county side, who moulded the future captain into a second row of international potential.

Bill's debut for England came in 1975, when he was called to Dublin at the eleventh hour as a replacement for Roger Uttley and, after touring Australia with the national squad the same summer, he commanded a regular position at lock with special duties at the front of the line-out. By the time he was made England captain, Bill had enhanced his rugby reputation with a succession of impressive technical displays, both for his country and, in 1977, for the Lions. In fact, he was hailed as the 'find' of that visit to New Zealand. Called out as a replacement when Nigel Horton was injured, Bill's scrummaging and expertise in the mauls won him a place in the Test side for the last three games of the series.

Bill was already held in high regard by his team when he was first appointed their captain in 1978. But the mark of the man was his knack for player-management. Never one to bawl out his colleagues, Bill set about developing a happy team spirit, believing that good results on the field required good relations off it. He possessed the type of personality that enabled such a spirit to grow in a climate of respect, camaraderie and

Bill Beaumont breaks from a maul during the 1980 match against Ireland.

fun. He encouraged his squad to excel, and the players in turn warmed to his example.

Results improved. Ireland and Scotland were defeated in 1978, the French were beaten in 1979, and Beaumont's rebuilding work was completed in 1980 when a team bursting with confidence won the Grand Slam.

Alas, less than two years later, Bill's special talents were lost to English rugby. Playing for Lancashire in the County Championship final, he was injured and wisely accepted medical advice to retire. That was a sad way for one of England's finest servants to have to depart from a game he deeply loved. Arguably, his equal has yet to be discovered.

Jeff BUTTERFIELD
(Northampton)

Anyone meeting Jeff Butterfield, now the proprietor of the Rugby Club of London in Hallam Street, would find it difficult to believe that he had been a top-class centre in the 1950s. Jeff's youthful looks belie the fact that the age of retirement beckons for him. He still appears as fit as a man twenty years his junior.

Indeed, fitness was the keynote of his playing career. He set himself high standards when he was a student at Loughborough Colleges and, throughout his days in first-class rugby, he worked long and hard to improve his stamina, strength and speed.

As a rugby footballer, the striking feature of his play was his skilful handling. He had the intuition of a natural sportsman and established himself as a centre with Northampton during his college days at Loughborough. Wingers loved playing outside him, for Jeff had the dexterity to take and give a carefully-placed pass in one smooth movement. Possessed of the rare gift of perfect judgement, he was able to sum up a situation in a second. If he sensed that his threequarter division was being pushed sideways, he had no trouble straightening the line of attack; if the moment cried out for a swift transfer to the wing, then Jeff could be relied upon to deliver his colleague a try-making pass.

When he first appeared in an England jersey, in winter sunshine against France in 1953, he also showed his capacity as a finisher, scoring a fine try in the closing minutes to cap an excellent debut. Three weeks later, he was a prime agent in a scintillating display by the England backs, scoring a try himself and having a hand in several of the other five notched against Scotland, in a win which secured the championship title outright. Altogether, he played twenty-eight times on the trot for England in a decade which produced a string of championship successes: a shared title in 1954, the Grand Slam in 1957, and outright champions again in 1958.

His midfield vision, not only as a creator of tries but also as a sound tackler, was a key element in England's domination of the Five Nations tournament in this period. During Jeff's career, England scored forty-three tries, twenty-one of which were touched down by the threequarters who orbited around him. He also crossed five times himself, and England's defence kept fifteen clean sheets with him in their centre.

His only weakness was his kicking. Yet it was a drop-goal off his left foot which opened the scoring in the 1955 Lions' decisive 9-6 third-Test win at Pretoria. That visit to South Africa found Jeff at the peak of his powers. He relished running on the hard grounds of the veldt, and the South African press hailed him as the best centre to visit their land in modern times.

After he had captained England in 1959, a thigh injury interrupted his progress on the Lions tour to Australasia later that year, and he retired from the game soon after returning from New Zealand.

Jeff Butterfield, England centre 1953-59, breaks against Ireland at Lansdowne Road, 1955.

Will CARLING

(Harlequins)

The public face of England's golden era between 1988 and 1992 undoubtedly belonged to Will Carling, the man appointed captain of his country by Geoff Cooke in the first of those years. Will was only twenty-two when he became leader, and thumbing through the record books revealed that he was the youngest player to captain England for fifty-seven years.

Will has skippered England ever since, missing only one game (against Romania in 1989) owing to an injury which also deprived him of a Lions tour of Australia. In charge for the back-to-back Grand Slams and the 1991 World Cup, he is now the most successful captain in international rugby history, with twenty-six wins in thirty-five games at the helm.

Yet the critics have never quite resolved the chicken/egg question of whether or not his captaincy has been the crucial ingredient in England's recipe for success. Certainly, tub-thumping has never been Will's style; he does not set out to motivate teams with inspiring speeches. Instead, as befits a psychology graduate, he has adopted an approach to the job which, so far anyway, has brought considerable reward. Working with Geoff Cooke, Will has engendered in his England sides a collective responsibility to adhere to the playing style and tactics decided in advance at squad sessions. He has presided over an international squad which has developed a purposeful, friendly atmosphere more commonly associated with successful club sides.

Like another famous England captain, Wavell Wakefield, Will Carling learnt the game at Sedbergh School, where he set his young heart on playing for his country. His chance came in January 1988, when he was pitched into a team which the experts predicted would be annihilated by France. England did lose, but only by 9-10, and those same experts were hard put to avoid eating humble pie. The team's results improved steadily during the season and, in March,they gave notice of their potential to play dazzling rugby when Ireland were demolished in a 35-point second-half spree.

Will Carling leads the way: England v Wales at Twickenham 1992.

The campaign saw Will establish himself as a world-class player. He showed a real flair for the outside break, that most demanding of moves for the ace centre to execute effectively, and he showed a perception in defence that was rare for one then so young.

Interestingly, the qualities of his threequarter play have never been called into question during his career, although there have been times when his captaincy has been criticised. These have followed occasional, narrow defeats: 9-12 against Wales (1989); 7-13 against Scotland (1990); and 9-10 against Wales (1993) when, with greater presence of mind, perhaps he could have changed tactics and turned defeat into victory. Yet the measure of the man who is so calm and confident both in public and on the rugby field is that he has managed both to ride these criticisms and to maintain his standing in the top flight of world centres.

He still has half-a-dozen or so years in which to parade his skills, and he has openly stated that he relishes the captaincy. No doubt he will continue to fill an influential role in his country's run up to the 1995 World Cup, and who knows what championship honours and records lie in store for him as England rebuild their Five Nations team around his leadership in the future?

Fran COTTON

(Loughborough Colleges, Coventry, Sale)

English rugby passed through its Dark Ages in the early 1970s, with the national side winning only six games in the Five Nations tournament between 1970 and 1976. Many reasons were suggested for this miserable run: selectors were blamed for inconsistency in choosing the team, and players were criticised for lack of commitment. The other Home Unions, tongues in cheek, even threatened to drop their fixtures with the dismal English. Yet several outstanding individual performers passed through the England XVs of those years; arguably, players of the calibre of David Duckham, Tony Neary, John Pullin and Fran Cotton would be automatic selections for any eclectic British team of the period.

Fran was the only member of this triumvirate who stayed in the England side long enough to participate in the subsequent revival which culminated in the 1980 Grand Slam. And while the celebrations of that achievement were savoured by the entire squad, Fran Cotton understandably had more cause than most to enjoy England's triumph.

He had entered the national side in 1971 after a promising junior career. John Burgess, his Lancashire coach, and Jim Greenwood, Fran's mentor.at Loughborough Colleges, were important influences in his early days. Greenwood, no tub-thumper, appealed to Fran's intelligence, making him physically fit enough to put scrummaging theory into practice for eighty minutes in the hurly-burly of international rugby. Burgess was the positive thinker who instilled in the young prop a sense of self-belief.

Fran was on the losing side in his first five England matches. Yet his down-to-earth attitude and his uncompromising rugby values enabled him to ride out the disappointments of his early international traumas, and he compensated for those disasters with two memorable performances against the world's best teams. In November 1972,he was the young captain of the North-Western Counties XV which became the first English provincial side to beat New Zealand and,two years later, he was the tight-head for the Lions when South Africa were beaten in a home series for the first time this century.

Altogether, therefore, Fran could be described as a young veteran in 1977 when, still under thirty, he was the cornerstone at tight-head of an England team which began to pull itself out of international obscurity. Scotland and Ireland were beaten thanks to the sterling qualities of the England pack, and Fran's quiet determination - his inner strength - together with his technical expertise helped his fellow forwards to win a wealth of possession.

The resurgence continued in 1978 but, without Fran's experience, England suffered setbacks in 1979. Then, in 1980, England accommodated Fran on the loose-head side, much to the surprise of the experts who contended that the Cotton physique was unsuited to the demands of the scrum's No. 1 position. He was 6ft 2in, and it was felt that he was too long in the back to be an effective loose-head.

But Fran proved the pundits wrong and put remorseless pressure on opposing props in England's best season for twenty-three years. He had the perfect temperament for front-row operations and played an important role in England's subdue-and-exploit approach during the Grand Slam campaign.

Yet within a year of his international career reaching its zenith, he had retired at the premature age of thirty-three. A heart attack scare during the 1980 Lions tour was diagnosed as pericarditis, but when he limped off at Cardiff in 1981 Fran realised that he was not indestructible and that he had played his last match. Typically, there were no bleats of self-pity from the man who had become his country's most-capped prop. But just what England might have achieved with powerhouse Fran up front in the early 1980s must remain a matter of conjecture.

Fran Cotton, with Peter Dixon in support, draws Jean-Pierre Rives into a tackle at Twickenham in 1977.

John CURRIE

(Oxford U, Harlequins, Bristol)

Distinguished playing partnerships in post-war English rugby have been uncommon. One thinks of Butterfield and Davies's centre pairing in the 1950s, Richard Sharp and Dickie Jeeps at half-back in the 1960s, and Rob Andrew and Richard Hill, also at half-back, in more recent times. But probably the most famous combination of all appeared in the heart of the scrum between 1956 and 1961, when David Marques and John Currie packed down together in the second row in twenty-two consecutive internationals.

Marques was the tall, slim one who jumped in the middle of the line-out, while John 'Muscles' Currie was the shorter and squatter of the two who carried out his duties in the more difficult, congested areas at the front. They were exact contemporaries who began their first-class careers as arch-rivals. John went up to Oxford from Bristol GS with a reputation as a powerful all-round sportsman and won his first Blue in 1954, marking David Marques who was at Cambridge. They played against each other in four successive Varsity matches but, by the end of their undergraduate days, they had joined forces, first for England and then for Harlequins.

John in fact had a qualification to play for Scotland, but he politely declined overtures to appear in a Scottish trial before taking his chance in the junior sides under Eric Evans in the 1955-56 England trials. Twice he gave Peter Young, a former cap and his opponent, such an awkward time at the line-out that he was selected to complement David Marques's effortless jumping in an England side which faced Wales in 1956 with no fewer than ten new caps.

For the next four seasons, there was scarcely a forward whom John or David looked up to. They were simply the best pairing in the business and provided Dickie Jeeps and the graceful, skilful English backs with gilt-edged possession which was invested in a Grand Slam in 1957, another championship title in 1958, and a second Triple Crown in 1960. That was the most successful run enjoyed by any post-war England side before the advent of Will Carling and Co., and the massive contribution of the two second rows cannot be overestimated.

Whereas David Marques's domain was aerial combat, John was the unflinching Mr Fix-it who ensured that the ball was recycled neatly at the mauls, although he was perfectly capable of holding his own at the line-out too. There was also an inscrutable look about John which effectively discouraged opposition upstarts from mixing it anywhere in his vicinity.

Not surprisingly for a cricketer good enough to play for Somerset, John was well-co-ordinated for a forward of the 1950s. He was athletic, and an accurate handler who would easily have suited the needs of modern-day forward play. He was also that rare bird, a lock who could place-kick. Indeed, in his first season in the England team, he shared the goal-kicking duties with Fenwick Allison, the full-back.

John was a Clifton-born Bristolian whose varied business career took him to clubs as far afield as Newcastle Northern and West of Scotland. But he eventually returned to Harlequins as a committee man in the 1980s, when he and his family finally settled in Buckinghamshire. Undoubtedly, it was his vision as an administrator that transformed the Quins into a force when the Courage League Championship began, and the changes he set in motion at the club arguably helped lay the foundation for the recent pre-eminence enjoyed by the English national side. John died suddenly in December 1990.

Wade DOOLEY

(Preston Grasshoppers, Fylde)

'Wade who?' they said when he won his first cap at twenty-seven in 1985. The big 6ft 8in Blackpool policeman had played only twenty minutes of representative football (for the North against Romania) before he answered England's call. Wade must be one of the few players to attract the critics' eyes for an action which occurred off the field: while on the replacements' bench that day for the North, he made light work of cleanly catching a kick into touch. Then he came on in place of Jim Syddall in the second half, and made the pundits and selectors sit up even further and take note of his height, mobility and line-out presence.

He proved to be the middle-of-the-line jumper England had badly needed since 1982, and he went on to dominate his country's second row until announcing his retirement at the end of the 1993 season.

The distinguished career of the man they called the Blackpool Tower brought him fifty-five caps in nine seasons. From small acorns great oaks grow, and Wade, though never small, planted strong roots when he first became part of the international set-up. In one respect he was a throwback, a reminder of the days when England teams were drawn from a club rugby circuit which was completely without structure. For he came from a minor club (Preston Grasshoppers) whose last England international player had been capped before the First World War.

That never bothered big Wade. He realised that the pace of international rugby was several gears up from the relative frolics of the Grasshoppers, and he set himself a tough training schedule to keep fit enough for the duties England expected him to perform. That determination was the characteristic that enabled him to keep his England place despite strong opposition early in his career. And the determination became the hallmark of the man.

How was it, for instance, that he managed to step up his game from the fourth division one Saturday to international standard the next? Sheer willpower, that's how. And a healthy competitive edge which never entertained the possibility of personal or collective failure. At times, mind, that aspect of his personality was his undoing. Never one to mix it with opponents unless

Mike Teague, Nigel Heslop, Brian Moore (No 2), Wade Dooley, and Jason Leonard pause for breath.

provoked, he was no shrinking violet when it came to defending himself and, at Cardiff in 1987, his act of reprisal early in a bruising encounter earned him a match suspension together with three other England colleagues.

Putting such incidents behind him, Wade held his place thereafter and, by the time Geoff Cooke began assembling his team of all the talents, the big lock was part of the nucleus of quiet, hard men who gave inspiration to the newcomers in the side. During the years of the back-to-back Grand Slams, Wade's line-out jumping was a key element in England's success. He usually took forty minutes to set his sights, but invariably cleaned out opponents with his second-half performances to provide the vital platform for victory.

In 1993, both he and England struggled under the new laws, but one of the most revealing statistics of recent times is that, between the Wales match of 1985 and the 1993 Calcutta Cup match, England were never beaten for line-out possession in the Five Nations tournament. No fancy epitaph could sum up more effectively Wade Dooley's contribution to English rugby.

Dooley contests a line-out with Donal Lenihan of Ireland.

Eric EVANS
(Sale)

There is always a tendency to put the heroes of the past on pedestals. But now, nearly forty years since his heyday, the mention of Eric Evans's name still evokes fond memories in the minds of his former playing colleagues - fair testimony to the regard in which one of England's most inspiring and successful leaders was held. Truth to tell, it was Eric who welded his England team-mates into a side which dominated the Five Nations championship in the late 1950s.

Eric made his England debut as a prop against the 1948 Wallabies, but his appearances in the international jersey were few and far between in the six seasons that followed. He twice broke his arm and sometimes fell foul of fickle selection policy. By 1950, he had made the transition to hooker, immediately earning respect as one of the best technical exponents of his art. But while players and critics alike regularly lobbied for his England inclusion, he was often inexplicably overlooked by the selection committee.

One of Eric's harshest critics was his father, who once chided him after a Twickenham international early in his career for not being fit. As a qualified PE expert, Eric appreciated the importance of physical fitness more than most and took himself off to Old Trafford, home of the Busby Babes and Manchester United, the team he had supported as a boy at Audenshaw Grammar School. Eric began training with the soccer professionals and raised his stamina to levels that would not look out of place in today's demanding regimes. He was even invited to take charge of the fitness sessions at Old Trafford.

His finest hour began somewhat unpromisingly in December 1955. In those days it was the custom of the RFU to hold three trials, culminating in a match between England and the Rest, prior to the Five Nations tournament. Eric, finding himself installed as captain of the junior side, wrote to those selected to play under him. He implored them to abstain from the festivities of the Christmas season which fell before the final trial, and put positive thoughts into their minds by indicating that the shortest route to selection for the internationals would be for the Rest to win the match. They did - by 20-3 - and Eric was duly promoted, aged thirty-four, to captain an England team containing ten new caps with nine players from the successful Rest side.

His enthusiasm rubbed off on his charges, and the players he had carried into the international side developed the greatest affection and respect for Eric. He set them high standards with his own personal fitness and forged the entire team,

Eric Evans (front row, second left) as a member of Bob Stirling's England team AO Lewis, DS Wilson, CE Winn, PD Young, N Gibbs, VH Leadbetter, JE Wood

both forwards and backs, into a formidable unit with a common purpose: to win. It was said that the England sides of the late 1950s would die for Eric Evans.

Defeat by Wales was the result of the first England match in which Eric was captain. But the team, showing minor alterations, came good in its next assignment, thrashing Ireland 20-0 with a dazzling second-half display to mark the beginning of a triumphant march through twelve games which produced only one England defeat.

Eric's team won the Grand Slam in 1957 and, in 1958, when he was considered too old to play for Lancashire, he led England to another championship title before retiring at the age of thirty-seven. Revered for his strength of character, discipline and,above all, fitness, he ranks as one of the most inspiring England captains of modern times.

ue Crown winners who shared the championship with Wales and France. Back: JM Kendall-Carpenter, uinn. Front: JE Williams, E Evans, DL Sanders, RV Stirling, M Regan, J Butterfield.

Jeremy GUSCOTT
(Bath)

British rugby can boast of an embarrassment of riches nowadays when it comes to selecting centre threequarters. Will Carling, Scott Hastings and Scott Gibbs have all made impressive marks on modern Five Nations championships, but the player whose vision and silky skills place him streets ahead of his rivals in the outside-centre position is the Bath player who has been a permanent fixture in England's international side since 1989, Jeremy Guscott.

One of the rare birds who has flown steadily from mini-rugby as an Under-7 through the various age-groupings to senior rugby, Jerry is the most exciting talent in British rugby today. Although he lags slightly behind Will Carling in his overall centre play, he has no superior as an attacker when given space in which to manoeuvre. He runs, passes and kicks exquisitely, but it is the clear-cut breaks that rip defences apart which have thrilled the Twickenham crowds and set up numerous tries, particularly for Rory Underwood, in England's recent honour-laden seasons.

In the course of his progress through the rugby ranks, he has become the target of Rugby League scouts (he has reputedly turned down offers worth nearly a million pounds) and an attraction for feature writers from *Rugby World and Post* to *GQ* magazine. It is said that all talented sportsmen need an arrogance in order to shine on the fields of their chosen game. Certainly, Jerry Guscott the rugby player strikes the onlooker as a confident exponent of his art, but the myth has grown up that he has the same arrogant persona off the field as well. Not so: he admits to having been an awkward cuss as an adolescent, but his lifelong association with Bath has provided him with role-models to enable him to work out the happy character balance between successful player and easy-going family man with a steady job working as an executive for British Gas.

Balance has also been the secret of his playing success. Some of his bursts through crowded defences have defied belief, and a recent strength has been his ability to deliver a pass of textbook rectitude without any perceptible loss of momentum - an extremely difficult skill for any player to execute when careering towards the opponents' try-line.

Jerry is now in his prime and, provided he remains tone-deaf to the overtures of Rugby League, he will continue to be an integral part of England's long-term plans. To date, his record is impressive. There have been twenty-eight full appearances for England; a partnership with Will Carling extending to twenty-seven matches, just one short of the world record set by the Scottish centres, Scott Hastings and Sean Lineen; and a total of sixteen tries, putting him in third place behind Rory Underwood (thirty-six) and Cyril Lowe (eighteen) on the list of England try-scorers. There have also been a couple of drop-goals to his name, one with each foot.

Finally, no reference to Jeremy would be complete without mention of his iron will to succeed as a Rugby Union footballer. If Geoff Cooke has achieved one thing more than any of his many predecessors as coach or selector, it is in imbuing his squads with a ruthless determination to win - a characteristic which, it is amazing to note, has not always been apparent in the spirit of past England XVs. Jerry's resolution has manifested itself in the vast improvement in his tackling since he joined the England set-up. He has stepped up his commitment to training during the past four years and now brings a much greater physical presence to his country's midfield. His shatter-proof defence will be an important foundation on which England will rebuild their international challenge in the coming seasons.

Jeremy Guscott.

Dusty HARE
(Nottingham, Leicester)

A chief accountant was needed to keep the records of Dusty Hare's points-scoring in order. The little Midlands full-back was the most prolific scorer in the history of the game and, even when he retired, statisticians differed with their final calculations of Dusty's total in all first-class matches. Suffice to say his tally lies somewhere between 7000 and 8000 points, no mean feat for any last line, especially one whose tackling and defence were a little short of the standards shown by Alastair Hignell, Peter Rossborough and Marcus Rose, three leading players of the day who challenged Dusty for the No. 15 shirt in the England side.

Yet behind attacking backs, a well-organised drift defence and dominant forwards, Dusty was the ideal goal-kicking full-back, a man who could win matches with place-kicks or drop-shots from anywhere inside opponents' halves. He had a metronomic action and, when he addressed the ball for an attempt at goal, his body language bore the mark of a confident player expecting to score more points for his side.

William Henry Hare (the nickname was a result of his speckled bare head and was bestowed on him by his father at birth) began his first-class career at Nottingham, whom he joined from Newark where the Hare family farm is situated. His consistent form as a kicker, plus a penchant for joining the threequarter line in attack, made England's selectors sit up and take notice of him in 1974, when he won his first cap in a winning side against Wales at Twickenham.

Dusty did little wrong, collected a hatful of points later in the year when the England Under-23 XV met the Tongans, but then found himself in the international wilderness for the next four years. Although recalled in 1978 and playing tidy matches against France and

Dusty Hare begins a counter-attack with Peter Squires in the background.

the All Blacks, he was again stood down, this time in favour of his young rival, Alastair Hignell.

But the man who was destined to make as many international comebacks as Dame Nellie Melba returned in 1979-80 for a lead role in England's first Grand Slam saga for twenty-three years. Everything went right for him that season, and his haul of 34 points gave his colleagues the cushion to launch adventurous attacks in the matches with Ireland, France and Scotland. Nevertheless, it was the vital last-minute penalty against Wales from the right touchline at Twickenham which counted as Dusty's most precious contribution. The kick enabled England to snatch a 9-8 victory from the jaws of defeat against their strongest Five Nations challengers.

Dusty was in and out of the national side several more times before announcing his retirement from international rugby after an uninspiring tour to South Africa in 1984. Dusty felt that his family and farm commitments were too pressing for him to continue to sacrifice so much time to the squad training that membership of the England team entailed. Yet he happily maintained his links with Leicester, whom he had joined from Nottingham in 1976, and continued accumulating points until bowing out after the 1989 Pilkington Cup final at Twickenham. England had failed to find a reliable goal-kicking successor who could overcome Dusty Hare's record-breaking full-back act: 240 points in twenty-five matches.

Peter JACKSON
(Coventry)

Facing Peter Jackson on the rugby field was a bit like trying to mark the Invisible Man. For a start, Peter's wan complexion in the all-white garb of England gave him an almost ghostly appearance, while his elusive running left defenders clutching at thin air as he spirited himself into the clear. His was a now-you-see-him, now-you-don't act.

Peter was the most exciting England winger since the days of Obolensky. Like the famous flying Russian prince, he could tear defences apart with his unorthodox style, and he had a particularly lethal cut-in which invariably wrong-footed his opponents. The only criticism one could lay at his door was that, quite often, his unpredictability bamboozled even his own playing colleagues. If he cut inside off his favoured right wing, there was no way of telling which way he would veer next. He was equally likely to thread his way across the field to score at the left corner flag as under the posts, or even at the right corner-flag. Beating players came instinctively to him.

Peter was no spring chicken when he entered the England team in 1956, six years after his first trial. He eventually took his chance as one of the 'possibles' in a team led by Eric Evans in the final England trial in January of that year. He was on the winning side, the juniors thrashing the established men 20-3, and was promoted to the England team to face Wales at Twickenham a couple of weeks later.

There were ten new caps in that England XV, and Wales won 8-3, with Peter's opposite number scoring a try. But he conceded only one more touchdown to an opponent in nineteen more internationals, and the next game, against Ireland, brought him the first of his six tries for his country. With the England forwards dominating the set-pieces, the backs had a field day, passing and running with gay abandon. Peter put in several dazzling runs, but it was simply his pace which brought England's first try of the match after a break by Jeff Butterfield.

England won the Grand Slam in 1957, by which time Peter had become firmly established in the side. Against Wales it was his strong defence, seen in a series of careful tackles, which saw him singled out for praise, while it was clear that his reputation as a tricky runner had marched ahead of him. His opposite number quite rightly ensured that Peter had as little room as possible in which to manoeuvre, but overstepped the mark fatally once in the first half: trying to close Peter down at a line-out, the Welshman was caught offside, and England's full-back kicked the only points of the match. Next, Peter's weaving, swerving run brought him the game's only try in Dublin. Then a side-step which sent a would-be tackler the wrong way enabled him to wriggle over at the corner for the opening try against France, and his pace gave him a clear run-in for a vital second try in the same match.

He continued to cast spells on his adversaries to help England to the championship title in 1958 and set off for Australasia with the Lions in 1959. There he was pure box-office. The New Zealand public raved about his elusive running and rolled out the red carpet for him at the end of a tour which brought him nineteen tries.

Yet, within three months, that same carpet was threadbare. He lost his place in the England side and made only one more international appearance in three seasons before returning, at thirty-two, to play in the side which won the Five Nations title in 1963. Although he did not score that year, he did make the running in Cardiff for a spectacular try by Malcolm Phillips in what was destined to be England's last win in Wales for twenty-eight years

Peter Jackson in 1963.

Dickie JEEPS
(Northampton)

On the rugby field, Dickie Jeeps was the busybody type of scrum-half every pack loves to have aboard. He never hesitated to stick his oar into the tide of forwards bearing down on him, whether at scrum, line-out or maul, and he made life hell for his adversaries. Jeeps's name became a byword for courage and tenacity and, between 1956 and 1962, he played twenty-four times for England before retiring as his country's most-capped scrum-half.

One of the small band of players who achieved Lions honours before appearing for England, Dickie won his spurs in South Africa with the 1955 tourists. Selected as the third scrum-half, it was to everybody's surprise that he won promotion to the Test side to partner Cliff Morgan. There was nothing fancy about Dickie's passing; that was why he got the Test job. He understood the importance of delivering quick ball to his fly-half. That was just what the Welshman wanted, and the Morgan-Jeeps alliance was the catalyst that brought the Lions an historic share of the spoils with the Springboks.

Yet when he returned to Britain for his first England cap in 1956, Dickie failed to click on his international debut and was hastily discarded in favour of Johnny Williams, the scrum-half who had understudied him in South Africa. Twelve months later, however, he was finally installed at the heels of a Grand Slam pack. The immaculate service he provided from the base of the scrum was of the type that most fly-halves dream about: fast and accurate. The late 1950s were a time of tight man-to-man marking in which defence usually triumphed against offence. But Dickie's tempting passes, just in front of the player so that the ball could be taken on the move, helped the England fly-half, Ricky Bartlett, to unlock tight defences and pave the way for his back division to run in the tries.

It was against Scotland at Twickenham in the 1957 Grand Slam match that

Dickie had the critics singing his praises. His short, sharp passes (his service was never noted for its length) were the source of his side's three tries, although it was his heroic defence when Scotland threw everything bar the kitchen sink at England in the first half that really impressed the experts. Dickie was their unanimous choice as player-of-the-season, and his exploits in another England championship year in 1958 were just as vital to his country's unbeaten run.

In 1960, after a successful tour of New Zealand with the Lions, he was appointed England skipper, a job he carried out with distinction for three seasons. It is a well-worn cliché to say that a player leads by example, but the phrase was particularly apt to his style of captaincy. No player tackled more resolutely than Dickie or displayed such second sight when covering; no man shrugged off with less fuss the hammerings he suffered. His courage rubbed off on others, and the tough little guy had the pleasure of leading England to the Triple Crown in his first season in charge.

Off the field, Dickie showed all the resilience and energy which made him into a star in the rugby firmament. An apple-farmer from the Fens borders, he served the RFU as selector and president, was a local county councillor and JP, and even did a stint as chairman of the Sports Council.

His international career ended in 1962 where it had started - in South Africa with the Lions. Soon afterwards, a Transvaal horse owner, who respected the Englishman, named a racehorse after Dickie. The horse, by all accounts, was a frequent winner - just like his namesake.

Dickie Jeeps fends off Jean de Gregorio (No 2) and Alfred Roques (No 3) at the front of a line-out at Stade Colombes in 1962.

Brian MOORE

(Nottingham, Harlequins

Hatred - hatred of losing, that is - has become the driving force behind Brian Moore, the hooker whose tough-mindedness and all-round skills have epitomised the new breed of England forward. Gone forever are the play-up, play-up-and-play-the-game days of not so long ago. Now England rugby teams perform with a ruthless efficiency which would have been difficult to imagine even five years ago. It is thanks to men such as Brian Moore, who play hard but strictly within the laws, that England have enjoyed such a sustained winning streak in the 1990s.

Brian was brought up in Yorkshire and, during his schooldays at Crossley and Porter Grammar School in Halifax, he showed youthful signs of the mental toughness and rugby ability that were to enable him to become the most-capped England hooker in the history of the game. He graduated first in law at Nottingham University and then into first-class rugby with the town's club.

Early representative honours were won with the England Students and Under-23 teams. He captained England B against Italy in 1985, and was called up for his first full cap in 1987 when Bath's Graham Dawe was dropped for disciplinary reasons after an ugly match against Wales at Cardiff.

Brian made an impressive mark in a remodelled England side which won that year's Calcutta Cup and, even in his debut match, the importance of winning was apparent in his approach. One sensed that to surrender a strike against the head, or to see the enemy steal a line-out against his throw, would have been a painful loss to Brian. It was no surprise then that his hooking technique compared favourably with his opponent, Colin Deans; and the line-out statistics for that match showed that England led by 20-4 in clean takes during the first half. Brian has never looked back since.

His role in England's recent resurgence has been a significant one. Will Carling has been the very public figurehead of the national team by reason of his captaincy; but make no mistake, Brian's contribution to the Grand Slam glory has been immense. Dominance up front has been the platform for England's successes, and Brian has been the catalyst who has whipped the tight forwards into a unit capable of subduing any pack in the world. For sheer energy and commitment, it would be difficult to nominate a superior. At critical moments in matches he is the player who has held the pack together, leading by disciplined example and exhorting his colleagues with a thoughtful mix of encouragement and advice.

Moreover, he has managed to keep his unquenchable thirst for success in perspective. After England were surprisingly and unluckily beaten by Wales in Cardiff in February 1993 - their first championship defeat in ten matches - Brian's generosity and sporting gestures were admired by Welsh players and critics alike.

Now thirty-one and a senior England squad member, 'Old Moore' has no intention of writing the last page of his rugby almanac yet. English spectators can be sure that, fitness permitting, he will return from the 1993 Lions tour as determined as ever to snap his country's forwards into a championship-winning outfit.

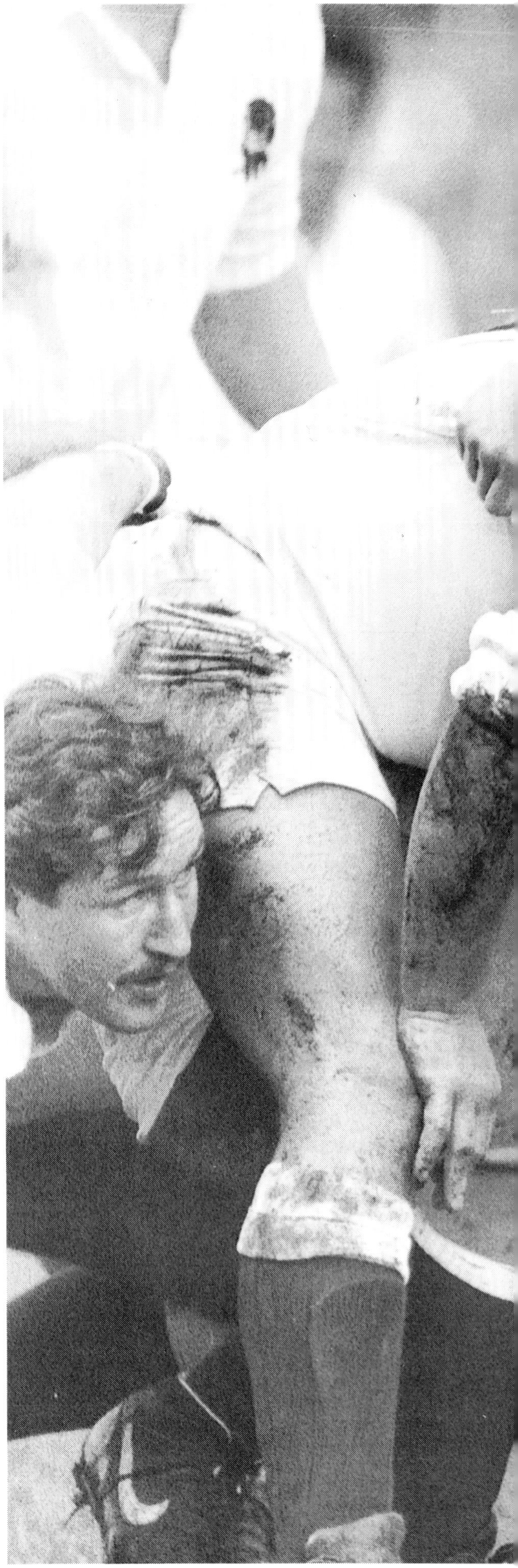

The England front row against Ireland, 1991: Brian Moore flanked by Jeff Probyn and Jason Leonard. Moore's tough-minded commitment has whipped the tight forwards into a unit capable of subduing any pack in the world.

Malcolm PHILLIPS
(Oxford U, Fylde)

They also serve who make tries for wing threequarters, and Malcolm Phillips, an England centre in the honours-winning sides of 1958, 1960 and 1963, was such an unsung hero whose straight running and strong bursts set up numerous tries for his fellow backs. Wingers love playing outside unselfish footballers who can give carefully-weighted passes that are perfectly timed, and Malcolm was the player with whom the England wingers of the late 1950s and early 1960s most wanted to play.

Well coached at Arnold School, Blackpool, by the former Lancashire centre Bill Howarth, Malcolm loomed large in Peter Robbins's Oxford side which won the 1957 university match. Within two months of that event, he was in the England side, making his debut in the match against Australia. Not only did he score a try himself from an outside break, but he also gave Peter Jackson the pass which sent the right wing heading for a famous last-minute touchdown in the south-west corner at Twickenham.

After such an auspicious start, a bright future was predicted for him, and he soon showed that his debut performance was no flash in the pan. In Paris one month later, he was a constant thorn in the side of a poor French back division. Malcolm was always at his best when given plenty of room in which to operate and, in fine conditions at the Stade Colombes, he was virtually awarded the freedom of the city to make any number of scything runs, two of which led to first-half tries for Peter Thompson.

England became champions in 1958, and Malcolm looked set for a long stay as one of the basic elements of a side which required rebuilding after Eric Evans and Jeff Butterfield retired in 1958 and 1959 respectively. Once again, Malcolm delivered when England expected.

The 1960 season belonged to Richard Sharp and England, but the quiet authority of Malcolm Phillips (now the Oxford University captain) was the linchpin of a relatively inexperienced England back line containing four new caps. Having played inside Sharp for a term at Oxford, Malcolm had developed a good understanding with the new fly-half, whose unpredictability in attack could otherwise have been a drawback for a centre unused to Sharp's exciting style of offensive play. But Malcolm showed no sign of loss of pace and he adapted carefully to complement his fly-half. His lightning dart set up the winning try for David Marques against Ireland; his decoy run in Paris drew attention away from Mike Weston, his co-centre, who scored an important try against France; and it was Phillips the creator (this time for right wing John Young) who had a loud say in England's last try of the Triple Crown and Calcutta Cup win at Murrayfield.

He was unfairly made a scapegoat for England's narrow defeat in a fast, open game at Cardiff in 1961, and it took him two years to regain his place in the centre. But when he did, he showed that all the guile and speed of his youth were still there in abundance. In a never-to-be-forgotten win in Cardiff in 1963, his double-act with Peter Jackson culminated in his scoring a spectacular try in a victory destined to be England's last in Wales for twenty-eight years.

He was an ever-present in that 1963 championship-winning team and bowed out of international rugby after gracing the England side for one more season. Nowadays he is still enjoying the game as a respected administrator at his former club, Fylde.

Both Malcolm Phillips and Peter Robbins were in the England XV which shared the title with France, 1960. Standing: Mr JAS Taylor, J Roberts, MP Weston, RAW Sharp, TP Wright, RWD Marques, JD Currie, WGD Morgan, RE Syrett. Crouching: SAM Hodgson, MS Phillips, REG Jeeps, PGD Robbins, CR Jacobs. Front: JRC Young, D Rutherford.

Peter ROBBINS
(Oxford U, Coventry, Moseley)

Knocking over outside-halves with hard, fair tackles was second nature to Peter Robbins, the out-and-out flanker who specialised on the open side of the England packs which dominated the Five Nations championship in 1957, 1958 and 1960.

An Oxford graduate, Peter was the perfect example of the 'banging' type of forward: he tackled like a thunderbolt and covered the ground with lightning pace. And it was while he was at Oxford that he first lined up for England, against Wales in 1956. Under Eric Evans's broad wing, Peter was one of ten new brooms brought in that year, many of whom, Peter included, survived to take part in a clean sweep of the Five Nations in 1957, a season which found the flanker at the peak of his powers.

Quite apart from his speed and strength in the tackle, Peter was a canny wing-forward who lured attackers into his web with subtle changes of pace. His methods were difficult to appreciate from ground level on the terraces, but watching from the lofty heights of Twickenham's stands it was clear that his track from the side of the scrummage was a complex curve of pursuit. He had the ability to change direction according to the velocity of his target and, as a result, he rarely overran his opponent in the way that less talented flankers who made beelines for attackers were prone to do. Like the Mounties, Peter always got his man.

Just look at the England record during their 1957 Grand Slam, their 1958 outright championship and their 1960 Triple Crown. In the twelve Five Nations matches of those three seasons (Peter was controversially dropped in 1959 when England achieved nothing), England's opponents scored just three tries. That statistic speaks volumes for the effective defensive work of the team, and of their flankers in particular.

One criticism that was levelled at Peter's play was that he did not push in scrums. For this reason he was overlooked for the 1959 matches, while palpably inferior players were promoted ahead of him. Yet 1959 was a Lions year, with the top thirty players from the Home Unions due to tour Australasia and, despite the accusations of his own selectors, Peter was considered too valuable to be left out of the party. Alas, however, he fractured his leg at Easter while touring with the Barbarians, and the coveted Lions jersey - unlike 99 per cent of his opponents - escaped him - as did the captaincy of England.

In 1957, his tactical awareness had been illuminated during his second year as skipper of Oxford. He transformed a mediocre side into one of the fittest teams ever fielded by the university, and his clever rugby brain enabled the Dark Blues to outwit a much-fancied Cambridge team. After that, critics canvassed him as a future England leader.

But the position was never offered to him and, in 1961, when a young Bedford open-side flanker named 'Budge' Rogers was drafted into the England back row, Peter's international career was virtually over. Almost certainly, he sensed it too. He made a switch to blind-side, and there was even a spell at No. 8 when new laws changing the offside lines at set-pieces were introduced in 1964. But his cap tally stuck at nineteen, a figure that was probably the same number short of the England appearances many experts believe he should have made.

An Oxford modern linguist, schoolmaster, rugby journalist, bon viveur, practical joker . . . there was no end to the list of his talents and activities. And, not surprisingly, his premature death at the age of fifty-three in 1987 brought sorrow to the considerable number of friends and acquaintances whose lives were touched by the boundless energy of Peter Robbins.

Budge ROGERS
(Bedford)

One story told about Budge Rogers illustrates the enthusiasm and dedication he brought to the game. Early in his career, he was criticised for being a decidedly one-footed player. Typically, the young Rogers set to work on his left foot to eradicate any deficiencies in his basic skills. The result? He became equally adept at kicking with either foot.

That approach was characteristic of his determination to become a successful rugby player. He had converted from scrum-half to open-side flanker as a teenager at Bedford School, modelling his game on Peter Robbins, his rugby hero. At the age of eighteen Budge was playing representative rugby for the East Midlands; he was still in his teens when he was invited to play in his first England trial and, in 1961, he replaced Robbins in the national side, scoring a debut try in Dublin when he charged down a kick by the Irish fly-half.

For the next four years, he was England's automatic choice as open-side, quickly gaining a reputation as one of the most destructive flankers in British rugby. For fitness and stamina he had no equal, his speed carrying him into those parts of the field which lesser back-row men could not reach.

'Death to the fly-half' was his motto, and he successfully blotted out the best the Home Unions and France could field in the Five Nations tournament. During his first three seasons in the championship, England conceded only one try through the backs - an extraordinary statistic which bears testimony to his exceptional talent as a snuffer-out of attacks. Arguably, home spectators witnessed him at his best in 1963, when England won the championship title outright. That season he was a key figure, terrifying fly-halves and bottling up the threats from flankers and scrum-halves on the fringes of the loose and tight.

Significant changes to the laws, designed to take the sting out of the activities of loose forwards, came into force in the mid-1960s and Budge temporarily lost some of his edge. He had been an expert at breaking full-pelt off the side of scrums and rucks to catch opposition fly-halves, but the revised laws decreed that flankers had to remain

Budge Rogers.

bound on to the set-piece until the ball emerged. Flankers had to reassess their tactics, and Budge (the nickname his grandmother coined when he was a baby) effectively transformed his game. True, he continued to harry opponents with all his old verve, but there was now a subtle difference to his lines of attack: instead of the beeline course which had been so devastating under the old laws, he adopted a drift approach which forced the fly-half to move or pass sideways. Of course, he continued to chop men down with hard tackles if a break was attempted, but more often than not he was best seen backing up colleagues who made tackles in midfield. For Budge was still invariably first to the breakdown and now built a new reputation as a constructive player who was an invaluable asset in setting up second-phase ball.

His distinguished England career ended in 1969 when he broke Wavell Wakefield's forty-year-old England cap record. Undoubtedly his country's player of the 1960s, Derek Prior Rogers's unselfish contribution to the game was recognised at the end of the decade when he became the first Englishman to be awarded the OBE for services to rugby. The honour was well deserved.

Richard SHARP

(Oxford U, Wasps, Bristol)

Richard Sharp's champions, 1963. Standing: Mr HB Laidlaw, DC Manley, BA Dovey, Seated: MP Weston, J Roberts, PB Jackson, RAW Sharp (captain), MS Phillips

At 4pm on the grey, dry afternoon of Saturday 16 January 1960, Welsh rugby men could be neatly partitioned into three subsets. If you were a Welsh international rugby player (particularly a back-row man), you were crying in your dressing-room. If you were an adult Welsh rugby follower, you were crying into your beer. And if you were a rugby-mad Welsh boy, you were just crying.

The cause of enough tears to end forever the fear of summer droughts in Wales was one Richard Sharp, the blond, leggy Oxford outside-half who had run rings around a bedraggled Welsh team containing seven of the 1959 Lions. He had entered the England side as an eleventh-hour stand-in for Bev Risman, another distinguished Lion, who had had to withdraw owing to a leg injury. Sharp wasn't even listed in the programme, yet his brilliant attacking play had every Fleet Street rugby journalist raving over his performance, and his name was printed in banner headlines in the Sunday and Monday newspapers.

Exceptionally tall for an outside-half, Richard constantly had the Wales back row and defence at sixes-and-sevens. His adventurous running and audacious breaks were a breath of fresh air to England rugby, which had been so stilted in 1959 that, for the only time in the history of the Five Nations championship, England had failed to register a single try.

Yet within forty minutes of becoming an international player, Richard had carved out several openings for his threequarters, and England's left wing had scored two splendid tries. England went on to win 14-6 - a hammering when low scoring was the norm in international rugby - and Richard kept his place in a side which was, uniquely, unchanged throughout a Triple Crown-winning season.

What set Richard apart as an outside-half was his predilection for taking risks. He had received a sound grounding in the game's basics at Blundell's School in Devon, where his mentor was the former England full-back, Grahame Parker. Parker had encouraged the schoolboy to attack and to enjoy his rugby. The pleasure Richard derived from the game was clear to see, and his uncomplicated style brought equal joy to those who savoured rugby played with a touch of panache.

But the dash he brought to the international matches of 1960 created difficult problems for him in the seasons that followed. England expected him to ignite the back division every time he played, and opponents, mindful of his offensive potential, singled him out for close marking. Twice in 1962, he was the victim of particularly heavy tackling. After a characteristically virtuoso Sharp performance in a 16-0 win against Ireland, the French mercilessly took him out of the game in Paris a fortnight later, their cruel treatment preventing him from playing against Scotland. Then, in South Africa with the Lions, he was the target of a high, late tackle in which he sustained a fractured cheekbone.

But he returned for his

s, JE Owen, BJ Wightman, NJ Drake-Lee, MF Turner.
rs, JD Thorne. Front: SJS Clarke, JG Willcox.

last Five Nations season in 1963 and captained England to a rare victory in Cardiff on their way to winning the championship title. His unpredictable genius for setting up flowing movements caused no end of anxiety for harassed defenders, and it was a typical piece of Sharp magic which rounded off the season and helped England to win the championship. Against Scotland he scored one of Twickenham's five-star tries, running diagonally from a scrum near the right touchline before dummying his way past three Scotsmen for a vital touchdown.

He retired at twenty-seven, although he made a fleeting but unsuccessful comeback a couple of seasons later. In thirteen Five Nations matches, Richard was on the losing side twice, four games were drawn, and a handsome seven were won. That record speaks for itself.

Bob STIRLING
(RAF, Leicester, Wasps)

Industrious was the word critics used to describe the old-fashioned virtues of strength and commitment possessed by Bob Stirling, England's prop in the first half of the 1950s. Had not the demands of service life disrupted the early part of his rugby career, he would almost certainly have doubled the number of caps he won for England. And who knows what levels of greatness he might have achieved with a longer commission of international duty?

As it was, Bob did not win a place in the England scrum until 1951. He was then 31 and had a distinguished service record behind him, having joined the RAF at Halton as an apprentice in 1935 after leaving Nether Edge Grammar School in Sheffield. For most of the Second World War he was stationed in India, and it was not until 1947 that he was permanently posted back to Britain, where he joined the Leicester Tigers. His first sporting honours had been won as a heavyweight boxer representing the RAF between 1948 and 1950, but a seminal meeting with George Beamish, the former Irish rugby international, Leicester stalwart and RAF bigwig, set Bob on the trail of an international rugby career.

With the blessing of the Leicester club selectors, Beamish persuaded Bob to transfer from the second row to prop. The move was an instant success. Bob was too short at 5ft 10in to progress in first-class rugby as a lock, but he had the ideal build to make his presence felt in the front row.

Called for his first England trial at Otley in December 1950, Bob made his international debut a month later in a team which was overwhelmed by a much-praised Welsh side at Swansea. England suffered two further defeats that year before overcoming Scotland 5-3 at Twickenham, a victory in which the home side's front row, comprising Stirling, Eric Evans and Wally Holmes, were singled out for special commendation - a rare plaudit for tight scrummagers in those days.

Bob was rarely prominent in the loose; indeed, it was widely held that he would not know what to do if given a pass in the open, but his ruggedness in the tight was the cornerstone of his country's forward play in the next three seasons. Together with Eric Evans, he formed the nucleus of the pack which carried England to the runners-up spot in the 1952 championship and to the Five Nations title in 1953.

Although Bob Stirling did not get into the England team until he was thirty-one, he went on to captain the side which three years later took the Triple Crown.

An RAF transfer brought him south during the 1953 close season, and he joined Peter Yarranton and several other RAF players at Wasps, where the average age of the 1st XV was only twenty-two. Yet Bob blended in perfectly with the youngsters and finished his England days on a high note, captaining a side which won the Triple Crown and shared the 1954 championship with Wales and France.

That was a fitting way for the modest, moustachioed man who knew his technical limitations to wind up a worthy career which had brought him eighteen consecutive caps. Certainly, no England captain better deserved a Triple Crown as a parting gift than Bob Stirling.

Rory UNDERWOOD
(Leicester, RAF)

Rory Underwood finishing off a threequarter move with a surge of pace and a dash for the corner has become a regular sight during England's recent run of success in the International championship. Time and again, Rory has turned a match England's way with his instinctive genius for popping up in the right place at the right time to take a vital pass.

Witness the twenty-five-metre run after a switch with Simon Hodgkinson in Dublin in 1991. England were trailing 6-7 with eight minutes to go when Rory launched himself at a packed defence and somehow spirited his way past would-be tacklers to score a near-impossible try. Those were probably the most important 4 points of an England revival which had started in 1988 under Geoff Cooke's management and Will Carling's captaincy. For, after they had narrowly failed to win honours in both 1989 and 1990, Rory's touchdown secured England's hold on the Triple Crown and brought within reach their first Grand Slam for eleven years.

Then another typical Underwood try, this time against France at Twickenham a fortnight later, paved the way for the Grand Slam. England had their backs against the wall when, on the half-hour, Rory took a pass from Hodgkinson after Dean Richards and Mike Teague had led a forward drive deep into French territory . Rory left Jean-Baptiste Lafond, no slouch himself, standing as he swerved outside the Frenchman to score wide out on the left. If you were to ask the pillars of that England Grand Slam side - Wade Dooley, Peter Winterbottom, Brian Moore, Uncle Jeff Probyn and all - to identify the instant when the years of struggling against criticism and disappointment suddenly became worthwhile, almost to a man they will point to one of Rory's many magic moments.

Rory has now completed his tenth consecutive season as an automatic choice on the England wing. At school at Barnard Castle in County Durham (where he was an exact contemporary of Rob Andrew), Rory displayed a precocious sporting talent that matured in the rugby colours of Yorkshire, the Northern Division and England B before he was awarded his first cap in 1984.

Down the years he has collected England rugby records with the quiet modesty that is the defining characteristic of rugby football heroes. To date he has collected sixty caps for England - more than any other player; and his thirty-six international tries place him top of the England honours board and third on the roll of the world's leading try-scorers. Although the small band of his detractors will harp on about his occasional and admittedly spectacular lapses in defence, the matches he has won for his country outnumber those where his errors have left something to be desired.

After announcing his international retirement in 1992, he revoked that decision later the same year

to line up for England against South Africa alongside his younger brother, Tony. Fittingly, it was Rory who provided the pass which created Tony's first international try, and playing in the same side as Underwood minor has given Underwood major (and the Underwoods' mum) obvious pleasure.

There were signs in the 1993 Calcutta Cup match that Rory is now enjoying a new lease of life, and his numerous admirers will hope that he scores plenty more tries in England's quest for future championship honours.

Rory Underwood arcs outside Ieuan Evans of Wales at Twickenham in 1992.

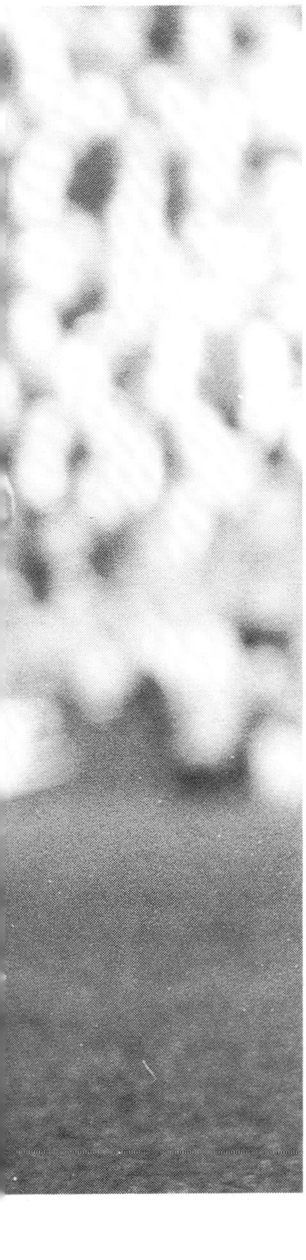

Peter WHEELER
(Leicester)

The world's top hookers who came eyeball-to-eyeball with him all agreed that Peter Wheeler was the best in the business between 1975 and 1984. He presided over his country's front row forty-one times during that period and was the man in the middle when England took their first Grand Slam for twenty-three years in 1980.

Yet, surprisingly, he was first called into the England side on the strength of his goal-kicking. Back in the early 1970s, he filled that role for his club, Leicester; but make no mistake, he had already shown that he had the makings of a first-rate No. 2.

Peter learnt the game at Brockley County School in south-east London (where he first played as hooker) and joined Leicester in 1969 when he was transferred to the town by his employers. He quickly established himself in the Tigers' first team and went on the Far East tour undertaken by the senior England squad in 1971. Caps did not immediately follow, however. While Peter honed his skills with a successful club side, he had his work cut out to supplant John Pullin as the England rake.

But the young pretender to Pullin's throne made a strong bid for international recognition in 1974. Always a livewire in the loose, Peter made front-row unions the length of the country sit up and take note when he scored a hat-trick of tries for the Barbarians against the East Midlands that season - an impressive display which was not wasted on the Lions' tour selectors,who put him on standby for the summer visit to South Africa. The following season, Peter leap-frogged Pullin to win his first cap against France at Twickenham, but a severe neck injury, sustained a fortnight later against Wales, allowed his Bristol rival to return to the side for the rest of the campaign and for the subsequent England tour of Australia.

By 1977, Peter was back in the national colours as first-choice hooker. A new determination gripped England's rugby at the start of the season, after several years of undistinguished performances in the Five Nations tournament. The talents of Peter Wheeler, a traditional right-footed hooker of the ball in the scrummage and an indefatigable mauler and rucker in the loose, were polished contributions to England's rehabilitation. 'Wheelbrace', as he was known, took his special ability on two Lions tours, in 1977 and 1980, after England's Grand Slam. It goes without saying that his all-round work was a mighty donation to a season in which England collected all of the silverware - tangible and intangible - that the Five Nations championship offers.

Peter should have gone on a third Lions trip in 1983, but Ciaran Fitzgerald (as captain) and Colin Deans were deemed more suited to the style of play preferred by the tour selectors. What poppycock - the Lions of 1983 had no style and, in the end, were to rue Peter's omission as they licked the wounds of a 0-4 mauling by the All Blacks.

For his final season in international rugby, Peter was rewarded with the richly-deserved honour of leading his nation. His captaincy began auspiciously with a win against the All Blacks, but the promise of that victory evaporated into thin air when three defeats followed in the championship. That was no fitting farewell for a player who was a credit to English rugby.

Peter Wheeler.

Peter WINTERBOTTOM
(Headingley, Harlequins)

If it moves,tackle it. That was the motto of Peter Winterbottom, the flaxen-haired flanker whose career spanned the years of decline which followed England's 1980 success until the golden era of the back-to-back Grand Slams in 1991 and 1992.

When he first came into the England side in January 1982, after a distinguished youth career with Rossall School and England Colts, Peter was known as 'the straw man' on account of his straight blond hair. But he was no man of straw - definitely not. He was a hard, super-fit specimen whose work on his uncle's farm complemented his rugby training and developed his upper-body strength.

In his first two seasons of international rugby, Peter acquired a reputation as an open-side who made an art of flattening opponents with vigorous tackles. He was hell-bent on winning possession, and anyone tracing his locus during the eighty minutes of an international match would rarely find him straying more than two or three metres from the ball while it was in play.

A formative summer spent in Hawke's Bay, New Zealand, in 1982 sharpened his aggressive defence, and it was no surprise when, one year later, he emerged from a disappointing Lions tour of a the same country as the stand-out British player of the visit. It was with remarkable foresight that the *New Zealand Rugby Almanack* concluded: 'This outstanding flanker seems assured of a long and meritorious career.' How right the editors were. Peter persisted thereafter with his 'strong man' game, based on an inner belief in his capacity to get the job done effectively without seeking praise. Despite periods of inactivity due to niggling injuries, he then experienced first-hand the phoenix-like rise of England's rugby from the ashes of despair in the mid-1980s to the heady heights of the early 1990s.

Peter's own adaptability to change was remarkable. He buckled down to the strict new training schedules set by the England team's advisers when Geoff Cooke became manager, and he comfortably made the transition from the cosy club atmosphere of Headingley to the slick city outfit at Harlequins, where he was twice appointed captain.

He was the rugby man who had seen it all and done it all. Apart from representing the Lions, Peter played provincial rugby in South Africa, New Zealand and Canada, and it was his experience, quiet demeanour and considerable achievements which filled his colleagues with respect when he returned to the international side in 1989-90 to take part in England rugby's most successful period of modern times. The hardness of his youth had not been altered by the passage of time, but it was now his contribution as a constructive flanker that made such a lasting impression on England's blueprint for success. Peter was the key player who invariably set up the rucks and mauls as the team went forward, providing the platform for second-phase possession which the backs used to score tries or dictate the tactical pattern of the match.

In 1993, he promised that he would retire from rugby after returning to New Zealand with Gavin Hastings's Lions. England's most-capped forward will be an extremely difficult act for anyone to follow.

For over ten years, until his retirement in 1993, Peter Winterbottom was one of England's key players.

SCOTLAND PLAYER PROFILES

Colin Deans.

Gary ARMSTRONG (Jedforest)

Comparisons, they say, are odious. But it was inevitable that Gary Armstrong should be compared with his predecessor at scrum-half in the Scotland side, Roy Laidlaw. Both Roy and Gary had similar border backgrounds and both played for the same club, Jedforest.

Yet Gary has become very much the axis of the Scottish side and, while Laidlaw certainly passed on many useful tips to his successor, few would argue that he played anything more than a secondary tactical role to John Rutherford during their long half-back partnership. By contrast, Gary Armstrong became the most complete scrum-half operating in the Five Nations championship. Tactically he played second fiddle to no one.

Gary entered the Scotland team in 1988 against the Wallabies when Ian McGeechan took over as national coach. He impressed immediately with his energetic breaks from the base of the scrum, and he formed an excellent working relationship with his back row. In fact, it has been Gary's ability to maintain the momentum of attacks by linking with his flankers, rather than the speed of his service to the backs, which has given Scotland's rugby a treasured extra dimension in offence since 1988. Moreover, his option-taking is shot through with class. Gary instinctively knows the right move to make at the right time - the talent of that *rara avis,* the player with perfect judgement.

He was Scotland's scrum-half in 1990 when, for the only time to date, Scotland fielded an unchanged side throughout the Five Nations season. If the gold medals for the Grand Slam that year were justifiably presented to the back row for their outstanding efforts, there were no doubts that Gary Armstrong deserved silver for his courageous deeds behind a winning pack.

His supreme effort came in the pulsating match with England in 1990. Throughout the campaign thus far England, who had accumulated 83 points in three games, had dictated tactically from half-back. Scotland had worked out an effective game plan to disrupt the English pack in the rucks and mauls and so cut off second-phase possession at its source, but equally damaging was Gary Armstrong's harassment of Richard Hill at the set scrums. Time and again the Scot put pressure on his opponent as England heeled the ball. Indeed, one of the crucial moments of the match for Scotland was a typical piece of aggressive defence by their scrum-half late in the match.

With England flexing every muscle in an all-out attempt to salvage the game, they won a scrum in a good attacking position deep in Scottish territory. Richard Hill was poised to launch his back line when Gary pounced, dispossessed the Englishman, and coolly thumped the ball into touch forty metres away. Legend has it that the Murrayfield roar that greeted that wonderful rescue act was heard as far away as Stornoway. The Scots sensed that Gary's kick was the final relieving action which lifted the siege and put their victory beyond doubt. It certainly did.

He has given great pleasure to neutral observers as well as to partisan Scots ever since. Injuries, however, in 1992 and 1993 restricted his opportunities to shine for Scotland and the Lions, and perhaps influenced his decision to give up his scrum-half role. After playing for his club at stand-off, there is still hope that Gary Armstrong may revert to his former outstanding position.

Peter BROWN (West of Scotland, Gala)

It is a long winter that brings no sunshine, and the winter of Scotland's longest rugby discontent lasted twenty-six years. After winning the Triple Crown in 1938, they had to wait until 1964 before winning their next championship honours. Even then they had to settle for a share of the spoils with Wales.

The willingness of Scotland's pack both to play a significant role in attack and to do their best to win their share of the set-piece ball was a definite plus in their bull run of 1964. Two new forwards, Peter Brown, whose father had been a soccer international goalkeeper, and flanker Jim Telfer were the important 'finds' of the season. Both were to have major parts in Scotland's championship challenge for several seasons, though only Brown survived to participate in the 1973 matches when Scotland were again joint champions.

Educated at Marr College, Troon, Peter graduated to the Scottish side via the West of Scotland club and the Glasgow District team. His physical appearance belied his ability. Long legs and long arms, allied to an ungainly gait, made Peter seem an improbable rugby footballer to critics who first cast their eyes over the 6ft 3in lock in 1964.

But his skills came as a revelation to the unsuspecting pressmen visiting Murrayfield that year. Peter displayed exciting talents as a runner and handler in the loose, and he won a lion's share of the line-out ball, specialising in delicate deflections to his scrum-half. He had excellent games against France (won 10-0) and the All Blacks (drawn 0-0) and set up the decisive try which took the Scots two scores clear of England in the Calcutta Cup match. On the stroke of half-time, he made a Sevens-type burst from a line-out to link up with the ubiquitous Jim Telfer, who gave Norman Bruce the pass which led to the try. Scotland's 15-6 win was their first victory against England for fourteen years,and Scotsmen had plenty to celebrate that night.

Peter made only intermittent appearances in the next couple of years, the Scottish selectors relying on bigger, heavier and tighter binders to supply second-row power to the scrums and line-outs. Then, after taking a rugby sabbatical to pursue professional qualifications as a chartered accountant, he made a comeback in 1969.

He was now cast in the unlikely role of goal-kicker. Unlikely, that is, because of his style. Never in the history of international rugby has there been a place-kicker with such an offbeat approach to the responsibility. Peter's routine preparation was: i) dot the ball on the ground with only a cursory glance at the goal; ii) wipe nose; iii) turn back on ball; iv) swivel, run up, and whack ball between posts. And those peculiar trajectories of his kicks would have made Sir Isaac Newton revise his theory of motion under gravity.

By the time he made his most famous conversion - against England for a last-minute win at Twickenham in 1971 - Peter was Scotland's captain and occupying the No. 8 shirt. He found a new lease of life as a back-rower, the position affording him the scope to play the open forward game off the back of the line-out that he positively relished.

His swashbuckling approach was invaluable when Scotland shared the 1973 Five Nations title but, at 31, the man whom one Welsh player described as built like a coat hanger, had reached the end of the line. It was not, however, the end of the 'Broons from Troon'. Peter's 'little' brother, Gordon, maintained the family sporting tradition for much of the 1970s, representing both Scotland and the Lions.

Finlay CALDER (Stewart's-Melville FP)

You could have excused Finlay Calder for thinking 'better late than never' when he answered the Scottish selectors' call to join five other new caps in the team to meet France at Murrayfield in 1986. At twenty-eight, he had spent five seasons in the wings watching his twin brother Jim collect twenty-seven caps as a flanker,and was resigned to seeing out his career as a first-class club player with Stewart's-Melville FP. But competition between brothers is often intense and, when Finlay now followed Jim into the Scottish back row, no doubt part of his motivation was to show that he was every inch as effective a player as his sibling.

Finlay succeeded in his quest, to the benefit of Scotland and, eventually, the Lions. He began his international career hell-bent on making up for lost years and immediately fitted into the patterned game practised by the Scottish side. Ideally built, Finlay was a rough predator who took to the rucking game propounded by Derrick Grant (and later Ian McGeechan) with ease. Best described as an out-and-out open-side, he had pace, hardness and resolution - qualities which made him an expert when it came to support play and setting up second-phase attacks at the points of breakdown.

The dictionary defines flint as a very hard mineral used to produce a spark. There was never any doubt about the relevance of the first part of that interpretation relative to the playing style of Finlay Calder; 'flinty' was an adjective frequently used to portray the Scot's character. And when, in 1989, he was promoted to national captain during Ian McGeechan's first season as Scottish coach, his captaincy style sparked off a recovery which was to extend to a revival of British rugby fortunes in general.

Finlay Calder was an inspiring leader whose quiet authority and personal example united a Scottish side which won two of its Five Nations matches that year and scavenged a scrappy draw against England at Twickenham. More than that, however, he instilled vital confidence in his team to the extent that, when the historians of the future look back at the Scottish record of the late 1980s and early 1990s, Finlay's contribution must be recognised. He worked closely with coach McGeechan to breed a strong sense of self-belief amongst the Scottish players.

Finlay's captaincy casebook had a new chapter added in Australia in the summer of 1989, when he became the first British captain this century to lead a Lions team to victory in a series having lost the first Test. His sound stewardship was particularly valuable in the Lions' win in the second Test, when he steadied the nerve of a British team caught up in several unsavoury incidents.

Although replaced by David Sole as national captain for 1989-90, he remained the initiator of Scotland's forward drives in the loose that season and was the main plank in the back row's policy of disruptive defence. Finlay's doctoring of England's mauls in the Grand Slam match at Murrayfield in 1990 was a masterful piece of rugby subterfuge; cutting off England's supply of possession was like denying oxygen to a flame.

Then he was gone - or almost. Having announced his retirement from international rugby after the 1990 Grand Slam, Finlay was coaxed by Ian McGeechan into exchanging his hearth slippers for rugby boots as Scotland made a brave bid for the 1991 Rugby World Cup. This time, though, England had their own plan to nullify the tactics of the greying, foxy Finlay, and he had to content himself with a final fling in a third/fourth-place play-off match against the All Blacks for his swansong.

Finlay Calder looking for support as Philippe Sella makes a tackle. Jean-Pierre Garuet and Gavin Hastings are in hot pursuit.

Sandy CARMICHAEL
(West of Scotland)

In 1973, Murrayfield throbbed with the energy of a nation celebrating its Rugby Union's centenary. That those celebrations extended to a share in the International Championship was thanks to the sterling work of a Scottish pack in which Sandy Carmichael was a pillar of strength at tight-head. Scotland's best season between 1964 and 1984 was also Sandy's only championship success in a long career which brought him fifty Scottish caps.

Named after his maternal grandfather, who had won eleven soccer caps for Scotland between 1904 and 1913, Sandy learned the rudiments of forward play under the sharp eye of international referee Jack Taylor at Loretto School. His early sporting prowess also included hockey and athletics, and the ball skills and strength engendered by these activities soon found expression on the senior rugby playing-fields, first with West of Scotland and later for the Glasgow District side.

His Scotland debut came as an eleventh-hour replacement for the durable

veteran prop, David Rollo, against Ireland in 1967. Sandy was not required for the subsequent Calcutta Cup match but, at the end of the year, he was selected again to face the New Zealanders, beginning a series of forty-nine consecutive international matches.

During the first full season of his record run, there was the formative experience of playing loose-head, to accommodate David Rollo on the starboard side of the front row. Rollo retired in 1968, enabling Sandy to move over and don the No. 3 shirt. Clearly, the subtle understanding of body positions that he had gained from propping on the loose head equipped him to make life extremely difficult for his opponents. He was an awkward cuss to scrummage against.

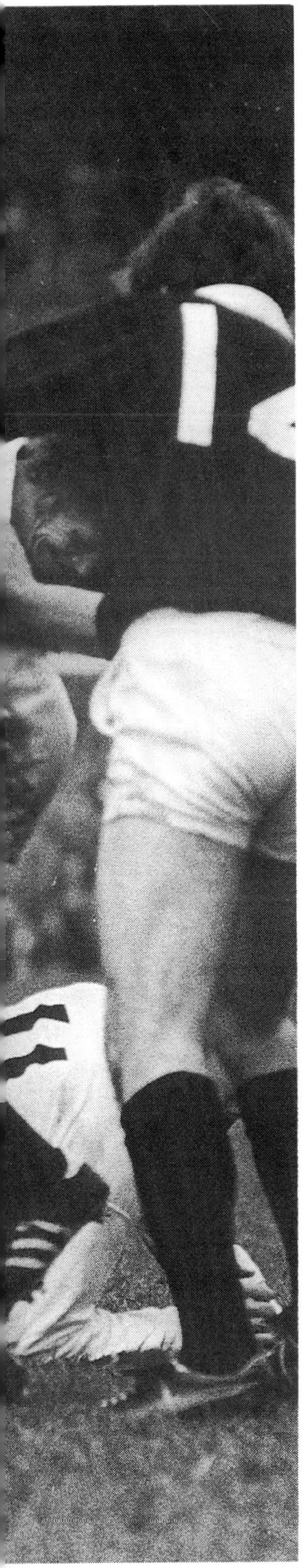

Sandy Carmichael (far left) playing against England at Twickenham, 1973.

That awkwardness made him the top tight-head prop on the 1971 Lions tour of New Zealand, but the All Blacks never had to face the Scot. A vicious assault by the Canterbury pack one week before the Test series opened left Sandy nursing grievous multiple cheekbone fractures and ruled him out of the rest of the tour. It was entirely in his character to take the unprovoked punishment without uttering any recrimination or seeking any physical reprisals .

No ordinary four-square prop, Sandy was a mobile man in the loose and a considerable snapper-up of trifles. He made a speciality of pinching tries from line-outs on the opposition line, used his 6ft 2in to steal valuable ball on the enemy's throw, and threw himself into tackles with the verve of a flanker.

It was to Scotland's good fortune that he was at his prime in 1973. After nearly a decade of French/Welsh domination of the Five Nations tournament, Wales were expected to continue their winning ways when they journeyed north to meet Carmichael and Co. at Murrayfield. But Sandy played his part perfectly in disrupting the much-vaunted Welsh pack. The Scottish plan was to impart a sideways force from the front row of the scrum and, by slewing the set-piece, to deny the Welsh clean first-phase possession. That Scotland succeeded in subduing Wales and establishing a match-winning lead early in the game was almost entirely due to the immense scrummaging power and technical know-how of both Sandy and his equally destructive colleague, Ian McLauchlan.

Sandy bowed out of the Scotland side gracefully in 1978, aged thirty-three. In over six-score years of international rugby, the country has never found a forward with more integrity, scrummaging nous and sheer guts than Alexander Bennett Carmichael.

Craig CHALMERS
(Melrose)

If ever Ian McGeechan pulled off a masterstroke during his tenure as Scotland's coach, it was in January 1989, when he introduced Craig Chalmers for the opening match of the Five Nations championship. The Melrose fly-half, who had previously been capped at four different age levels for Scotland, made a dream debut against Wales and became a permanent fixture in McGeechan's sides.

Craig quickly showed himself to be a gifted all-rounder. A balanced runner, a poised kicker and a cool defender, he forged an effective link with Gary Armstrong at half-back. As a pair, they were seen as successors to Scotland's 1984 Grand Slam halves, John Rutherford and Roy Laidlaw. However, Craig has quite different qualities from his predecessor. Both have shown remarkable skills as punters and drop-kickers, but there the similarities end. Craig's preferred route in attack is direct; subtle swerves and pretty side-steps (the hallmarks of John Rutherford) are not weapons in his armoury. Instead, it is his scrum-half who makes the openings near to the scrum, leaving Craig to practise his belief that the shortest distance between two points on a rugby field is a straight line.

It is a philosophy which requires a good deal of courage and plenty of strength and, in his short career to date, Craig has certainly demonstrated no shortage of these virtues. Although he is not a particularly big man, he has learned how to ride tackles, and there is no loose forward yet who has managed to contain him in an international. As you would expect of a player who so clearly enjoys the physical side of the game, he is an heroic tackler and staunch defender, a real glutton for punishment.

Craig was an influential figure in Scotland's Grand Slam season in 1990. Tactically, he was happy to be nursed by the confident Armstrong in the curtain-raisers to the showdown with England. Yet his roles in the victories against Ireland, France and Wales should not be overlooked. In the euphoria of the clean sweep it was easy to forget that 1990 was the year in which Gavin Hastings lost his place-kicking nerve. Without Craig Chalmers to assume those important duties, Scotland would never have collected the first tricks on the Grand Slam trail.

Just look at Craig's record up to the England match: a penalty and conversion against Ireland (in a 13-10 win); two conversions and two penalties against France (Scotland won 21-0); and three penalties in the 13-9 defeat of Wales in Cardiff. Even in the crucial encounter with England, where his defence work and sniping runs from second-phase possession were worthy parts of Scotland's great team effort, he kicked three penalties in the 13-7 triumph.

In 1993, two setbacks held up Craig's progress. The law changes affecting the rucks and mauls have led to a version of rugby in which only fly-halves with a huge appetite for trench warfare are likely to make any headway. There is a current tendency for any number of flankers to fan out from the fringes of the second-phase struggle, so that not even the Craig Chalmers of this world find the battles of attrition rewarding. Then, of course, he suffered a painful double fracture of his forearm during Scotland's Triple Crown bid at Twickenham. The injury almost certainly ended Scotland's hopes of carrying off the prize and deprived the 1993 Lions of their likely Test fly-half.

Colin DEANS
(Hawick)

Every cloud has a silver lining. Ask Colin Deans, the Scotland hooker who toured New Zealand with the 1983 Lions and should have played in the Tests. The Scot's disappointment at failing to dislodge Ciaran Fitzgerald, the Lions captain, from the Test side led to a steely resolve to prove a point when the 1984 Five Nations championship began.

Colin, Jim Telfer (the Lions and Scotland coach), and seven other veterans of the 1983 tour were the masterminds who guided Scotland to the Grand Slam in 1984. Embracing New Zealand forward methods, they romped to wins against Wales, England and Ireland which suggested that greater Scottish representation had been deserved on the ill-starred Lions visit. Effective rucking backed up by a swift, destructive back row were the defining features of Scotland's triumph, and Colin Deans was the ideal hooker to fit into the jigsaw pattern cut out by coach Telfer.

Weighing in at $12^1/_2$st and standing 5ft 10in, Colin was a dedicated player who, unusually for a hooker, placed great emphasis on acceleration, taking part in frequent sprint training. In 1984, he was super-fit and at the peak of his form, ready to play a big part in the Grand Slam challenge. He was a mobile forward who had the speed to carry him quickly to the scene of the breakdown in the loose and set up the rucks which became the trade mark of the Scottish forwards' game.

But, above all, it was his inch-perfect throwing at the line-out, providing the vital launch-pad for the Scottish back row, which represented his most valuable contribution to the 1984 Grand Slam. One of the major criticisms that had been levelled at Ciaran Fitzgerald, Colin's Lions rival in 1983, was that his line-out throwing was poor; Colin now demonstrated that the lobby who had supported his own inclusion as the Lions Test hooker had been absolutely right. His ability to pick out Jim Calder, Iain Paxton and David Leslie with unerring accuracy was a fascinating sideshow for the statisticians who charted Scotland's four victories, in a year which saw Colin become his country's most-capped hooker.

Colin was one of the host of internationalists produced by Hawick High School, and

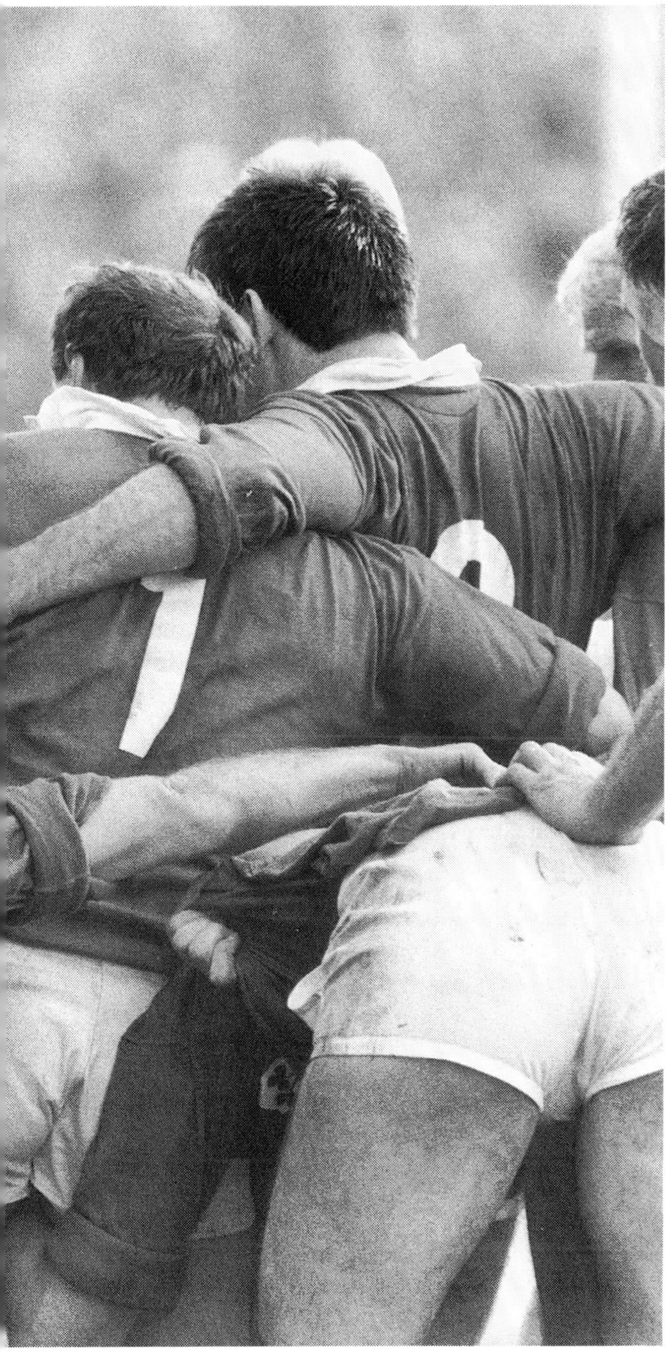

Colin Deans flanked by Iain Milne and David Sole against Ireland, 1987.

he began his long career in the Scottish team in 1978. Scotland's pack in the late 1970s was in decline, as tight forwards Sandy Carmichael, 'Mighty Mouse' McLauchlan and Alastair McHarg were fast approaching their dotage. It was a baptism of fire for Colin in his first season as Scotland hooker. He successfully made the strike on his own loose head, but frequently had the unpleasant experience of back-pedalling as an ageing scrum was pushed back off the ball. Typically, Colin responded by working conscientiously to eradicate any deficiencies in his own hooking style.

Not long afterwards, a succession of team changes necessitated by retirements and loss of form left him as the senior forward of the Scottish side at a relatively young age. Yet his undoubted technical ability, his irrepressible loose play, and his unshakeable faith in his colleagues, earned him the respect of Scotland's rugby players and followers alike. And when he wound up his career as captain of his country at the 1987 Rugby World Cup, his many admirers felt that that was a fitting finale for the man who remains the undisputed king of Scottish hookers.

Peter DODS (Gala)

Scotland have been well-served by full-backs in the past twenty years. Remarkably, there have been only four No. 15s called upon by the Scottish selectors in their eighty-four Five Nations matches played between 1973 and 1993: Andy Irvine, Bruce Hay, Gavin Hastings and Peter Dods.

Peter Dods, a native of Gala, became the sixth in the distinguished line of full-backs from his club who have played for Scotland. He made his international debut in 1983 after an impressive spell in the Scottish District Championship with the South of Scotland side, during which he accumulated an equally impressive collection of points. And he quickly settled in the groove for Scotland, kicking 33 points in his first Five Nations season.

Injuries to Andy Irvine had opened the door to the Scotland XV for Peter in 1983. By the middle of 1984, however, Irvine was restored to full fitness and challenging the Gala man strongly for his position as the last line of defence. But through his reliability, accurate kicking and unpredictable runs on the counter-attack, Peter fully justified his selection ahead of Irvine in the Grand Slam season.

With the benefit of hindsight, it is easy to see the immense contribution Peter made to Scotland's 1984 successes. The plaudits rained down on the pack and the halves but, without Peter's ability to land difficult kicks at telling moments, the Grand Slam would never have become even a remote possibility.

Events proved that Wales were one of the most creative sides in the championship in 1984. But Scotland were lucky to face them on the opening Saturday of the season, before the Welsh selectors had managed to get the right blend of players in their team. Even so, 6-9 down after an hour, Scotland had their work cut out to overhaul the home side at Cardiff. It was then thanks to a Peter Dods penalty that the Scots drew level, and his conversion of Jim Aitken's try, ten minutes from no-side, was an important psychological blow which meant that Wales would have to score twice to win the match. They did not even score once, as Peter stood firm under the high punts of the Wales halves.

His steadfast defence on a miserable day against England at Murrayfield similarly denied the Auld Enemy a try in an 18-6 win, and he finally came of age as an international player with a model performance in Dublin. Here he played a cameo role in attack to silence his detractors, who had claimed that Irvine's speed and broader vision in open play outweighed Peter's more mundane full-back strengths. Besides, the Gala man scored 16 vital points, including a try, in the match which brought Scotland's first Triple Crown win for forty-six years. A fortnight later, he scored 17 points out of 21 in the Grand Slam decider with France, equalling the Scottish individual record for most points in a match.

With the advent of Gavin Hastings two years later, Peter found himself relegated to bench duties but he returned in 1989 to kick the kind of goals which people never forget, and so competent were his Five Nations displays that, even when Hastings was declared fit for the Lions summer tour to Australia, Peter was taken as second-choice full-back.

For the rest of his career, Peter had to be content with playing second fiddle to big Gavin. His final caps for Scotland were token appearances during the 1991 Rugby World Cup, but any player who gathers more than his weight in points at international level, despite spending half of his career as an understudy, can be justifiably proud of his record.

Gavin HASTINGS
(Watsonians, London Scottish)

In international terms, Gavin Hastings demonstrated that life begins at twenty-four. For it was only a couple of weeks after celebrating his first two dozen years that the big man with the boot to match played in his first Test for Scotland. In a memorable debut against France in 1986, Gavin kicked six penalty goals - all of Scotland's points in an exciting 18-17 win at Murrayfield. His feat equalled the then world record for most penalties in a match and created a new Scottish record for most points by a player in an international. He has never looked back since.

After such a debut, you might have expected the player to rest on his laurels and bask in the glory of his achievements for a couple of months. Not a bit of it. During his first season of Five Nations rugby, Gavin went on collecting points as prolifically as a train-spotter gathering engine numbers at Clapham Junction. In an inch-perfect demonstration of place-kicking, he landed eight goals against England for a haul of 21 points, improving on the record he himself had set against France. And by the end of the season he had amassed a stunning 52 points, a total which remains the highest by a Scottish player in a championship season.

Besides his kicking, Gavin has had a wonderful calming effect on Scottish sides since 1986. Of course, it has given a massive boost to his team-mates' confidence to know that such an efficient kicking machine is ready to supplement their efforts. But his presence as a firm defender and his perception in attack have also been considerable assets to an improving side. Naturally, he has been compared with Andy Irvine, his illustrious full-back predecessor. To many, however, there is no contest: the more measured approach that Gavin takes to his offensive duties contrasts starkly with the frenetic solo efforts which characterised

Gavin Hastings: safe as houses under the high ball.

Irvine's sorties out of defence. For Gavin has a vision which enables him to contribute more as a link-man than Irvine ever did. While Andy was undoubtedly a faster runner and a more spectacular finisher, one sensed that, when he was caught, that was the end of any threat to the opposition's try-line.

Moreover, in the realms of defence, Gavin is streets ahead of his rival. Those bone-jarring tackles of his would have warmed the evil heart of Vlad the Impaler, and there is not one player in the Five Nations who would relish taking on the big Scot in a head-to-head confrontation.

Injury interrupted his career during the winter of 1988-89, but he recovered in sufficient time to travel with the Lions to Australia that summer. He was a key figure in their Test series win and, after his return, he emerged at the peak of his powers for Scotland's Grand Slam season in 1990.

Despite entering a spell of indifference with his place-kicking, the solid foundation of his defence imbued those in front of him with the spirit of enterprise which is an adjunct of most successful teams. He was also the author of the move which brought Scotland the Grand Slam in the magnificent showdown with England at Murrayfield in 1990. Gavin it was who made the break and placed the perfect chip ahead for Tony Stanger to gather and score the decisive try of the match.

After captaining Scotland in 1993, Gavin was selected as captain for the Lions tour to New Zealand, the highest distinction rugby football can bestow on a Five Nations player. The honour was thoroughly well-deserved.

Scott HASTINGS
(Watsonians)

The Popeye factor was a big influence on Scotland's rugby rise in the late 1980s. Several players who would have been measured as no better than good club performers in England and Wales were transformed into superhuman beings when playing for their country. To a Scotsman, pulling on the navy blue jersey was the equivalent of Popeye eating his spinach.

Scott Hastings is one who has been placed in this category. Very much a players' player, he has given 100 per cent commitment in every one of nearly fifty international matches since making his debut with brother Gavin in 1986 against France. For sheer determination to succeed, he has had no superior.

Hard tackling is a Hastings family trait, and Scott marked his arrival as an international player with a wonderful all-round display in defence. There were moments in that 1986 match against France when Sella, Estève and Berbizier threatened to steal the winning try in a see-saw match, but time and again Scott made telling tackles to snuff out France's scoring attempts. He effectively padlocked the middle of the field, setting a combination which the opposition utterly failed to unpick.

The following season, he was paired for the first time with Sean Lineen at centre. Together they went on to set a world record for a centre partnership, with their reign bringing Scotland the Grand Slam in 1990 and a semi-final appearance in the 1991 Rugby World Cup. Yet it was an unusual alliance because of the similarity in styles of the players. Usually, great centre combinations complement one another, but Sean Lineen was almost a carbon copy of Scott.

Neither was a creative genius, though Scott has shown a feisty attitude in attack, both for Scotland and the Lions. A big man at 6ft 1in and $13^{1}/_{2}$st, he is a powerful runner who generates considerable momentum in his direct approach. When held up, he gives the maul or ruck exactly the impulse his supporting forwards require in order to recycle the ball to the backs for second-phase attacks. He is not renowned for his handling, but it is an interesting statistic that the wingers who have played outside Scott since the Watsonian came into the national side have collected more than thirty tries.

Scott's role in the 1990 Grand Slam was crucial. Once again, it was his midfield defence which underpinned the hard-earned Scottish triumphs against Wales and England. In performances worthy of comparison with the top hit-men of American football, Scott's crunching tackles on Welsh forwards intent on impersonating battering rams held the Scottish line together long enough to protect a narrow 13-9 lead. That win set up Scotland's showdown of the century against England at Murrayfield.

Scott Hastings.

In the battle of Hastings and Guscott, itself a microcosm of the Grand Slam game, it was first blood to the Bath player when, early in the action, an uncharacteristic dip in Scott's concentration led to England's try. But for the rest of a pulsating match, the defensive stand of the Scotsman - in particular, an astonishing tackle on Rory Underwood from behind - blotted out the threat of Messrs Carling and Guscott, and was an underlying reason why the Anglo-Saxons were sent packing, empty-handed, when the Five Nations' holy trinity of Grand Slam, Triple Crown and Calcutta Cup had beckoned.

Even if he never makes another tackle in anger, Scott Hastings deserves a place in the small pantheon dedicated to rugby's most heroic defenders; those players who win matches with selfless displays of courage in the face of adversity.

Andy IRVINE
(Heriot's FP)

When Bill Dickinson restored credibility to Scottish rugby in the early 1970s, it was a combination of patterned forward play and the dynamic attacking style of full-back Andy Irvine which brought the crowds flocking to Murrayfield to enjoy the long-overdue revival. Andy's skills were amazing. He was the swiftest runner ever to play full-back for Scotland, and his love of enterprise made him the ideal player to back up an improving team in the early years of the Australian dispensation law restricting kicking to touch.

Andy was a distinguished threequarter at George Heriot's School in Edinburgh and joined the former pupils' club when he left to study at Edinburgh University. He was still a student when he began to make his mark on the Heriot's 1st XV and won his first cap at the age of twenty-one against the 1972 All Blacks.

Immediately, he caught the eye with his mazy runs from deep defence. At full tilt, exuding all the joy he felt for the running game, he was a sight to behold - the perfect study in balance. His first campaign as an internationalist was a year in which Scotland shared the Five Nations title. No coincidence there: Andy's bold, arcing runs were instrumental in committing defences to tackles, and although he did not score any tries in the championship - he would certainly make up for that in subsequent seasons - the extra dimension he created as an auxiliary threequarter took the pressure off his colleagues and thrust it instead upon opposing defenders.

Then there was his place-kicking. He adopted a no-nonsense round-the-corner technique which was to bring him a record haul of international points. He won several matches for Scotland almost off his own bat (or perhaps that should be 'boot') and the French, who more often than any other side in the Five Nations succumbed to Andy's talents, had the highest regard for the full-back's potential.

Yet for all his statistical achievements, he remained a modest character with a disdain for records and a desire to see the game's laws revised. Ten years before it became encased in statute, Andy expressed a wish for the value of the try to be raised to 5 points. And he has long campaigned for less importance to be attached to the penalty goal, the scoring action which brought him the majority of his world-record

Andy Irvine - always looking for an opportunity to attack - playing here against Wales, 1977. Left to right: Alastair McHarg, Irvine, Bobby Windsor, Allan Martin, Mike Biggar and David Burcher.

points tally.

It was inevitable that he should be compared with that other great running full-back of his age, JPR Williams. Andy was certainly a faster, more elusive runner than JPR; but the Welshman had no equal in defence, while Andy lacked the 'they-shall-not-pass' attitude in his tackling, and under the high ball his fielding was occasionally insecure.

His enthusiasm and brilliance sustained Scotland for a decade until an Achilles tendon forced him to miss the internationals of 1983. Shoulder injuries plagued him after that but, by February 1984, he was back in Scotland's squad as bench substitute to Peter Dods in the side that went on to win the Grand Slam for the first time in fifty-nine years.

It was ironic that the player who had probably contributed more than most to the rise of Scottish rugby should find himself sidelined during his country's finest hour. No one would have begrudged Andy, then Scotland's leading cap-winner, one more appearance, albeit as a replacement, in that Grand Slam side.

John JEFFREY
(Kelso)

'Farmers make the finest flankers' would be a fitting slogan for Scotland's post-war selectors. Two of the best produced north of the border since 1945 were Doug Elliot, who played twenty-nine times during the bleakest years of Scottish rugby, and John Jeffrey, the rangy Kelso loose forward who succeeded Elliot as his country's most-capped flanker, notching up forty appearances between 1984 and 1991.

Many distinguished flankers make their names on the strength of one particular area of expertise in their game. Some are brilliant constructive players; others are renowned for their destructive talents. Look at the records of international flankers, and you will see that their position, more than any other on the field, is the one in which national selectors are inclined to chop and change personnel most frequently in accordance with the shifting priorities of their strategy at any given time.

John Jeffrey was the glaring exception to this rule, simply because he was such an outstanding all-round player. During his apprenticeship with Kelso and the South of Scotland, he mastered the elements of creative loose play and also preyed on players in possession with the ruthless efficiency of the Scottish Border reivers of old.

It was under the reign of Ian McGeechan as Scotland's coach that John flourished. The Scots perfected a classic approach to the game based on speed, support and direct attack, and John's credentials for this style of play were ideal. No quarter was asked and none was given by the uncompromising blond-haired flanker who was aptly named the 'White Shark'.

His stirring deeds for Scotland in 1990 during the Grand Slam campaign were the stuff of legend. During the crucial final match of the season against England at Murrayfield, no one did more

Farmers make the finest flankers: John Jeffrey of Kelso.

to ensure that Will Carling and his confident glory-seekers were sent packing. The way in which John disrupted the visitors' mauls that day struck at the very heart of England's power game. Somehow, he managed repeatedly to sandwich himself between the English and the ball, whether it was on the floor or in the hands. Frustrated of their prime source of second-phase possession, and bottled up by the cracking tackling of the entire Scottish back row, England were unable to exert any tactical grip. John gave an astonishing display, full of courage and skill, and memorable for his magnificent strength and stamina.

There were other occasions during the Grand

John Jeffrey, the uncompromising 'White Shark'.

Slam when his powers in attack were invaluable. The typical John Jeffrey break was a straight charge; then, when challenged, he would dip the right shoulder to ride the tackle or screen the ball to set up the ruck. Rarely did he lose possession, and he would probably have been equally at home playing under the new ruck/maul law which has tantalised so many of the leading British forwards since its introduction in July 1992.

As one of the fastest forwards of the past decade, John, not surprisingly, reaped handsome dividends in the form of eleven tries - a Scottish record for a forward, shared with his former back-row colleague, Derek White. Now that he has retired, Scotland are certainly finding that John Jeffrey's boots are extremely difficult to fill.

David JOHNSTON
(Watsonians)

The jury was out for some time deliberating whether or not the Watsonian player, David Johnston, was the most talented Scottish centre of the 1980s. But there was always plenty of evidence to suggest that he was one of the most skilful ball players of his generation. Besides winning honours with Scottish Schools as a rugby footballer, David also found the time to make a name for himself as a part-time professional soccer player. There were spells at Hibernian and Hearts, and he was even offered a contract with Glasgow Rangers.

Injuries and the demands of his studies at Edinburgh University, where he read law, influenced his decision to turn his back on soccer, and the round-ball game's loss was rugby's gain. David joined his school's former pupils at Watsonians and enjoyed a meteoric rise which projected him into the Scotland side when he was barely twenty-one.

Immediately, he was hailed as the most exciting attacking player to grace the Scottish midfield for many seasons. He had the ability to kick with either foot and relished using his sharp acceleration to carve out openings. In his first Five Nations year (1980), he swept through international rugby like a breath of fresh air at a time when British centres were obsessed by crash-ball moves. David was a delight to watch, reminiscent of the classic centres of old.

A persistent hamstring problem forced him to miss the Five Nations championship in 1981, but he was back at the heart of Scotland's attack when Jim Telfer's side gave early warning of its Five Nations potential with a thorough rout of Wales at Cardiff in 1982. In perfect conditions, David led the kick-and-chase from half-way which produced Jim Pollock's decisive score early in the second half. Later in the match he took a short pass from John Rutherford on the Wales 22, tucked the ball under his right arm and, with a wiggle of the hips, bemused the Welsh defence to run through, untouched, for the best solo try of the championship.

In the 1984 Grand Slam he filled the star part again, this time in the win in difficult conditions against England. On a day when it was obvious that scores were not going to result from orthodox handling, David resorted to his old footballing skills to dribble the ball twenty-two metres for the try which sent Scotland on their way to an important 18-6 triumph.

Yet not all critics shared total admiration for David. Witnesses for the defence attested to his courage and versatility as a tackler and fielder under pressure, and certainly his blistering pace was an asset to Scotland when opponents' tactics compelled him to turn and retrieve a ball kicked over his head. But the prosecution case that really told against David concerned his passing and angles of running in threequarter movements. While he had the ball in his hands he put the fear of God into the centres who faced him but,once drawn into a tackle, his threat was minimal, for he never mastered the subtle art of giving a carefully-weighted pass to his wing. As long as defenders managed to shadow David Johnston, there was very little chance of them conceding a try in the corner.

One sensed that David himself was fully aware of his shortcomings. As his career developed, he tried to camouflage the effect of his wayward distribution by moving sideways towards his winger to reduce the length of his pass. But in so doing he merely crowded his partner, and the final verdict on David's career was that he would have been more likely to achieve lasting fame as a winger himself.

Roy LAIDLAW (Jedforest)

The great improviser - that was the judgement on Roy Laidlaw, Scotland's scrum-half in the 1984 Grand Slam team. He was a gutsy, bustling competitor, imperfect in his execution of some of the game's basic skills but a dangerous and penetrative player when he chose to attack from the base of the scrum.

Jedburgh-born, bred and educated, Roy served a long apprenticeship as understudy to Alan Lawson and Dougie Morgan. He was the resident No. 9 for Scotland B when those fixtures began in the mid-1970s, and it appeared that he was destined to be permanent bridesmaid to the senior team until, after nine seasons of first-class rugby, he finally won his full cap in 1980.

After that, he never looked back. Lucky, maybe, to find such a tactical genius as John Rutherford as his partner, Roy nevertheless positively flourished behind an improving scrum. Faults, specifically with his passing, and a tendency to delay the delivery of the ball to his backs, were never completely eradicated during his long international career, but somehow the players who depended on him managed to accommodate such peccadilloes.

The greatest of Roy's strengths was his readiness to take on opposing back rows. With almost total disregard for his personal safety, he launched himself at forwards of all shapes and sizes. His strength in the tackle meant that, unlike his predecessors, Lawson and Morgan, he was well able to make the ball available to his own loose forwards and so maintain the momentum of his drive.

Never was his value to Scotland better demonstrated than on that spring day in 1982 when Scotland took Wales's wonderful unbeaten home record, scoring five tries into the bargain. Roy's probes and chip-kicks were instrumental in bringing down the curtain on nearly fourteen years of Welsh dominance at Cardiff. He was no great respecter of opponents with puffed-up reputations and,in his characteristic, businesslike manner, he instigated several of the audacious raids which brought Scotland their tries.

After touring Australia the same year, he returned to captain Scotland in 1983 when both Andy Irvine and John Rutherford were unavailable because of injury. The responsibility sat heavily on his shoulders, and his game at international level deteriorated. Unfortunately, he was no great tactician - a burden he had never needed to carry when John Rutherford was around to call the shots. After Scotland laboured their way to three successive defeats that year, Roy was relieved of the leadership for the visit to Twickenham. Reunited with Rutherford and playing under the inspiring captaincy of Jim Aitken, Roy once again hit peak form and was involved in both of Scotland's tries in a rare win on English soil. The victory was Scotland's only one of the season and ensured that England were left holding the wooden spoon but, more important, it brought together the nucleus of the team which eventually won the Grand Slam in 1984.

Naturally, Roy played a vital role in that first Scottish clean sweep for fifty-nine years. His alertness and imaginative decision-making supported the tactical direction given by Rutherford, and he integrated splendidly with the rucking style of a skilful pack. Altogether, his career took in forty-seven caps, a record for a Scottish scrum-half, but his most brilliant performance for his country lasted only forty minutes. Against Ireland in the 1984 Triple Crown decider, he completely dominated the first half, scoring two tries to take his side into an unassailable 22-0 lead. Though he was forced to leave the field concussed at half-time, no one will ever forget his part in Scotland's first Triple Crown win for forty-six years.

Roy Laidlaw, in true gutsy style, kicks for position against Ireland in 1987.

David LESLIE (Dundee HSFP, West of Scotland, Gala)

There were no doubts about rugby's player-of-the-year in 1984: David Leslie won the contest hands down. The Scottish flanker, enjoying a second lease of life at thirty-one, was the most constructive forward in the Five Nations tournament and gave his team's line-out an added dimension with his manoeuvres at the tail. There were several factors cited as crucial to Scotland's Grand Slam that season but, arguably, the individual play of David and his combined work with his back row colleagues were the most important influences in the long-awaited triumph.

Educated at Dundee High School, Glenalmond and Dundee University, where he qualified as an architect, David was playing fourth-division rugby for Dundee HSFP when he broke into the Scottish side as a No. 8 in 1975. For two seasons he played his part in the steadily improving national team, but then a cruel series of injuries restricted him to only two appearances in the following four years.

Meanwhile, he joined Gala in the cauldron of border rugby and switched from No. 8 to flanker. The change was as good as a long rest for David. People began to sit up and take notice of his all-round ability on the side of the scrum, and with his lack of inches - he was only 6ft 1in - there was less pressure on him to win line-out ball, as Scotland called in bigger men such as Iain Paxton and John Beattie to dominate the back of the line in the No. 8 spot.

Furthermore, the relaxation of pressure brought an unexpected bonus. David was an athletic player with innate ball skills, the legacy of a schoolboy spell as an outside-half. Whether as blind-side or open-side in the Scottish pack, he managed to win a statistically significant share of line-out ball jumping against opponents who were invariably two or three inches taller.

Half-way through the 1981-82 season, David broke his leg playing for Gala. He took the injury philosophically, adding that the enforced lay-off would give him welcome time to spend with his family. But his off-the-cuff remark was seen by the more conservative alickadoos of rugby football as a swipe at the increasing commitments that leading players were expected to undertake in an amateur game. It is impossible to gauge how much damage was done to his reputation by the comment, but one wonders whether the 1983 Lions' selectors regarded his words as an indication that he would be unable to submit himself to the pressures of an eighteen-match tour. Whatever the reason, his omission from the Lions party was an unfair reflection on his undoubted ability.

That oversight spurred him with renewed determination to succeed in 1984. Advancing years had somewhat diminished the pace of his youth, but his appetite for the game remained voracious. Coach Jim Telfer wanted the Scottish forwards to concentrate on rucking the second-phase ball, and so David spent the entire season magnetised to the loose ball, proving himself to be the ideal player to implement Telfer's plans. Whenever fifty-fifty situations arose in the loose, David was invariably the first player at the breakdown to set up the quick ruck ball Scotland's halves wanted. Not only was he a ubiquitous force around the field, he also showed that he had lost none of his effectiveness as a first-phase attacker from the back of the line-out. He cleaned out Welshman Richard Moriarty in the championship opener at Cardiff, made marvellous contributions in difficult conditions against England and Ireland, and dominated Jean-Luc Joinel in the second half of the Grand Slam win against France. Player-of-the-season in 1984 was a much-deserved honour for the Scot whose drive and ball-winning potential put him in the class of the all-time greats.

Ian McLAUCHLAN (Jordanhill)

Inspiring leadership and advanced front-row skills were the two outstanding qualities that defined the contribution which Ian 'Mighty Mouse' McLauchlan made to Scottish rugby during the 1970s - a decade of dramatic change in the organisation of the game north of the border. In between appointing Bill Dickinson as their first national coach and introducing a revolutionary league structure for club rugby, Scotland made the 'Mighty Mouse' their international captain.

It was an enlightened move. Ian was a respected and established internationalist with an impressive rugby c.v. when he became skipper in 1973. His first match in charge was at home against a formidable Wales XV, who were favoured to win. But Ian instilled in his side a belief in itself and, sticking to a carefully-devised game plan, Scotland carried the fight to their distinguished opponents.

The plan was to disrupt Wales up front by crabbing the scrummage on the Welsh put-in and so disrupt a vital source of Welsh possession. Only a prop of Ian's unusual stature (he was just 5ft 8½in and under 14½st) and technical know-how could initiate the disruption by taking physically near-impossible sideways steps to offset the effect of the Welsh shove.

What were small steps for Ian were giant strides for Scottish rugby, and the side beat Wales and Ireland that year to win a share of the Five Nations championship. Under the leadership of the Jordanhill prop, and helped by the wise counsel of Bill Dickinson, Scotland went on to make Murrayfield something of a fortress against visiting sides. Ian captained his country eight times at Murrayfield in the Five Nations tournament: only one of those games was lost.

As a forward, he was a fascinating player to watch. Even the most naïve threequarter, ignorant of the mechanics of scrummaging, could see and appreciate the effect Ian had on the doughtiest of opponents. And the rugby intellectuals among the game's press corps had sufficient material to write whole textbooks extolling Ian's approach.

The enduring intrigue of 'Mighty Mouse' was that, for one of so compact a frame, he could absorb so much pressure from the shove of his opponents, yet transmit so much of the power coming from the locks who packed down behind him. His ability to remain firm on his own side's put-in and become disruptive on the opposition's feed was the crucial building-block on which Scotland's successful packs of the 1970s were based. His speciality as an undercover agent in the front row was to burrow underneath his enemies, neutralising their thrust.

The old adage that the best props, like the best ports, mature with age was never better illustrated than in the glowing example of Ian McLauchlan. When he became the first player to be capped from his club (Jordanhill College) and the first former pupil of his school (Ayr Academy) to play for Scotland, in 1969, he was already twenty-six. More than a decade and two trail-blazing Lions tours later, he was still the best loose-head prop in Britain. Since his retirement, the teacher-turned-media man has had many imitators who have helped Scottish rugby to maintain the high profile that Ian helped to create during his playing days. No player could ask for a better epitaph

Iain MILNE (Heriot's FP, Harlequins)

Scrum it, ruck it and run it was the forward plan Scotland successfully adopted under Jim Telfer, the coach whose drafts for victory became best-sellers in 1984. Iain Milne, the broad-beamed bear of a tight-head prop in the Grand Slam side, was the perfect embodiment of Telfer's ideas. He was the ideal specimen for the front row: bulky, mobile and immensely strong. He was well-versed in the rucking game which was Telfer's preferred platform at the second phase; and he could provide the vital link if required when the Scottish pack went on the rampage in the loose.

The son of a doctor, Iain won his first cap when he was a twenty-year-old stripling studying biochemistry at Heriot-Watt University and playing for Heriot's FP. Rave reviews greeted his opening international performances, and it was crystal-clear that, given freedom from injury, Iain would be an automatic choice in the Scotland XV for a long time. He worked hard to improve his game, especially his loose play, and became an integral part of a Scotland side which was largely unchanged for several seasons leading up to the 1984 Grand Slam.

That continuity, granted to Iain and several others in the squad, was a key element in the building of what became recognised almost as a happy club set-up. All for one and one for all could well have been the battle-cry of the Scottish front three, Jim Aitken (an inspiring captain), Colin Deans and Iain, when they locked horns with the Wales front row at Cardiff in the opening match of the Grand Slam campaign.

Iain had played once before at Cardiff, in 1982, when Scotland broke Wales's record fourteen-year unbeaten home run. Scotland's play in the second half of that famous victory had been a revelation. They totally outscrummaged the Welsh pack, and four of the scores in an astonishing 34-18 win stemmed directly from set-piece ball won by Iain and his friends.

So Cardiff held no great fears for him when he returned there in 1984; and again he emerged with credit for his part as an unsung hero in the front row skirmishes in a battle Scotland never once looked like losing. In fact, they never looked like losing to England or Ireland either, as Iain convinced the critics that he had superseded Graham Price

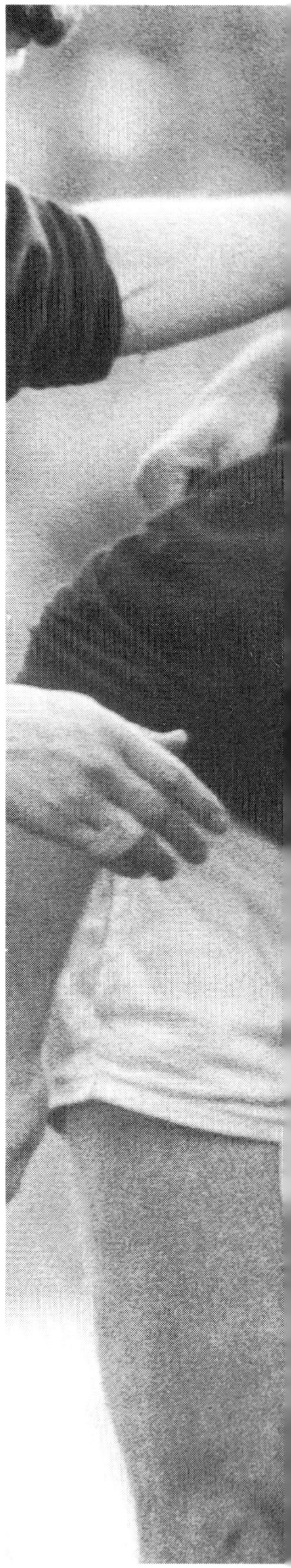

as the leading tight-head in the Five Nations.

With the Triple Crown neatly packed in their sporrans, the Scots then faced France in a Grand Slam showdown in front of the kilted hordes at Murrayfield. Here, Iain enjoyed his finest

hour, after Scotland had withstood a torrid first quarter against a French side which played as if the Grand Slam was a formality. The visitors led 9-3 before the Scottish front row, with Iain giving a technically perfect display of tight scrummaging, began to exert pressure on the French forwards. The upshot was a famous victory, in which Iain was mentioned in despatches by coach Telfer for a demonstration of resource and character which helped Scotland to their first Grand Slam in fifty-nine years.

A move south to London followed, where he joined the Harlequins (much to the disgust of a certain Alastair McHarg, the London Scottish coach), and Iain finished his Five Nations career as reserve to Paul Burnell in the 1990 Grand Slam, when his younger brother Kenny was national hooker.

Iain Milne, a regular member of the Scottish pack in the 1980s.

John RUTHERFORD (Selkirk)

Scottish rugby advanced steadily during the 1970s to reach its zenith with a Grand Slam season in 1984. There had been strong packs in the early 1970s, and enterprising backs in the latter part of the decade. Yet ne'er the twain did meet until a settled side of talented threequarters and competent forwards was welded into good working order by a smooth half-back partnership comprising John Rutherford and Roy Laidlaw.

John Rutherford was the outside-half of the combination. Clever tactical kicking and elusive running were the hallmarks of the player who became his nation's most-capped No. 10.

John, who was Selkirk-born and educated, went on Scotland's Far East tour in 1977 before breaking into the international side in January 1979. From the start, there was a calm assurance to his play. He had a penchant for breaks close to the scrummage and developed a good understanding with his back rows. Early in his career, however, the quality of his tactical kicking left much to be desired. Yet it was entirely typical that John should work on this weakness of his game and, by the early 1980s, he had become one of the most feared tormentors of full-backs in international rugby.

One of his most memorable displays was

against Wales at Murrayfield in 1981, when he made the veteran full-back, JPR Williams, look fallible. (In fact, the great Welshman was dropped by his country after that.) But it was against England in 1984 that John experienced his finest hour in a Scottish jersey.

The match, staged in awful conditions, was the second leg of the Grand Slam for Scotland, while England were riding high after beating the All Blacks at Twickenham. The strength of Scotland's approach in the early 1980s had been the plundering in the loose and the playing of an expansive game from the set-piece. For

John Rutherford makes two kicks for the coaching textbook.

a number of reasons, however, this style had to be reassessed for the England match. The wet weather was a hindrance to the passing game and, without Andy Irvine (who was injured), fewer options were available to Scotland in attack. But John came to his country's rescue with as masterful a display of tactical punting as any ever given by a Scotland fly-half.

That day he shunted the English forwards around the field with his touch-kicks, and poor Dusty Hare, the England full-back, suffered the same fate that had befallen JPR Williams before him. Just to prove that he had arrived as a star of the first magnitude among the prominent constellation of outside-halves, John also demonstrated his safe handling when he miraculously scooped up a scruffy pass from Roy Laidlaw to send one of his centres over for an important score.

John remained the best all-round outside-half in British rugby for a few years more after the euphoria of Scotland's Grand Slam died down. A severe injury sustained during the inaugural Rugby World Cup in 1987 finally brought the curtain down on the career of the man who was undoubtedly the most complete Scottish outside-half of the post-war years.

David SOLE
(Bath, Edinburgh Acads)

Scottish coach Derrick Grant and chairman of selectors Robin Charters took a gamble in fielding six new caps for the opening Five Nations match against France in 1986. Scotland had lost six consecutive internationals since the 1984 Grand Slam success, and a change in personnel as well as a tactical rethink had become long overdue.

Enter scrum left David Sole, the Bath loose-head, who was to become the icon of a new-look team which put the accent on speed around the field. A product of Glenalmond School, where he had been a more than useful centre, David's three years at Exeter University had put him in the right place at the right time to join Bath as the club began its steady climb to the foremost position in British rugby.

As a thoroughly modern forward - master of the game's basic skills, a technical expert on the loose head, and a force to be reckoned with in open play - David typified the mobile, all-round player Scotland needed in the build-up of a side which, in 1990, would become Grand Slam winners.

He emerged with credit from his first two internationals in 1986. In a tense match at Murrayfield, Jean-Pierre Garuet, an old warhorse if ever there was one, needed all his experience to keep David in check. French indiscipline, the result of their inability to overcome their frustration at being disrupted by the Scottish pack in the tight, permitted the home side to sneak home by 18 points (six penalties) to 17, so ending that long, demoralising run of defeats. A new spirit was born in Scottish rugby that afternoon, and the determination of the two Hastings brothers, David Sole and Finlay Calder (all international freshmen) was to sustain that spirit for the best part of the next five years.

David returned to Scottish club rugby in the late 1980s, joining Edinburgh Academicals at historic Raeburn Place. Practice, fitness training, and the intense competition of the National League sharpened his playing reflexes and, by 1989, he had firmly established himself as the leading loose-head in the Five Nations. He paraded with courage that year in the red garb of the Lions in Australia, when the tourists came from behind to win the Test series 2-1, and returned from the trip to find himself installed as captain of Scotland for the 1989-90 season.

The Five Nations campaign that year was, arguably, the most exciting in the colourful history of the competition. England, hyped up after cracking victories against Ireland, France and Wales, came to Murrayfield as hot favourites to dispose of the Scots. David Sole, however, had a different view of the match. His team were unbeaten too, and the entire Scottish nation, united by a common desire to teach the invaders a lesson, rallied to support the proud prop as he marched his men out defiantly to do battle with the cocky English. It was Bannockburn all over again. England were destroyed, and David's inspirational example and intelligent leadership made him Scotland's most popular folk hero since Robert the Bruce saw off the English in the 1314 version of the Grand Slam.

David went on to lead his country to a semi-final in the 1991 Rugby World Cup, and set a fresh record by captaining Scotland twenty-five times before retiring at the relatively young age of thirty in 1992. In a valediction to Scotland's most successful captain, Ian Robertson quoted David as saying: 'It is not the registration of the model which counts in my case, but the number of miles on the clock.' Not a single British rugby enthusiast would have objected if a mechanic had somehow managed to wind back that clock - just a few miles, perhaps - to see David perform a little longer at international level.

David Sole, a hero in the 1990 Grand Slam season.

Tony STANGER
(Hawick)

Mention the name Tony Stanger, and the phrases 'decisive try' and 'Grand Slam decider 1990' come immediately to mind. Tony's try at the beginning of the second half of the match against England that year was the moment that mattered most on Scotland's way to only their third-ever Grand Slam. He wrote his name indelibly in the big book of Five Nations history by following up a kick ahead by Gavin Hastings; the ball bounced high on the England goal-line, Tony jumped, collected it above his opponent Rory Underwood, and dropped over the line for the touchdown which took Scotland 13-3 ahead. It was the killer blow: England just could not get back into the game after that score.

For Tony, the match marked a perfect end to his first season in international rugby. A background as a strong-running centre in the Hawick High School and Scottish Schools teams equipped him with the talent to forge a way as a hungry winger when he made the transition to first-class rugby as a teenager. Yet few players ever dream of making the debut run which Tony enjoyed in 1989-90.

He was on the winning side in each of his first six Scotland matches, collecting five tries in his first two appearances, and could have been excused for thinking that international rugby was a mere bagatelle. However, while he has become his country's second most prolific try-scorer in Tests, the Scotland side has never since matched its wonderful achievements of 1990.

Tony has now scored fifteen tries in Tests. Neither quick off the mark nor particularly blessed with evasive skills, he needs a metre or two to move into top gear. Once into full stride, however, he is a rugby sight to behold. His graceful, raking stride generates the pace which takes him flying to the line when he is set up for a clear run-in. Moreover, he is not averse to taking on defenders when his path is less obvious. Indeed, at 6ft 2in and 14st, Tony is a leviathan among wingers and certainly takes some stopping. He uses his height and weight intelligently to put would-be tacklers under pressure, and he has the priceless ability to stay on his feet to ride weak tackles. Often he creates his own space by stepping clear from close-range marking to work up momentum and dash away to score.

Tony has made the Scotland right-wing berth his own and, at twenty-five and with thirty consecutive caps in the trophy cabinet, he could easily overtake Iwan Tukalo's record number of appearances by a Scottish wing (thirty-seven). Besides, if he maintains his impressive scoring strike rate he should go on to challenge Ian Smith's all-time Scottish career record of twenty-four international tries.

Yet, even if he never scores another try for Scotland, his place in his country's sporting folklore will always be guaranteed, thanks to that March day in 1990.

Tony Stanger celebrates the Scotland win in the 1990 decider against England at Murrayfield.

Derek WHITE (Gala, London Scottish)

Bad news for Scotland's opponents in the Grand Slam campaign of 1990 came in the shape of three dynamic back row forwards: Finlay Calder, John Jeffrey and Derek White. Derek was the quiet, conscientious No. 8 whose Scottish career began when Calder and Jeffrey were nothing more than mere twinkles in the Scottish selectors' eyes. And those same selectors were happy to continue to play him after his two illustrious colleagues had chosen early retirement.

Dunbar-born Derek made his Scotland debut in 1982, as a flanker. It was then not until the 1987 Rugby World Cup in New Zealand that he returned to the Scotland side. After Ian McGeechan took over as national coach in 1988, Derek became the automatic choice at No. 8 in a breakaway unit which played together seventeen times, the Scottish record for a back row.

In the search for the reasons behind Scotland's rise under Ian McGeechan, Derek White's name features boldly. He was the perfect embodiment of the all-round loose forward: effective at disrupting the delivery of opponents' ball in the loose; a useful strike force from the back of the scrum; and a battering ram who softened up defences with his charging runs in second-phase attacks.

The rest of Scotland's tactics in these years hinged on the success of Derek's endeavours in concert with his back row colleagues. When the tartan trio stepped gaily on their way, the day went well for their country. Nobody present in Dublin in 1990, when the Scots began their build-up to the Grand Slam with their first away win in the championship for four years, would disagree with that view. Scotland struggled for an hour before the Irish were put to the sword. Then it was a sustained period of Scottish forward pressure led by Jeffrey, White and Calder which sent the men in green faltering through first gear and neutral into rapid reverse. Derek was the man who finally penetrated the defence, going on the rampage from a scrum ten minutes from time and scoring the match-winning try with two defenders clinging desperately to him.

Twice more that season, Derek played his heart out for Scotland. He performed an effective double-act with John Jeffrey against Wales, when the pair invariably arrived first at the breakdown to set up vital second-phase ball against a Welsh pack picked specifically for its mobility. England, in *the* Calcutta Cup match of the century, were an entirely different kettle of fish, but once again the big, fair-haired No. 8 showed his mettle and versatility. While his covert operations in the rucks and mauls gave pleasure to connoisseurs of forward play, there was no such joy for the England pack as they found Derek and his cronies disrupting their supply of possession to their threequarters.

That 13-7 triumph against England was arguably the summit of a mountainous career in which Derek scored eleven international tries, earning an entry alongside his comrade, John Jeffrey, for the most tries scored for Scotland by a forward. His country has yet to find an adequate replacement.

Derek White prepares to help Craig Chalmers in Scotland's match against England, 1991.

IRELAND PLAYER PROFILES

Ciaran Fitzgerald.

Ollie CAMPBELL
(Old Belvedere)

The East-versus-West confrontation of outside-halves is a phenomenon well-known in Wales, where the rival claims of two outstanding performers from opposite ends of the South Wales rugby cradle has often been an interesting problem for the selectors to solve.

The closest Ireland have come to producing a brilliant side in the past twenty years was in the early 1980s, when their selectors, too, were faced with the difficult decision of choosing between the merits of two different but exciting outside-halves: Tony Ward from Munster in the West, and Ollie Campbell of Dublin in the East. Both were expert kickers; both could hoodwink defences with a shuffle of the feet or a convincing dummy; and both had their champions.

But it was Ollie Campbell who occupied the pivot position when it really mattered, in 1982 - Ireland's Triple Crown season. Tony Ward, it was argued, was too individualistic to bring out the best of a talented Irish back line. Ollie, by contrast, was more than just a kicking machine: he was an instinctive genius who loved to run, and he took as much pleasure from freeing a threequarter with a delicately-given pass as he did from thumping over a fifty-metre penalty with a casual sweep of the right instep. He was also an enthusiastic tackler - a rare trait in an outside-half.

Ollie was calm where Tony Ward was erratic, and Ollie was a tactical thinker where Tony was an impulsive opportunist. They contrasted in personality and appearance too. Ollie was the shy, red-haired perfectionist who had immersed himself in rugby since his school-days at Belvedere College, the Jesuit academy that gave the world Tony O'Reilly and Ireland's first great rugby captain, Karl Mullen, as well as Terry Wogan. Ward was dark, played off-the-cuff, and was more broad-minded in his interests. For example, it was alleged that he once raised the eyebrows of the Irish selectors when he said that he preferred to attend a Football League game in London instead of watching a club rugby match.

The single feature of Ollie's approach to rugby which eclipsed all others was his dedication. He practised his kicking until all hours in all conditions all the year round. Selected for his first cap against Australia in 1976 he missed four goal-kicks and was immediately discarded. It looked for a while as if the hours of devotion he had given to the game would be the wasted time of just another of rugby's legion of one-cap wonders.

But Ollie's resilience and steadiness were rewarded in the summer of 1979, when he leap-frogged Tony Ward to kick Ireland to a share of a two-Test series with the Aussies. Another sound performance, this time in the Irish trial in early 1980, took him into his first Five Nations championship. After that, Ollie never looked back.

He was a prolific collector of points and set a

Ollie Campbell (right) in usual immaculate kicking style, whilst (below) he illustrates his instinctive love of running from the tightest of positions.

new championship scoring record in 1980, gathering 46 points. He equalled this mark in 1982, setting a new individual match record with six penalties and a drop-goal when Ireland - or rather Campbell - beat Scotland 21-12 for the Triple Crown. And he pulled clear of Tom Kiernan's national points record in 1983, before finishing on 217 points from twenty-two matches. Illness and a much-needed rest took him away from the Irish side in 1984 and, to the regret of his country's supporters, he never returned.

Willie DUGGAN (Blackrock College)

The book of Irish Triple Crown victories is, admittedly, a thin volume - the Irish have only won the mythical trophy six times in their history. The list honouring the players who have partaken of these few-and-far-between prize-givings is short too, but it does include some notable back-row men. One Charles V Rooke, who was in the first Irish side to win the Triple Crown in 1894, is regarded as the father of modern wing-forward play. Des O'Brien, Jim McCarthy and Bill McKay were the breakaway trio whose exploits helped their country to successive triple triumphs in 1948 and 1949. And it was another combination of loose forwards, John O'Driscoll, Fergus Slattery and Willie Duggan, who were synonymous with Ireland's 1982 crowning efforts.

Willie Duggan, a native of Kilkenny, was a rich rugby character in the finest tradition of Irish sport. His forceful play on the field was equalled only by his strong personality and big sense of humour off it.

Willie learnt to play at Rockwell College in Tipperary, but chose to join the Blackrock club in Dublin after leaving school. For Willie, a 150-mile round trip to the capital for a match was not a long way to go: throughout his long first-class career, he was a one-club man who never once complained about the demands rugby made on his business as an electrical contractor.

His stubborn defence and menacing charges from broken play were qualities which he first showed playing for Leinster between 1972 and 1974, and which ultimately earned him promotion to the Ireland team in 1975. Once there, his game improved in leaps and bounds. Willie himself was a quick learner who benefited from the advice of Roly Meates, one of Irish rugby's best-ever coaching gurus. The wily, wiry Willie added a line-out dimension to his talents, and his tail-gunning from the back of that set-piece became a useful strike weapon in Ireland's armoury in the late 1970s.

The value of his unyielding style of play was never higher than in 1982. Despite a tendency to give away penalties for offside or handling the ball on the floor (signs of his keenness to get on with the game), Willie's shuddering tackles and barnstorming runs in the loose were important factors which relieved the pressure on the Irish team in their march to the Triple Crown. And how his colleagues missed him when he had to withdraw on the eve of the Grand Slam game in Paris. Without Willie to bottle up the threat of the French back row, Ireland's season ended with a 9-22 defeat at Parc des Princes.

He was on top with Ireland again in 1983, when the title was shared with France and, in January 1984, he went into the Paris match in an Irish pack which broke all manner of records: the eight were playing together for the eighth time; their mean age was 31 years, 10 months; and Willie was appearing with Slattery and O'Driscoll for the nineteenth time in his country's back row. Alas! Irish rugby has never been famed for its half-measures. After two wonderful seasons, 1984 found them whitewashed in the championship, and Willie was one of several members of the old brigade whose services were dispensed with for 1985.

Ciaran FITZGERALD
(St Mary's College)

Irish rugby was on the verge of its longest losing streak as the 1982 Five Nations championship loomed. Under Fergus Slattery, Ireland had lost seven Tests on the trot in 1981. But then came something completely different, and a remodelled Irish team, fashioned around a new captain, exposed the flying circus of unpredictability which hovers over Five Nations rugby. That year, Ireland were catapulted from wooden-spoonists to champions.

The credit for the change in Irish fortunes went jointly to Ollie Campbell, who called the tactical tune from fly-half, and Ciaran Fitzgerald, the new skipper. Ciaran was a seasoned hooker who had followed in the well-trodden footsteps of Ray McLoughlin. He had learned the game at Garbally Park in his native Connacht, and had captained the province as well as St Mary's College, the Dublin club which he joined when he took up a career in the Irish Army. First selected for his country in Australia in 1979, he had won six consecutive caps before giving way to Pat Whelan at the outset of Ireland's ill-starred 1981 season.

From time to time, the Irish find a born leader to take a grip on their rugby team, and Ciaran proved to be such a find. He was implacable in the face of adversity,although his leadership skills were tested to the full when he first found himself in charge of the national side in January 1982. Wales led 9-4 just before half-time, but Ireland's new captain chivvied his men with a hands-on approach that brought out the hitherto latent talent of the team. The result was that Ireland won by 20-12 and, at Twickenham a fortnight later, Ciaran's inspirational and busy captaincy was a significant factor in another triumph. The skipper was regularly seen urging his colleagues to give of their best. Enthusiasm oozed from every pore of his body, and every member of the Irish team appeared to respond to his encouragement.

It was at Twickenham, too, that the various aspects of his forward play were brightly illuminated. He had a technically sound game against Peter Wheeler, the best hooker in the Five Nations, and his example in the loose was unforgettable. Indeed, his ferocious mauling near the end of the match wrestled the ball free to set up Ginger McLoughlin's vital try - moments which have become enshrined in Irish rugby's folklore. Victory against Scotland followed to leave Ireland holding the Triple Crown for the first time since 1949.

Ciaran possessed a seraphic face, but it masked his steely determination to keep Ireland at the top of the rugby tree. For sheer drive he had no equal among contemporary captains and, after leading his country to a share of the Five Nations title with France in 1983, he was selected to lead the Lions in New Zealand.

It was an unhappy tour. The Lions were whitewashed, and Ciaran was the target of a hostile campaign waged by some parts of the British press. His leadership was criticised and, when he returned to Dublin, he was first injured and then dropped from an Irish side which was similarly whitewashed in the 1984 Five Nations.

Never one to overstate his achievements or to dwell on his disappointments, he bounced back in 1985 to lead another Irish championship-winning side. That must have given Commandant Fitzgerald, then aide-de-camp to the President of the Irish Republic, warm satisfaction. One year later, he led Ireland for the nineteenth and final time. But he will be forever remembered as the icon of one of the most successful periods in Irish rugby history.

Ciaran Fitzgerald (centre) discusses a tactical point with Michael Bradley. Des Fitzgerald (right) awaits instructions.

Michael GIBSON
(Cambridge University, NIFC)

To a man, the contemporaries of Mike Gibson, and those from the generations that preceded him, will agree that he is the player they would pick in midfield if selecting an all-time World XV.

Mike filled the lead part for Ireland in one of the longest-running shows in international rugby. His classical qualities brought massive audiences to watch him perform for an unprecedented fifteen years on the highest stage.

He was an outside-half who had such an encyclopaedic knowledge of rugby patterns that, like the grand masters of chess, he foresaw complex passages of play several moves before they unwound. This was an obvious gift in defence but, when he applied his perception in attack, the results were invariably tries to savour. Nothing flashy; just the products of elegant designs planned in the mind of a rugby genius who was blessed with the beautiful balance and sound technique needed to execute them at speed.

Oddly, the only flaw of his uncomplicated game derived from his quickness of mind. By thinking ahead, his concentration at any given instant was marginally compromised. In this respect, he resembled the brilliant mathematician who trips up by making an elementary arithmetic slip in an otherwise seamless proof. Mike Gibson's occasional error was a dropped pass early in a match.

It was at Cambridge in the Michaelmas term of 1963 that he first attracted the attention of the critics and the Irish selectors. An unorthodox outside-half, Mike was none the less an effective and elusive runner who had a convincing dummy to help him to open tight defences. He made a dream debut against England in 1964, guiding his country to their first win at Twickenham for sixteen years. After that, he was an integral part of the Ireland XV.

Between 1968 and 1975, Irish rugby enjoyed a rare run of success. The wearers of the green lost only one Five Nations match at home in this period, and the team shared the championship title in 1973 before winning it outright in 1974. Mike Gibson operated as a centre during these years, having transferred to the threequarter line when big Barry McGann was introduced at outside-half in 1969.

Mike Gibson the centre was an even better proposition than Mike Gibson the outside-half. The uncluttered view of the game he had from the middle of the threequarter line gave him more scope to study lines of attack, and increased his own freedom to choose his options.

The splendid vision he had in reading the play, as

well as his speed off the mark and sparkling side-stepping runs, gave an edge to Ireland's back line in the successes of 1974. A vintage Gibson performance was always worth travelling many miles to see, and those present at Twickenham in 1974 saw two tries which illustrated the different facets of Mike's genius. A simple dummy opened up England's defence for him to score his first, and his acute sense of anticipation and intelligent running off the ball were the talents behind a later try when he popped up unexpectedly on the overlap.

Mike Gibson finally called it a day in 1979, having become the world's most-capped player. But since his retirement, no British back has come anywhere near the quiet Ulsterman's claim to the title of best all-round post-war footballer.

Mike Gibson was just as brilliant in his Cambridge shirt as he was in the green of Ireland.

Moss KEANE (Lansdowne)

There nas never been much love lost between the Rugby Union and Gaelic football factions in Irish sport.

Writing one hundred years ago, Jacques MacCarthy, the vitriolic correspondent of the *Irish Times*, noted: 'Football in Ireland may be said to consist of three parts. In Rugby, you kick the ball; in Association, you kick the man if you cannot kick the ball; and in Gaelic, you kick the ball if you cannot kick the man.'

For their part, the Gaelic football authorities banned their players from rugby - or any other code of football, for that matter - for years. Then, in the 1960s, the ban was lifted and, in 1974, one Maurice Ignatius Keane, late of the Gaelic football stronghold that is County Kerry, went into the annals of sporting history as the first former Gaelic rules man to represent his country in international rugby.

Apart from this distinction, Moss, as he was known, went on to earn his

place in Irish rugby's hall of fame on the strength of his forward play in the teams that won the championship title outright in 1974 and again in 1982, when the Triple Crown became Ireland's possession for the first time since 1949. Very much in the Willie-John McBride mould, both in build and style of play, Moss assumed the great man's mantle from 1975 and went on to win fifty-one caps as a lock before retiring in 1984 after gracing forty-four consecutive Five Nations matches in eleven seasons - a remarkable tribute to his durability and fitness.

Moss Keane blocks Sandy Carmichael in a line-out during Ireland's match against Scotland, 1977.

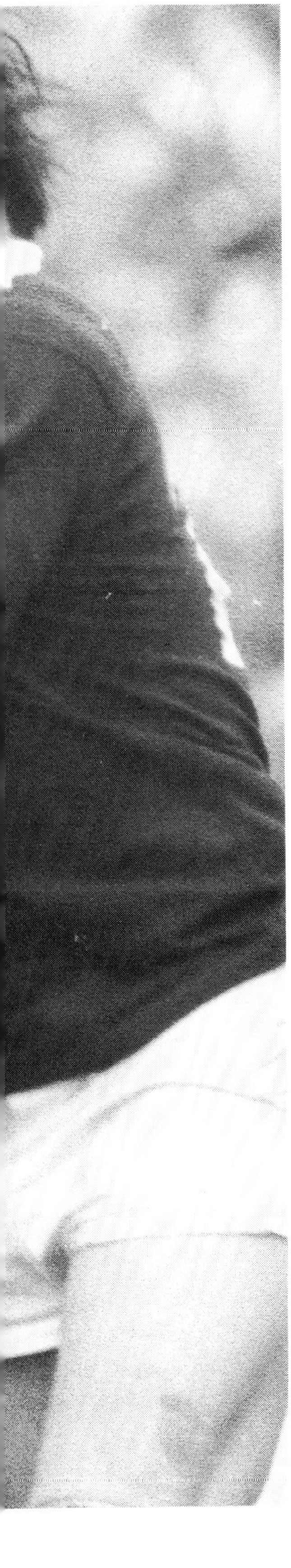

Although he was a trifle green when he first packed down alongside Willie-John against France in 1974, Moss demonstrated with something to spare that the selectors' faith in him was justified. Ireland were beaten 6-9 in the last minutes that day in Paris, but young Moss revealed the commitment and spirit for which Kerrymen are renowned. He was prominent in several of the rushes which gave the French such a fright and, by the end of the season, he had slotted in perfectly to the traditional scavenging, disruptive role which comes so naturally to successful Irish forwards. And the Irish *were* successful in that campaign, winning the championship outright for the first time for twenty-three years. Moss had arrived in the side at the right time.

Moss had studied agricultural science at UC Cork before taking up a post with the Department of Agriculture in Dublin and, when he arrived in the Irish capital in the 1970s, he made a beeline for the Lansdowne club. It was a move he never regretted: the skills he learned at the club, allied to the natural athleticism which had first found expression on the Gaelic football field, stood him in great stead throughout his long career.

Perhaps his biggest service to Irish rugby was as the bulwark of the scrum which paved the way for the 1982 Triple Crown and championship. At the age of thirty-three, he scrummaged with all the power of his youth and the accumulated wisdom of several years' top-class experience. He was at the core of the sides which outplayed Wales and England to set up the Triple Crown game with Scotland, and who among the crowd in Dublin on that momentous occasion will forget the stirring sight of Moss and his seven colleagues time and again 'walking' the Scottish pack back several yards?

By then he had become the resident wit of the Irish side. One of the best tales told about Moss relates to a trial match in the early 1980s, when he was on the senior side in a 30-19 win. After the game, he turned to Ollie Campbell and announced: 'Between us we did all the scoring.' Campbell had scored 26 of the points.

Moss was in the Irish side that shared the championship in 1983, but 1984 proved a bridge too far for a pack that was tagged with the 'Dad's Army' label. The Irish were whitewashed in the championship, and Moss bowed out of international rugby, second only to Willie-John McBride on the list of the world's leading locks.

Ken KENNEDY
(CIYMS, London Irish)

There was a time in the 1960s when international players appearing in matches against Ireland wondered if kissing the Blarney stone was a prerequisite of becoming an Irish forward. For the men in green invariably fielded a couple of pack-men who kept up a constant harangue, both of colleagues and opponents, throughout the eighty minutes.

Noel Murphy was renowned for his babble in this way, and so was the Rochester-born hooker who became a permanent fixture in the Irish front row - Ken Kennedy. But Ken did more than just talk a great game; he was the model of fitness and agility who helped define the modern No. 2's role. Changing laws in the 1960s demanded that all forwards should be capable of making useful contributions in the loose, particularly at rucks and mauls, and the days of the Toby-jug hooker became numbered after the introduction of the Australian dispensation law in 1968-69.

Ken Kennedy had the physique and stamina of a loose forward to complement his technical skills as a rake. He perfected a swift, sweeping motion to strike quickly for the ball in the tight, and owed his long career at the top (eleven seasons in the Irish side) to his litheness, tenacity and determination to stay fit. Exceptionally well co-ordinated for a front-rower, he brooked no nonsense in the hurly-burly of battle, yet managed always to keep his head when others lost theirs.

Raised and educated in Ulster, he broke into the Irish side in 1965 while he was a medical student at Queen's University. His first season coincided with Ireland's surge from bottom to near the top of the championship table, and he was one of several players in key positions who stayed healthy and in form long enough for their country to keep the nucleus of a developing side together and press for championship honours. Ireland thereby established the continuity which so often runs hand in hand with rugby success. Ken was the bonding agent who did much to ensure that a club atmosphere prevailed in the team, and his example to colleagues was inspiring.

Ireland's reward, after establishing an impressive home record between 1968 and 1971, came in 1973 and 1974. Ken retained the competitive edge to remain first-choice hooker in a very experienced front row which also included Ray McLoughlin and Sean Lynch. That trio were the foundation on which was built the Ireland team that shared the Five Nations prize in 1973 and won the championship title outright in 1974. No opposition front row disturbed the Irish when Messrs McLoughlin, Kennedy and Lynch were on duty.

As opponents came and went, Ken seemed, like Tennyson's brook, to go on for ever. When he did bow out, against Wales at Cardiff in 1975, he had gathered forty-five caps, a record for an Irish hooker which stands to this day.

Michael KIERNAN
(Dolphin, Lansdowne)

Michael Kiernan belongs to one of Irish rugby's leading dynasties. His uncle Tom was Ireland's full-back in fifty-four Tests between 1960 and 1973; and another of his uncles, Mick Lane, was a threequarter in the 1949 Triple Crown team.

Michael entered the Irish team as a replacement against Wales in 1982, at a time when a mood of hopelessness was about to give way to a spirit of optimism, and his contribution to his country's resurrection after seven defeats on the trot was not inconsiderable. He had an enthusiasm for the game which comes naturally to Irishmen, and he brought the pace of a former Irish sprint champion to the team. Not all gifted track athletes transfer their talents effectively to the rugby pitch but, from the moment he entered the Ireland side, Michael demonstrated his potential as an attacking centre of silky skills. There was a beautiful balance to his running, yet he also showed that he had the vision to create try-scoring chances for his wingers. Look at the statistics: in his first five championship campaigns, a dozen tries were laid on for Ireland's wings whereas, by contrast,it had taken Michael's predecessors twice as many seasons to supply their wings with as many scoring opportunities.

Clever support play and an uncanny positional sense were other hallmarks of his game, and he must have thought that international rugby was a mere bagàtelle as he prepared to pack his bags for the 1983 Lions tour to New Zealand. For after only two seasons in the Irish side, he had already been a part of a team which had won the championship outright in 1982 and shared the title in 1983.

However, the New Zealand tour was a disappointment for all the British and Irish backs who appeared in the Test series, and Michael looked jaded

Michael Kiernan, playing for Ireland against Scotland in 1986, watches his penalty-kick as Phil Orr covers his eyes.

when he returned to Ireland. A career move from Cork to Dublin prompted a transfer to the Lansdowne club, but in the final Irish trial in 1984 his form was indifferent, and he lost his place for the two opening matches of the Five Nations tournament.

That wasn't a bad season to be in the wings: Ireland were whitewashed. But, by the start of the next season, Michael was back to his best and provided the backbone of Ireland's young team which regained the Triple Crown and championship title. Elevated now to the important role of place-kicker, he landed 47 points for the unbeaten Irish side - a tally which left the Irish coach, Mick Doyle, laughing into his beer since he had told the press at the outset of the campaign that Ireland had no expert goal-kicker! Certainly,the gods had smiled on Michael and his country in the final match of that season, against England in Dublin. In a nerve-racking game, Michael kept his cool to kick two penalties and, in the dying moments, he dropped Ireland's winning goal after the visitors had led 10-7 during the second half.

The light continued to shine on Michael for several more seasons. Although his pace waned in later years, his experience and invaluable place-kicking efforts enabled Ireland to hold their heads high throughout the 1980s. Whenever Michael Kiernan was in the side, the Irish were never considered a pushover on the rugby field.

Jack KYLE
(Queen's U Belfast, NIFC)

Few incidents on the rugby field excite spectators' interest more than a fly-half tearing defences to shreds with will-o'-the-wisp breaks. The player whose elusive runs did wonders for Irish esteem in the immediate post-war seasons was Jack Kyle, a young medical student at Queen's University, Belfast.

But Jack was far more than a mazy runner. His contribution to Ireland's two Triple Crown seasons (1948 and 1949) and three championship titles (1948, 1949 and 1951) was beyond measure. How he managed to take a game by the scruff of the neck, and how he instinctively knew the tactical moves most likely to benefit a team of limited ability, were phenomenal talents. Ireland had an intelligent pack, and Jack would be the first to acknowledge the splendid service he received from two skilful scrum-halves, Eric Strathdee and John O'Meara, during the years of Irish dominance. But his own spontaneous skills in the pivotal role were the keys that unlocked Ireland's potential for honours.

He could land a tactical kick on a sixpence, he could sniff out an opening where ordinary bloodhounds would be senseless, and his uncanny positional intuition enabled him to pop up at unexpected moments in defence and make try-saving clearances.

Like many of rugby's extraordinary performers, his persona off the field was merely ordinary. Many stories were told of his unflappability: how he would nod off on the bus to big matches when others were uptight; or how occasionally he would become absorbed in a book and nearly miss a team talk or training session. If Kipling had been born some fifty years later, Jack Kyle might well have been the inspiration for the immortal lines: 'If you can keep your head when all about you . . .' Even when he was controlling tactics in the hurly-burly of an international, Jack was the model of stability.

Although there was no Triple Crown for them in 1951, the Irish were champions that year. In the opinion of many leading critics, the side was the best of the three that won championship honours and, needless to add, Jack was the perceptive guide who took Ireland to the brink of a Grand Slam.

With wins against France, England and Scotland under their belt, Ireland found themselves 0-3 down to Wales at Cardiff in March. Then a flash of Jack's genius gave the packed Arms Park a try to live in the memory. From a line-out in the Welsh 22, he looped around his inside centre to receive a return pass. Next, he overlapped his outside centre and, tucking the ball under his right arm, he accelerated through a gap to take him up to the Welsh full-back, whom he left standing with a side-step off his right foot. Any one of three Welsh defenders might have tackled him, but Jack's try squared the match. And, minutes later, the defensive qualities of the great fly-half were seen when he terminated a sprint by Ken Jones, the Welsh wing, with a try-saving tackle ten metres from Ireland's line .

Jack Kyle went on thrilling crowds with his wonderful feats until 1958, when his international career finished on a then world record of forty-six caps for his country. He also played six Tests for the Lions. The modest Ulster doctor carried on playing rugby for fun and served his club, North of Ireland, for several more seasons as a full-back in the 3rd XV. There he seemed to draw just as much enjoyment from the game as when he had weaved through international defences with the easy confidence of a slalom racer.

Jack Kyle's mazy runs contributed much to Ireland's three championship wins just after the war.

Donal LENIHAN
(UC Cork, Cork Constitution)

He reminds me of a young Willie-John McBride,' said Tom Kiernan, the Irish national coach, of the twenty-two-year-old Donal Lenihan in November 1981. Donal, a student at University College Cork, had just completed his first full international for Ireland, against the Wallabies, and, in the decade that followed, he would go on to confirm the wisdom of his coach's observation. Donal played fifty-two matches in his country's second row, packing a spring in his heel to win good-quality line-out possession as Ireland's number one jumper. His total of caps for Ireland is only exceeded by one lock - that man Willie-John McBride.

Yet such distinction never entered the mind of the modest youngster when he embarked on his inaugural Five Nations campaign in January 1982. True, he had become only the fourth Irishman to win schools, Under-23 and B international honours before winning his senior cap, yet he was very much the stripling among the men in an Irish pack whose mean age was thirty. There were doubts about his physique: he appeared to be too thin, too light to be successful at the predatory game favoured by Ireland's forwards. Certainly, he had plenty to prove as he lined up against Wales for his first championship match.

Donal came through his test with flying colours, so much so that he was hailed as the most exciting new forward Irish rugby had produced for several seasons. Apart from the glut of ball he supplied at the line-out, he stampeded around the open spaces of Lansdowne Road with the spectacular effect of a wildebeest on the African grasslands. It was a sight that was to stir Irish teams and crowds throughout the 1980s and set up not a few decisive Irish scores.

His championship entry coincided with Ireland laying to rest the bogey of seven consecutive international defeats, and Donal could be forgiven for thinking that rugby at this level was a piece of cake. Before his twenty-fourth birthday he had been on the winning side in six of

his first eight Five Nations matches, while Ireland had been Triple Crown winners in 1982 and had shared the title in 1983.

Without any shadow of a doubt, his finest season was in 1985. Fuller of figure, he was now better able to parry the disruptive efforts of awkward line-out opponents and had developed the subtle knack of using his colleagues to lever himself higher off the ground. He had turned himself, too, into a more than useful mauler.

Most of Ireland's 'Dad's Army' pack had been pensioned off after the championship whitewash in 1984, leaving Donal as one of the senior officers in Ciaran Fitzgerald's scrum. Much depended on the young banking executive from Cork, and he did not let his country down. Donal's dominance at the line-out, power in the tight and surges in the loose were instrumental in putting Ireland back at the top of the northern hemisphere's rugby tree. And arguably his greatest moment in a green jersey came in the final seconds of the match with England in Dublin. With the scores level, Donal fastened on to the ball to make one of his do-or-die charges into England's 22. Egged on by all Ireland, he committed the England forwards to a maul, the ball was fed back, and Mike Kiernan dropped the goal that brought Ireland the match, Triple Crown and championship points.

Although the Irish were never to reach such lofty peaks again, Donal lived up to the great expectations critics and colleagues had of him as the genuine successor to Willie-John McBride.

Donal Lenihan jumps for the ball during a line-out against France in 1987.

Hugo MacNEILL
(Dublin U, Oxford U, Blackrock College, London Irish)

After the introduction in 1968-69 of the Australian dispensation law restricting kicking to touch, the selection of running full-backs with a flair for attack became almost *de rigueur* in international rugby. Yet the only Irishman to take to the role like a natural in the past twenty-five years was Hugo MacNeill, who missed only three Five Nations matches in a career which brought him thirty-seven caps between 1981 and 1988.

Ireland have rarely been quoted as favourites to win the Five Nations championship and, when they have, wooden spoons have usually been the only prizes with which they have finished. The burden of top seeding sits awkwardly on their reluctant shoulders. It was such an Irish team which found itself in this bewildering role when Hugo first entered its ranks against France in 1981. And, sure enough, Ireland finished bottom of the heap that year with four defeats in four games. Hugo, however, emerged as the find of the season.

Even in the despair of the whitewash, he managed to show off his abilities in attack. On his debut, he revealed his pace when he timed perfectly a break into the threequarter line before slipping through the tackles of Roland Bertranne and Serge Gabernet, two of the most experienced hands then in international business, for a super try.

In that first season on the championship stage, he also showed that, left home alone in his own half by a defensively feeble back line, he could tackle bravely. His only weakness - one which he later eradicated - was a tendency to overstretch himself and thus fail when kicking for touch.

It was typical of the fickle Irish to win the Triple Crown and championship the next season when they started (surprise, surprise) as underdogs. The campaign was one which saw Hugo grow in stature. Sound positioning, an increasing confidence to run at opponents from the depths of his own territory, and a marked technical improvement in his fielding and line-kicking, indicated that he had come of age as an international player. Pundits hailed him as one of the players-of-the-season. Mind, he did have the benefit of excellent advice in this respect: Tom Kiernan, the Irish coach, had filled the No. 15 jersey with distinction for a decade under the traditional laws, and knew well the basic elements of full-back play. In the 1982 Triple Crown match against Scotland in Dublin, Hugo graduated with honours in Kiernan's eyes. The young full-back was the model of steadiness under the high ball in a swirling wind which caused his celebrated opposite number, Andy Irvine, no end of problems.

So it was Hugo MacNeill who was the automatic choice at full-back for the 1983 Lions; and it was Hugo whose immaculately timed incursions created important scores on the path to another Triple Crown and championship for Ireland in 1985. And now it is for a full-back of Hugo's ilk that Irish rugby yearns during the most barren period of its history.

Willie-John McBRIDE
(Ballymena)

He wasn't the best line-out expert in the world, he wasn't the quickest forward in the loose, and he wasn't the perfect technician in the scrummages. But for strength of character and sheer physical power, it is doubtful whether British or Irish rugby will see his like again.

Willie-John McBride was the forward who dominated rugby in the northern hemisphere when he was at his peak between 1966 and 1974. On the world scene, his only serious rivals for the title of best lock were the tough-as-teak Springbok, Frik du Preez, and the New Zealand legend, Colin Meads.

Willie-John owed his natural fitness and immense strength to his upbringing and early working life on the family's fifty-acre farm at Moneyglass in County Antrim. He did not begin playing rugby until he was seventeen, but he took to the game like a bird to the air. Never one to shirk a challenge, Willie-John completed a rapid rise to the top within four years of his first school match at Ballymena: before his twenty-second birthday in 1962, he was an Irish international and a Lion.

But it was his ability to adapt to the changing needs of forward play in the 1960s, allied to that natural strength of his, which kept him to the fore in international rugby. As rucking and mauling became the vogue, so he applied his power to the task of winning vital second-phase ball. His legs pumped like pistons to supply drive at the heart of rucks, and he used his mighty arms to prise the ball free at mauls. As the demand for running, handling forwards increased, he even showed that he could join in the frolics of open play with the best of the pack.

Of course, the skills and labours of scrummaging remained important, even though law changes shifted the game's emphasis ever more towards continuous open play. The imperturbable Willie-John was never found to be anything but the solid backbone of the Irish scrum, going on to serve his country in sixty-three internationals spanning fourteen seasons.

Yet, above all, he will more likely be remembered for his charisma. He had first shown his leadership potential with the successful 1971 Lions in New Zealand, where he assumed the duties of pack-leader when Ray McLoughlin's tour was prematurely finished through injury. Willie-John had always had the respect of his colleagues; now he inspired their confidence and won their affection. He was the leader whose followers genuinely warmed to his calm control: players wanted to do well for him.

However, he came to captaincy late in his career, taking over from Tom Kiernan in 1973, when Ireland shared the Five Nations title. The following season, his never-say-die attitude paid off when the Irish were outright champions for the first time in twenty-three years. After two matches, his side had been languishing in fourth position on one point. But, on the eve of the England game at

Twickenham, he was quoted as saying that it was quite pointless going into any international unless there was a belief that winning was possible. His side duly beat England - and Scotland a fortnight later - and finished as the most improbable champions for decades.

In the minds of most rugby men, it was Willie-John's performances for the Lions, and particularly as captain of the all-conquering 1974 team to South Africa, that etched the Ulsterman's name among the game's eternal greats. And when the big-boned brave from Ballymena retired in 1975, more than a dozen top international locks let out a huge sigh of relief.

Willie-John McBride escapes the clutches of Andy Ripley at Twickenham in 1974.

Ray McLOUGHLIN (UC Dublin, Gosforth, Blackrock College)

Ray McLoughlin, a graduate of UC Dublin who later studied at Newcastle University, was the thinking man's ideal prop. He applied the analytical powers which brought him first-class university honours to solve the essential mechanics of scrummaging and, later, he was just as thoughtful in his approach to captaincy.

Irish rugby had drifted aimlessly during the decade or so since their Five Nations title in 1951. Meanwhile, Ray's growing reputation as a successful captain at Gosforth, the Newcastle club he had joined while studying for his doctorate, attracted the interest of the Connacht selectors in his native province. Now Connacht have always been regarded as Ireland's Cinderella team but, under Ray's leadership, the players were persuaded to plan more carefully and prepare more seriously for matches. His strategy worked wonders with the province; could his methods be transferred to the national side?

The answer was a resounding yes. He injected the spirit of purpose into the Ireland team. At a time when the word 'coach' in the rugby context meant nothing more sophisticated than a mode of transporting teams to matches, Irish internationals were called by their captain to team meetings at which tactical options were explored. Senior players were invited to contribute to discussions, and even the opinions of selectors were sought. Ray succeeded in motivating his teams to concentrate on victory and, in the psychological and physical preparation of an international side, he was probably five years ahead of his time.

He had first appeared in the green jersey on the same day that Willie-John McBride made his debut, against England in 1962. Three years later, Ray was the Irish captain and seeking his country's first Triple Crown since 1949. A draw with France and victories against England and Scotland set up the showdown of the 1965 season, when Ireland visited Cardiff to meet an unbeaten Wales XV. But Ireland's failure to press home a distinct first-half advantage cost them dearly, and Wales went on to win 14-8. Though many were satisfied with the huge improvement Ireland had made in moving from wooden-spoonists to championship contenders, shrewd critics felt that their captain should have manipulated the tactics more firmly to give his side the edge when Wales were reduced to fourteen men in the early stages of the Cardiff match.

The following season, Ray was relieved of the captaincy when a poor Irish team performance resulted in a disappointing home defeat by Scotland and, after travelling with the Lions in Australasia in 1966, knee injuries and increasing business commitments kept him out of the Ireland side.

Five years later, he made one of the most astonishing comebacks in international rugby history. He had switched from tight-head to loose-head, but all of the old scrummaging expertise was still there. The strong back, aligned low and parallel with the ground, put opponents under tremendous pressure. Enjoying a new lease of life, Ray confirmed the maxim that good props really do come of age in their thirties.

For five more seasons he burrowed away conscientiously, becoming the cornerstone of the Irish scrums which paved the way for the championship honours won in 1973 and 1974. He finally quit at the top in 1975. After forty caps at prop (a then world record shared with David Rollo and Sandy Carmichael of Scotland), he had earned his rest. Certainly, his international opponents welcomed the respite which his retirement brought for them.

John MOLONEY
(St Mary's College)

The most disappointing Five Nations campaign since the war was 1972. Not because the standard of rugby was low - far from it - but there were political overtones which disrupted the schedule of fixtures. Troubles in strife-torn Ulster were at their height, and threats made by terrorists prevented Scotland and Wales travelling to Dublin to fulfil their matches with Ireland.

Ironically, it was Ireland's rugby players who had most reason to feel cheated by the cancellation of the games. Tom Kiernan's team, including John Moloney, a young half-back from St Mary's College, among its five new caps, was one of the best ever produced by the country.

Johnny Moloney had been the pretender to Roger Young's scrum-half throne for a couple of seasons. Then, when Young emigrated to South Africa, Johnny stepped up to fill the No. 9 shirt with pride. He had a sound record of achievement at club and provincial level behind him, and he took his international chance with open arms.

At the Stade Colombes, he made a dream debut when, in the ninth minute, he squirmed past several French defenders to open the scoring. Few newcomers can have scored their first international try in so short a time, and Ireland went on to their first win in Paris since 1952 (and, to date, their last). Another win, against England at Twickenham, set up the mouth-watering prospect of a Grand Slam decider between Ireland and Wales in Dublin. Alas, that particular contest never materialised, and the duel between Johnny and Gareth Edwards had to be put on ice for twelve months.

Johnny was one of those exciting scrum-halves who loved to run with the ball in club rugby. He was an accomplished player, cast in the same mould as many of his outstanding Irish predecessors: intelligent, resourceful and even-tempered, with a good eye for openings.

When Ireland shared the championship in 1973, he played very much in the shadow of his burly half-back partner, Barry McGann. Ireland's tactics that year comprised little more than the kick ahead and chase. But, by 1974, McGann's star had finally set, and Johnny carried a heavier tactical responsibility on his shoulders, playing in concert with Mick Quinn. For the first time at international level, Irish supporters saw the scrum-half show a clean pair of heels to his opponents, and Johnny's run for the line at Twickenham was one of the bright spots that illuminated Ireland's first outright Five Nations title win for twenty-three years.

In the second half of the 1970s he had to vie with John Robbie, Donal Canniffe, Robbie McGrath and Colin Patterson for the Irish scrum-half place. He had a full (but unsuccessful) season as captain in 1978, before finishing his career with two appearances on the wing in the 1980 Five Nations matches. That positional move was no surprise to those who had closely followed the career of Johnny Moloney the sportsman. For although he looked an unlikely speed merchant, he was in fact a fine athlete who was ranked in the top flight of Irish 200m sprinters.

Karl MULLEN
(Old Belvedere)

Karl Mullen was the man who boldly took Ireland where no captain had gone before: to the Grand Slam. And no Irish leader has yet emulated his feat.

Irish rugby's *annus mirabilis* was 1948 and Mullen, as hooker, was the modern game's first captain to think deeply about the preparation and tactical approach of an international championship team. For once, the Ireland players were persuaded to abandon their happy-go-lucky reliance on the rub of the green as they found themselves commanded by a general who planned his campaigns with military precision.

The failing of Irish rugby between the wars had been its tendency to run out of steam and capitulate in the last quarters of matches. But, under Karl Mullen, the Irish played a patterned forward game based on ball retention before letting Jack Kyle create tries in opponents' halves. The expert hooking of the captain himself was an important cog in the team's wheel of fortune for, without plenty of possession, clearly the Irish could not shut out their challengers.

The strategy was not pretty to watch - except when Jack Kyle occupied centre stage - but it was extremely fruitful. Dr Mullen's prescriptions worked a treat for Ireland: further Five Nations honours were achieved in 1949 and 1951, as the men in green became a very awkward hurdle for other teams to overcome.

The teenaged Karl Mullen had made the Irish selectors pencil his name into

Karl Mullen, seen here flanked by Sir W Tyrrell an

their notebooks during the 1945 autumn tour to Britain and Ireland by the famous Kiwis, the New Zealand Army rugby team. Karl also played in the popular series of victory internationals that season, and was the inevitable choice as hooker when Ireland resumed full internationals in 1947. Measuring 5ft llin and scaling 13st, he was a robust figure in the loose, but it was for his expertise as a striker of the ball at the scrums that he really won his spurs. He was nimble on his feet, tough as teak, and found support from rock-solid props. No wonder that, during his run of twenty-three consecutive Five Nations matches for Ireland, he rarely conceded a strike against the head.

Captaincy came naturally to him - he was only twenty-one when he took charge at Twickenham in 1948. Years ahead of his time in his thoughtful approach to leadership and team preparation, he also had the priceless gift of being able to adjust his tactics depending on the state of the game. That is an art which has eluded many rugby captains, but his capacity to detach himself from the hectic fray of front-row play in an international match and calmly reassess playing options was a vital element of Ireland's successes. For example, look at the closeness of their wins in 1948, 1949 and 1951, and the value of Karl Mullen's steely-nerved stewardship will be appreciated. Not surprisingly, he was nominated Lions captain for the 1950 tour of Australia and New Zealand.

Without his intelligent lead in 1952, when the captaincy passed to Des O'Brien, Ireland were less difficult to beat. He bowed out of the side the same year, but maintained a high profile in Irish rugby, becoming a national selector between 1961 and 1964, and looking after the Irish Wolfhounds, the well-known invitation side.

ay, captained Ireland to a unique Grand Slam in 1948 plus two other championships in 1949 and 1951.

Brendan MULLIN
(Dublin U, Oxford U, Blackrock College, London Irish)

There is no force known to man that will keep an Irishman away from a heated argument. The topic that provoked numerous rugby discussions in the bars and clubs of Ireland during the early 1990s was the enigmatic case of Brendan Mullin. Depending on which camp you belonged to, Brendan was either the hero who broke George Stephenson's long-standing Irish try-scoring record, or he was the overrated centre who never achieved his full rugby potential. There were no half-measures, no sitting on the fence. You either loved him or hated him.

Brendan made his international debut against Australia in November 1984, and his incisive offensive style was to become a potent weapon in Ireland's Triple Crown-winning campaign in 1985. He had all the attributes of a brilliant centre. Fast enough to break the Irish senior men's 110m hurdles record, Brendan also brought panache to the back line. His smooth running and handling skills complemented nicely the strong tackling and shrewd kicking of his co-centre, Michael Kiernan, and as a pair they played twenty-three times for Ireland. Like all good threequarters, Brendan was also well able to take advantage of the odd bit of luck, and his opportunism against England that year brought the only Irish try of the Triple Crown match. Always quick to follow kicks which put opposing full-backs under pressure, on this occasion he was up on Chris Martin in a flash. As Martin shaped to find the security of the touchline, Brendan lunged, charged down the attempted clearance, and gathered a kind bounce to waltz over for the first of his fifteen international tries.

Yet the gamekeepers-turned-poachers of Irish rugby - former players who contributed trenchant columns to the leading Irish newspaper groups - seemed to have it in for Brendan. He became the subject of unpleasant and sometimes unreasonable digs, and even his former coach, Mick Doyle, took a metaphorical swipe at him in a hard-hitting article. The crux of the technical criticism of Brendan's play was that he was not delivering the type of international performance for which he was selected. His ability to create and score tries for Ireland was not considered sufficient compensation for the deficiencies in other aspects of his game, a view that was not subscribed to by neutral pundits.

At the end of the day, Brendan did lose form. Whether the strong criticism affected him deeply or not, it was difficult to tell. But in March 1992, aged only twenty-eight and by then Ireland's most-capped centre, he suddenly announced his retirement from the game, citing family and business commitments as the reasons for his withdrawal. Weeks later, Ireland slumped to their heaviest-ever defeat in the Five Nations championship. Brendan was too patriotic to allow himself to share the wry laugh enjoyed by the majority who regarded him as one of Ireland's all-time great players.

Brendan Mullin, having evaded John Rutherford and David Johnston, is about to step out of a tackle by Roger Baird.

Desmond O'BRIEN
(London Irish, Cardiff)

You could be excused for thinking that someone was taking the mick if they suggested that one of the best Irish forwards to turn out in the green and white of his country was named Desmond O'Brien, and that he was an executive with the brewers of Guinness, the lifeblood of the Irish male.

But Desmond O'Brien did exist. He was an active participant in the lively Irish back row of the immediate post-war era, making an unbroken run of appearances from 1948 to 1952, a period

in which Ireland won the Five Nations title outright three times. And he did work for Guinness, joining the company as a trainee brewer at Park Royal in 1941, shortly after leaving school at Belvedere College, Dublin. During the war years he turned out as a flanker for Wasps, featuring at Sudbury in the regular matches put on by Neville Compton for servicemen on leave and those like the young Des who were in reserved occupations.

When normality returned to the rugby world after the war, Des moved to London Irish and switched to the No. 8 position. Within two years of the change, he was picked to make his Ireland debut against England at Twickenham. Sound displays in that match and the subsequent game with Scotland established him as a fixture in the side, and Karl Mullen, the Irish captain, appointed him his first-lieutenant. While Mullen was very much in charge of the team, Des O'Brien's counsel as pack-leader from the back row of the scrum, where he was better placed than his hooker captain to make overall judgements on the effectiveness of tactics, was much appreciated.

A tall, angular man, who was definitely not user-friendly to would-be tacklers, Des was a skilful dribbler who was in the vanguard of the rush which led to Chris Daly's try against Wales when Ireland won the Triple Crown and Grand Slam at Belfast in 1948. That exquisite moment in Ireland's rugby folklore - it was their first Triple Crown of the 20th century - was immortalised by its scorer when he said to O'Brien: 'If there's no further scoring, I'll be canonised'.

In 1950-51, his company moved Des to South Wales as a member of their sales group. Flogging beer to the Welsh was a doddle compared with breaking into the 1st XV at Cardiff. Nevertheless, the experienced Irishman served his time in the reserve ranks before taking his place beside several Welsh caps in the club's senior team.

The intensity of Welsh club rugby sharpened his reflexes, and his forthright play in Ireland's championship win in 1951 was hailed as a revolution in modern back-row tactics. Working closely with Jim McCarthy and Bill McKay, two speedy flankers, Des formed a tight defensive cordon which closed down the attacking options of opponents; and Ireland, who were unbeaten, conceded only four tries. But the achievement of the season was a win with only fourteen men at Murrayfield, when full-back George Norton was seriously injured early in the match and Ireland had to play with seven forwards. O'Brien and McCarthy performed wonders in bottling up the Scottish halves, and in the second half Des showed his nose for a try when he crossed for the winning score after a Kyle break.

After one season as Ireland captain, in 1952, he retired from serious rugby, but showed himself to be a man of many parts in subsequent years. He won representative honours at squash and hockey, and pursued numerous academic interests. His association with rugby football was never forgotten, however, and in 1966 he found the time to managc thc Lions tcam which toured Australia and New Zealand.

Des O'Brien (top) was a vital member of Ireland's great post-war team.

John O'DRISCOLL (London Irish, Manchester)

The roster of Irish rugby internationals is littered with the names of famous players who were members of the medical profession. The man who brought a clinical approach to Irish back-row play in the early 1980s was Dr John O'Driscoll - a Dublin-born, Manchester-educated, London Irish stalwart.

It was during his successful run as captain of the Irish exiles in 1980 that John became a fixture in the international side. A player of superb vision, he was a driving blind-side specialist who had the perfect physique for blocking duties in defence. There must be something about doctors' mentalities that makes them near-reckless when it comes to self-preservation on a rugby field; perhaps they know better than most the physical limits to which the human body can go. For John, like his famous fellow doctor, JPR Williams, positively relished the clatter of bodies in contact. He was a fearsome sight charging forward with the ball, and his crunching tackles stopped would-be attackers dead in their tracks.

A double Lion, he toured South Africa in 1980 and New Zealand in 1983, but his finest hours on the rugby field were as part of the firm of Slattery, Duggan and O'Driscoll, loose forwards to the Irish teams that won the Triple Crown and Five Nations title in 1982 and who were joint champions with France in 1983.

Apart from his classical contributions as a flanker, he had a useful fourth dimension to his play as a mopper-up of trifles at the tail of the line-outs and, in Ireland's Triple Crown wins against Wales, England and Scotland in 1982, he was mentioned in despatches for his control of the rear of that department. In a season of Irish wins which owed much to a precise tactical style mapped out in close detail (a rare piece of advanced preparation by Irish standards), John shone like the moon on a clear night. One of the cleanest forwards of his day, he hustled and bustled, bothered and smothered his opponents at rucks, mauls and on the fringes of the set-pieces. He was a great man to have on your side - a pain in the *gluteus maximus* to play against, the ideal exponent of the disruptive pressure game practised by his country.

Considering the commitment John showed on the field, it was a minor miracle that he suffered relatively few injuries during his hectic career. There was a rib cartilage injury which interfered with his progress through New Zealand with the 1983 Lions, and he was laid up by illness in the autumn of 1984 - a setback which in fact cost him his place in the Irish side.

But John was always a selfless team man, whether playing for Ireland in a vital Test or for London Irish in a friendly club match. After losing his international place he continued to turn out for the exiles, regularly making the round trip from Manchester, where he had taken up a post at one of the city's hospitals. His 6ft 3in, 15½st presence was sorely missed in the Irish team, and the hard-pressed national selectors, currently struggling to regroup after the longest losing streak in their history, must yearn for a player of John's standing now to bolster their ailing side.

Phil ORR (Old Wesley)

There must be something about Irish loose-head props and the exact science of mathematics. Between 1971 and 1987, two first-class honours graduates in the subject provided Ireland's stable equilibrium for scrums in eighty out of eighty-four internationals. Ray McLoughlin filled the No. 1 shirt until 1975, and Phil Orr succeeded him in 1976, going on to set a world record for appearances by a prop in internationals - fifty-eight caps for Ireland and one Test for the Lions. Phil provided the crucial support for Ciaran Fitzgerald's packs in the successful campaigns of 1982, 1983 and 1985, when Ireland were twice outright champions, won the Triple Crown twice and shared the Five Nations title once.

Phil was the Mr Dependable of the Irish team for more than a decade. Never a flashy player, he toiled earnestly as a tight forward at Dublin High School before enjoying three seasons in the Trinity College side while studying for his degree in pure mathematics.

It was in the autumn of 1974 that he first made the Irish selectors sit up and note his potential. Twice in the space of seven days, he showed against the All Blacks the sturdy independence and strength in scrummaging which are the essential requirements of the international loose-head. He propped up the Combined Universities in a 3-10 defeat by New Zealand in Cork and made his provincial debut for Leinster a week later, when the All Blacks scraped home by 8-3 in Dublin.

Yet his chance for Ireland owed more to luck than to his undeniable ability. Ray McLoughlin had retired at the end of the 1975 Five Nations campaign, and Phil

Phil Orr reaches for a loose ball, despite the attentions of the French pack, Dublin, 1977.

was understudy to 33-year-old Paddy Agnew for the Irish trial the following season. Agnew played against Australia, but Phil was named as a replacement for the championship opener with France in Paris in 1976. On the eve of that game Agnew withdrew, Phil came in and never looked back.

The young loose-head became the very staff, the very prop Ireland needed to fill the void left by McLoughlin's departure. By 1982, he was in his prime - just the type of raider needed to complement the work done by the loose forwards in open play; and just the cool, calculating technician to hold up Ireland's much-vaunted scrum. His endeavours during that Triple Crown season left both selectors and spectators best pleased.

The softly-spoken prop with the intellectual approach to scrummaging went on to play foty-nine internationals on the trot for Ireland, before he was dropped for two matches in 1986. A modest man, he accepted demotion with the same urbanity with which he had received praise. Somehow,a life time in the front row and a career as a loyal clubman at Old Wesley, one of the less fashionable of the Dublin sides, had prepared him for the ups and downs of top-class rugby.

But Ireland soon discovered that his talents could not be overlooked. In his absence at Twickenham, the Irish pack found themselves humiliatingly shunted back at the scrums. When Phil returned for his fiftieth cap, the tightness returned to Ireland's front row, and he stayed around long enough thereafter to pass Graham Price's world record of Test appearances at prop, and to see his country through to a quarter-final date with Australia at the inaugural Rugby World Cup.

Trevor RINGLAND (Queen's U Belfast, Ballymena)

Mick Doyle, that wily coach who was charged with the task of raising Irish rugby from the dead in 1985, made a dream start to the job. Although declaring that his side was committed to playing an expansive game, even the optimistic Doyle could not in his wildest imaginings have hoped for the kind of Five Nations entrance that his experimental side made.

Playing against Scotland, the Grand Slam holders, Ireland, the wooden-spoon holders, achieved a sensational last-minute win, thanks to their adherence to open play and the brilliant finishing of their right wing, Trevor Ringland. From a ruck on the left, the ball whistled down the line at 3:59pm to Ringland, who raced over in the corner for the score that put Ireland ahead. It was the Ulsterman's second try of the match and set his country off on the trail to their second Triple Crown win in three years.

Trevor was the automatic choice on the right wing for Ireland in thirty-four major internationals between 1981 and 1988, setting a new record for test appearances by an Irish wing. He was an elegant runner who relied on his pace and an instinctive shuffle of the feet to beat his opponents. Tries resulting from wide-arcing runs outside defences were clever Trevor's speciality, though he was not averse to following up the odd deftly-placed kick ahead. Altogether he chalked up nine tries in internationals, the first four of which flagged important Irish wins in their Triple Crown successes of 1982 and 1985.

Educated at Larne Grammar School, he was a law student at Queen's University in Belfast when he first entered the Irish side against Australia in 1981, and was one of three new Irish caps that season (Donal Lenihan and Mike Kiernan were the others) to participate in the Triple Crown success. With the ball in his hands he was a constant threat to defences for, apart from his speed around would-be tacklers, he relished physical contact to an extent rarely found in wing threequarters. This meant that Trevor never allowed the ball to die in attack, but was adept at making it available in the maul following a tackle. Occasionally, too, his robust approach paid dividends when faced by limp tackling: against Wales in 1982, for instance, he brushed through a feeble Welsh defence for the try which set Ireland's Triple Crown wagon rolling.

Yet strangely for one who was never backward going forward, his own defence was rather suspect. He had a tendency to pull up in his tracks when the ball was chipped behind him, and he sometimes 'bought' dummies which were palpably below the standard set by the Trades Description Act.

A miserable afternoon spent marking Chris Oti at Twickenham in 1988 brought down the curtain on Trevor's international career. England's winger ran in three tries, exposing the Irishman's defensive failings and loss of form. Trevor thus bowed out with a whimper, but the great and the good of Irish rugby will always remember him as the man who ran in the vital tries of famous Triple Crown wins.

Fergus SLATTERY
(UC Dublin, Blackrock College)

It is nigh on impossible to describe the ideal post-war flanker. Frequent changes in the laws of the game have arguably had more dramatic effects on the duties of flankers than on any other position on the field. For instance, look at the numbers of international appearances made by players who have specialised on the flank. Very few have sustained fitness and form long enough to join what might be called the really useful group who have accumulated thirty caps or more.

The flanker who heads this select company is one Fergus Slattery, a product of Blackrock College and University College, Dublin. 'Slats', as he was known to his companions, won a record number of caps for a flanker (sixty-five altogether for Ireland and the Lions) and stayed in the Ireland side long enough to enjoy the spoils of two outright championship titles and two shared titles.

Fergus came into international rugby in 1970, one season after the dispensation law restricting kicking to touch was introduced. The new rule kept the ball in play for so long that many teams amended the traditional roles of flankers. It now became the vogue for back-rowers to play left and right in order to share the burden of the extra work in the loose, rather than to act as out-and-out open-side and blind-side wing forwards.

The distinction did not unduly worry young Fergus. He was so fit and strong that he managed to keep running for the full eighty minutes of an international, irrespective of the side of the scrum on which he operated. His powers of anticipation were in the extrasensory class; he was quick to the breakdown of play in the loose, and he tackled vigorously in defence. The only blot on his otherwise perfect copybook was against his handling, for occasionally his passing was misdirected.

At his peak in 1973 and 1974, when Ireland were champions, Fergus was an open-side specialist. On the field he resembled a skirmishing Viking, his puckish face framed in a helmet of long, tousled hair. He was the scourge of outside-halves, and nothing gave him greater pleasure than detaching quickly from a scrum to wreck the plans of opposing backs. Ireland excelled at the spoiling game which, though not particularly pretty to watch, was highly effective.

John Taylor, the Welsh open-side flanker, had pipped Fergus to the Test spot with the 1971 Lions but, in 1974, the Irishman was an automatic choice in the best back row in Lions history. Yet that tour and Ireland's busy centenary season in 1974-75 were to prove his undoing in mid-career. Fergus was simply overplayed. He looked out of touch with the game when he resumed duties in 1975-76, and found himself out of the Irish XV for the first time since his debut.

A season and a half passed before his speed, imagination and sound method were deemed essential to inject new pride into an ailing Ireland side. The culmination of his comeback was a Triple Crown win in 1982, by which time he had switched to a tighter role on the left side of a workmanlike Irish back row. In his final full championship campaign in 1983, he capped a fine performance against England with a try that helped Ireland to a share of the title with France. That match was his last international appearance at Lansdowne Road: it was a memorable end to a memorable career.

Fergus Slattery of Ireland, the Lions and the Barbarians.

WALES
PLAYER PROFILES

Graham Price leaps high in a line-out against France.

Dewi BEBB
(Carmarthen TC, Swansea)

A rash of retirements forced the Welsh selectors to introduce seven fresh faces to a remodelled team for the 1959 Five Nations campaign. The new left winger was an unknown Welsh-speaker from Bangor who was to become a fixture in the Wales XV. His name was Dewi Bebb and he made a fairy-tale debut, scoring the winning try in a mud-bath at Cardiff against England. Eight years later, as Wales's most-capped left winger, he marked his thirty-fourth and final international appearance with another try against the same opposition.

Dewi truly relished taking on the English. 'They are the team I especially liked to play against,' he said. 'It's hard to explain, but it always brought out that extra something.' In fact, he scored six tries in eight matches against England at a time when wingers received few passes in internationals, the tendency being for sides to play to their packs in the early 1960s.

It was at Carmarthen Training College, where he was a student, that Dewi Bebb's prolific try-scoring first attracted the interest of the Welsh Big Five. Blessed with long legs and a raking stride, he used his speed intelligently on the field. Indeed, had he not found success as a rugby footballer, there is little doubt that he would have become an international sprinter - he was an even-timer over 100 yards.

Yet, ironically, fewer than half of his eleven tries for Wales were down to his sheer pace. Dewi had to be inventive to make up for the chronic shortage of passes which came his way while playing for his country and many of his tries were conjured from virtually nothing. He perfected a duet with his line-out jumpers: throwing in near opponents' try-lines, Dewi's quick reflexes were tuned to collect a swift tap-down; then he would dive over at the corner for a try. Probably the most important score for Wales fashioned in this way was his touchdown against the Irish in 1965, when the Five Nations title was at stake for both sides. The try stretched Wales to a secure position two scores ahead of Ireland, and it helped to win the Principality's first Triple Crown for thirteen years.

Weaknesses? In 1963, on a frozen pitch at Cardiff, his faulty handling - a very occasional affliction - cost Wales an early lead against an England side which went on to achieve a famous victory. Dewi was dropped for the next two months. And, three years later, it was his defence which was called into question when a beefier left winger was drafted in for the 1966 Championship bid. Wales were unexpectedly beaten, however, in Dublin; Dewi's opportunism was missed, and he was immediately restored to the team which beat France to take the Five Nations title.

After an effective tour of Australia and New Zealand with the 1966 Lions, he enjoyed another full season in the Wales XV. Then, in September 1967, citing as his main reason the hard slog of training solo in Cardiff, where he lived and worked while playing for Swansea, he retired at the age of twenty-nine. Wales thus lost one of its all-time quickest wingers; a player who loved his country and showed unwavering loyalty to Swansea, the only club he served after leaving college.

Dewi Bebb.

Phil BENNETT
(Llanelli)

'The king is dead; long live the king,' they said in Wales in 1972 when Barry John retired prematurely. For the canny Welsh knew well that there was a young prince waiting to sit on the outside-half throne after Barry's abdication, and Phil Bennett, the man who disintegrated defences with his bewildering jinks, duly stepped up to partner Gareth Edwards. Together the pair passed the John/Edwards record, playing in twenty-three Five Nations matches, and they guided the 1974 Lions through the unbeaten tour of South Africa.

Phil was one of the most gifted of all Welsh outside-halves. Playing against him was a tricky business. Apart from his elusive running, he was a natural ball player: he had good hands, a quick brain, and the priceless ability to create time and space for himself.

Yet when he became a permanent fixture in the Wales side in 1973-74, the dark, quiet, unassuming man from Felinfoel had his critics. True, he was the catalyst behind the great try scored by Gareth Edwards, featuring the 'magnificent seven' when the Barbarians beat the surly,

sixth All Blacks that year; but he seemed to lack the confidence to take on players in the claustrophobic atmosphere that surrounded Wales's Five Nations matches. And, true, the cultured right foot which packed a huge spiralling kick to send dejected opponents trudging back to their corner flags was an asset that made him the best outside-half in the Home Unions - not to mention the cool, efficient place-kicking which amassed countless points for Wales. But these offerings were insufficient to sustain the greedy Welsh hordes who craved tries from their international team, and Phil was unceremoniously dropped twice in 1975 - at the beginning of the year and again at the end.

Sadly, a string of personal tragedies which would have completely shattered a lesser man then befell him. In the span of three seasons, he was made redundant, he and his wife lost their first child at birth, and a congenital back weakness was diagnosed (which, he was told, would end his playing days).

Phil took it all philosophically and, when he was reinstated in the Welsh side, he was a different man. Gone were the old inhibitions; perhaps the private traumas had put the relatively unimportant matter of playing for his country into perspective. Whatever the reason, Phil now ran the ball with all the abandon that had thrilled the Tanner Bank at Llanelli, and a crowning period in Welsh rugby history began in 1976.

He equalled the Welsh Five Nations record, scoring 19 points - including a typical Phil Bennett solo try - against Ireland in the 1976 Grand Slam. The following season, he was appointed national captain and scored a picture-book try at Murrayfield to set the seal on a second successive Welsh Triple Crown. The same year, he took off as captain of the Lions to New Zealand.

The matches against Ireland and France in 1978, when Phil was Grand Slam leader, were physically and mentally demanding. After Wales had struggled to retain their invincibility, the players emerged drawn and relieved, like men who had just overcome serious illness. The effect those matches had on the senior players was impossible to tell but, within seven months, Phil had followed Gareth Edwards and Gerald Davies into retirement.

Phil Bennett seeks an opening against England at Twickenham in 1974. Dusty Hare, on his international debut, is the England full-back.

Gerald DAVIES
(Cardiff, London Welsh)

How do you describe the tricks of a magician? The problem is intractable. Gerald Davies, the rugby wizard who learned the game at QEGS Carmarthen and Loughborough Colleges, could easily have passed for a direct descendant of the good sage Merlin of Arthurian legend. Certainly,in the mythology of the second Welsh golden era, Gerald's deeds defied analysis.

One extraordinary try scored when playing in a representative match for England - yes, England - against Wales gives an idea of this particular wizard's wheezes. While he was at Loughborough, Gerald appeared in the English Universities team against their Welsh counterparts. At college he had come under the far-sighted influence of John Robins, and Gerald, the perceptive son of a miner from the little hamlet of Llansaint, had harnessed his basic skills to the application of Robins's theories on attack. Now, during the universities international, Gerald gathered a Welsh kick at goal and, sensing a scintilla of a chance launched an ambitious counter-attack from his own dead-ball area.

His sharpness off the mark took him clear of the first wave of opponents; at half-way, a couple of stabbing side-steps turned the midfield cover inside-out; and his exceptional pace then took him on a wide arc beyond the reach of the last line of defence for a spectacular score. More than 100 metres, and not a finger had been laid on him.

There was something of that remarkable try in every one of the twenty (a national record) he scored for Wales. He was considered unlucky not to accompany the 1966 Lions as an uncapped player before a teaching appointment took him to Cardiff that September, and he became an automatic choice at centre for his country later in the season. His initial tries for Wales'

Despite the attention of two defenders, Gerald Davies looks to pass out against Ire

973.

were scored in 1967 against England. First, Gerald showed his blistering speed to finish Dewi Bebb's touchline break by touching down under the posts. Then the famous Davies shimmy, a shuffle of the feet to take him clear of an opponent, created the opening for him to sprint diagonally to the south-east corner of the Arms Park for the final try of a breathtaking match.

Off the field, he was very much a renaissance man, and his love of literature and the arts led him to Cambridge University in 1968 to read English. The demands of study on his time forced him to withdraw from the Welsh set-up in 1969-70. But he returned refreshed in 1971, and playing in a different position. Before concentrating on his studies, he had toured New Zealand and Australia with Wales in 1969. There he had been successfully converted into a winger and it was in that role that he once more proved the scourge of the English when he resumed his Five Nations duties. On a filthy day in Cardiff, he demonstrated the geometer's axiom that the shortest path between two points is a straight line, darting to the south-east corner again for two superb tries.

With Gerald on the wing for seven more seasons, Wales always held an advantage over their opponents. When he was in possession, the threat was obvious; but even without the ball, at least two pairs of defenders' eyes needed to be trained on him. For a small man - 5ft 8½in, 11½st - he also made a sound contribution in defence. He perfected an astonishing pick-up off the ground without reduction of velocity, and he timed his smother-tackles on opponents as exquisitely as a black-belt throwing a challenger at judo.

He announced his retirement in September 1978, and his equal has yet to appear for Wales. Nowadays his wizardry with words, as Welsh rugby correspondent of *The Times*, brings some consolation to the many admirers who mourned the passing of a truly great player.

Mervyn DAVIES
(London Welsh, Swansea)

There is a tendency nowadays for international No.8s to be converted locks or displaced flankers. But Mervyn Davies, the world's most-capped Test player in the position, was a thoroughbred who never entertained the thought of playing first-class rugby in any other role. He was ever-present in the Wales side between 1969 and 1976, and he was first-choice for the successful Lions of 1971 (in New Zealand) and 1974 (in South Africa). Altogether he appeared in forty-six Tests, including thirty-one Five nations matches.

Jet-black curly hair, tightly wrapped in a thick white headband, was the trade mark of the Swansea schoolmaster whose father had played for Wales in the series of Victory internationals in 1946. Mervyn's climb up the ladder to Welsh honours was a relatively short one: he came into Clive Rowlands's team to meet Scotland in 1969 within months of breaking into the London Welsh 1st XV.

Inevitably, he was compared with Alun Pask, the archetypal modern Welsh No. 8 but, by the end of his first season in the senior XV, Mervyn had stamped his own

authority on a Triple Crown pack. He played by instinct at a time when other British No. 8s largely did their stuff by numbers. There was an uncanny sense of anticipation about his loose play; with the ball in his hands, he displayed all the dextrous skills of a Harlem Globetrotter; and, in defence, his tackles cut men down with the finality of a scythe slashing through long grass.

Lean almost to the point of being skinny, he dominated the back of the line-out for the Welsh teams of the 1970s. Wales had never adequately competed in that department since Pask's retirement but, with the advent of Mervyn Davies, suddenly their possession from the tail of the set-piece increased threefold, creating exactly the kind of attacking opportunities Gareth Edwards relished.

One of the areas of Mervyn's game that was often overlooked by critics was his scrummaging. His presence in the loose and line-out caught the notice of casual observers, but the purists were at pains to point out the vast contribution he also made in the tight. Wales frequently (and effectively) used the eight-man shove to disrupt opponents' scrummage heels during Mervyn's day, and the impetus for those surges came from the drive which his long legs transmitted along his back and up through the heart of the pack. For a big man he was nimble with his feet too, and he was adept at controlling the release of the ball from the back row.

He took over as leader of the Welsh team in 1975,during John Dawes's first year as national coach. Captaincy did Mervyn a power of good, bringing to light hitherto unknown aspects of his character. His confidence increased, and his tactical reading of games was close to infallible. Much debate rages in rugby football about which position on the field is ideal for leading teams; but, if all No. 8s possessed both the insight and ability of Mervyn Davies, there would be no doubt that they should automatically assume command.

Probably his hardest and sweetest victory as captain was his last match for his country against France in Cardiff in 1976. As Wales withstood frantic French pressure, Mervyn's will to win despite carrying a leg injury imbued his entire team with a grim determination to succeed, and his leadership ultimately saw them through to the Grand Slam.

Yet, within a month of his finest hour, he was fighting for his life and his rugby days were over. He had given up teaching and had returned home to Swansea in 1972. Playing for the club now against Pontypool in the WRU Cup semi-finals in 1976, he suffered a brain haemorrhage and had to be rushed unconscious to hospital. For several days, it was touch and go as to whether he would survive. Thankfully, he recovered, but his rugby career was cut off in its prime.

Mervyn Davies about to take the ball in a match against France, 1976.

Gareth EDWARDS
(Cardiff TC, Cardiff)

Where do you begin to pen a portrait of a young man who was quite simply the best rugby player in the world? Words alone are inadequate to capture the marvellous achievements of the scrum-half from Gwacn-cac-Gurwen.

The facts of the matter are that Gareth Edwards played in every Five Nations match for Wales between April 1967 and March 1978 - a run of forty-five consecutive championship games. That record alone speaks volumes for his strength, resilience and determination to stay at the top. But just look at the honours that came Wales's way during the Edwards years: three Grand Slams, five Triple Crowns, five outright championship titles, and two shared titles.

What a huge debt Welsh and British rugby owed to the man who groomed Gareth for greatness, Bill Samuel. He was the PE and rugby teacher at Pontardawe Technical School, which Gareth attended as a teenager. Mr Samuel sensed that his young charge was exceptionally gifted and set to work on all aspects of Gareth's game. He converted the boy from a centre to a scrum-half and strove continually to improve his skills and strengthen his adolescent physique. Systematically, Gareth developed his passing, tactical kicking and breaking from loose play. There was no respite from Mr Samuel's regimen in the summer either: weights, athletics and gymnastics were essential components of his programme of study.

Gareth lapped up the daily doses; no boy ever worked more conscientiously at his rugby. As his reputation grew, he sought out constructive criticism so that he could improve his game still further. Even after he left Pontardawe to take up a place at fashionable Millfield School, he regularly returned to Mr Samuel for advice. Quite simply, Gareth dedicated himself to reaching the summit of his sport.

The assault on his international Everest began as a teenager in the Wales sides of 1967, led by David Watkins. Gareth struck up his partnership with Barry John the following season - 'You throw them and I'll catch them,' was Barry's reassuring comment on his scrum-half's slightly wayward service when the pair first met. Gareth had established base camp by 1969, when he was a key figure in the Wales Triple Crown side coached by Clive Rowlands. Finally, he reached the top after Barry John's retirement in 1972 and stayed there for six gloriously successful seasons, during which Wales were beaten only five times in twenty-four Five Nations matches. Gareth assumed Barry John's mantle as tactical controller, and found in Phil Bennett another talented consort to exploit the now long, bullet-like Edwards pass.

Yet for all his shining deeds, there is one incident in Gareth's crowded career which eclipsed the myriad miracles he performed. Who will ever forget that wonderful try he scored against Scotland in 1972? He made a blind-side break from a maul deep inside his own half - wasn't that, according to Mr Samuel, the best place to attack from, just when the opposition least expect to be under pressure?

A powerful burst, every muscle in his sturdy frame straining, took him beyond the Scottish back row into no-man's land at half-way. Then a little chip over the full-back hinted that Wales would force a throw-in on Scotland's 22. But no, the ball bounced unpredictably over the try-line near the corner flag. In the death-or-glory race for the touchdown, those hours of training and sacrifice paid off: Gareth dived into the sludge in the muddy corner to earn the longest ovation of his life. Somewhere up in the stand, a schoolmaster could be excused for thinking that that try was 'made' on the playing fields of Pontardawe Technical School.

Gareth Edwards passes out, evading the attentions of Andy Ripley, in a Wales v England match.

Barry JOHN (Llanelli, Cardiff)

Barry John was the fly-half whose majestic powers were perfectly appraised by the following piece of black humour that did the rounds of South Wales in the early 1970s. The heavenly Welsh (coached by Carwyn James) are playing their English counterparts on the Elysian fields. Unhappy with the unsatisfactory performance of the Welsh No. 10, a supporter on the touchline turns to his all-knowing friend and asks: 'Who's the Welsh fly-half?' 'Ah,' begins the reply, 'that's God, but he thinks he's Barry John.'

The portrait of the artist as a young god in West Wales, where he grew up in the same village and attended the same school as Carwyn James, depicted Barry as a wraith-like scarlet runner with Llanelli. Master of the drop-kick and the whole gamut of tactical punts, he fleetingly displaced David Watkins in the Wales team in 1966-67. Next season he moved to Cardiff, beginning a long and productive partnership with scrum-half Gareth Edwards. When Watkins went north in October 1967, the pair had first claim to Wales's half-back berths and went on to play a record eighteen times together in Five Nations matches.

At first, Barry found the Edwards service slightly erratic,and he developed a habit of catching the ball standing still before choosing his options. To the horror of the purists, his first motion with the ball was sideways, and there was a lazy unorthodoxy to his distribution; but he was an instinctive footballer whose subtle skills on the end of Gareth's long pass still enabled him to create openings from nothing.

The second golden era for Wales dawned in February 1969, with Barry putting the final nail in Scotland's coffin with a lovely solo touchdown in the closing moments of the match. And it was a weaving run, his hands swinging the ball tantalisingly to and fro like a hypnotist's watch, that had the English spellbound when Wales overwhelmed the old enemy 30-9 in Cardiff. That try completely demoralised the visitors, put Wales in the driving seat towards the Triple Crown, and epitomised the spectral elusiveness of Barry John's running. Jokers meeting him in the flesh after that display expressed mock disbelief when he opened doors; they expected him to spirit himself through the walls.

Barry's star was at its zenith in 1971, and a fresh string was added to his bow when he was nominated place-kicker in the Welsh side. He kicked his goals with an almost blasé swing of the instep, a legacy of years of taking corner-kicks on the football pitch. (The teenaged Barry had attracted the interest of Coventry City's scouts.) Wales collected the Triple Crown and Grand Slam that year, and an unlikely element of Barry's repertoire had an airing in Paris. It was said that only wild horses could drag him to tackle, but he answered that particular criticism with a brave effort against the giant French forward, Benoit Dauga. Barry stopped a certain try despite breaking his nose.

He was crowned 'king' by the adoring New Zealand crowds during the triumphant tour by the 1971 Lions, and he returned home a popular hero, having been the guiding genius and top try-scorer in a team coached by his guru, Carwyn James.

While he preserved his dignity with the hordes of back-slappers, the excesses of their praise did embarrass him. The pressure to maintain his high playing standards and to fulfil numerous public engagements increased relentlessly. Then, out of the blue, Barry announced his retirement, aged twenty-seven, in May 1972. It was a decision he never regretted.

Barry John ghosts past Fergus Slattery of Ireland at Cardiff in 1971.

Roy JOHN
(Neath)

The biggest forward to emerge from the Five Nations in the first decade after the Second World War was a tall, dark Welshman named Roy John from Crynant near Neath. Measuring 6ft $3^{1}/_{2}$in, he broke into the Wales team in 1950 as a late replacement for his club mate Rees Stephens and, for the next four years Roy lorded it over the best line-out players in the world.

It is rare for a lock forward to be described as one of rugby's great entertainers, yet those who watched the game forty years ago retain warm memories of Roy John's spring-heeled jumping and clean two-handed catching in the line-out: none of your sloppy taps or frantic deflections. Contemporary photographs show vividly that he rose - literally - head and shoulders above his opponents to ensure that Wales took complete control of the throw-ins.

His value to the Welsh sides of the early 1950s was abundantly evident. Wales needed plenty of possession to practise tactics which depended on close co-operation between forwards and halves. Without Roy dominating the line-out, Wales could not have exercised the tight control of matches that was central to their successes in the Grand Slam seasons of 1950 and 1952.

Yet it would be wrong to portray him simply as a ball-winner. He had a unique positional sense and frequently turned up unexpectedly in the loose to provide a vital link in attack. His storming rugby in Dublin in 1952, when Wales won the Triple Crown, revealed that he was one of the fastest forwards of his generation. And who present on that day will ever forget the perfect dummy he sold before sending Clem Thomas over for the final try of the afternoon?

To achieve heights that none of his predecessors had reached at the line-out, Roy was supported and protected by solid props, well-versed in the skills of lifting and blocking. (Yes, such tactics were allowed under the laws of the immediate post-war era.) Wales and Roy were particularly well served in this department by Dai Davies, Don Hayward, John Robins, Billy Williams and Cliff Davies, pillars of strength who toiled largely unseen during a mini-boom for Welsh rugby at this level.

After giving international opponents plenty to think about for five seasons, Roy played his last game for Wales in 1954 at Twickenham. He lost form after that and had to concede his place to Rhys Williams.

The International Board - rugby's law-givers - supplied a flattering postscript to Wales's successes in Roy John's time. New legislation, making it illegal for a jumper to use another player as a jack to reach line-out ball, was introduced for the 1954-55 season. The view in Wales was that this change was deliberately made to put a direct check on Welsh line-out supremacy. Roy John's skills could have had no better epitaph.

Roy John used his height to great advantage, and became the best line-out player of his day.

Ken JONES
(Newport)

Schoolboys who grew up in Wales in the early 1960s revered Ken Jones. They were too young to have seen him play on the wing for Wales, but his wonderful international records - most tries and most caps for his country - were vital facts that no self-respecting junior rugby buff could afford to ignore. Ken was looked up to as the fastest Welsh wing since the golden era of Teddy Morgan and Willie Llewellyn by the lucky generations who did see him perform in the flesh - all 12st of it in his prime. He had Olympic pace, flypaper hands, and the talent for rugby indigenous to the Welsh.

On the field he resembled a refugee from a Lowry painting temporarily out of his civvies and garbed instead in the distinctive scarlet jersey of his country. But despite his tall, match-stick appearance, there was nothing frail about the rugby football played by Ken Jones. Apart from his speed, the secret of his prolonged success as a player was his sense of balance. He was the perfect study in concentration as a runner: every muscle and tendon was stretched in the effort to achieve maximum velocity. He had a tendency to tuck the ball under one arm but, like the tight-rope walker, he raised his free arm to a carefully-measured angle to preserve his equilibrium.

Ken Jones weaved his magic web on the wing for Wales in forty consecutive Five Nations matches, starting at Cardiff as a 25-year-old in 1947. When he was dropped for the first time, against England a decade later, the programme for the match still displayed Ken's photograph and biography with a tribute to his exploits - or perhaps the publishers just did not believe that the Welshman could be omitted from the side and carried his portrait through force of habit.

He was at the peak of his career in the Welsh Grand Slams of 1950 and 1952. Indeed, without his vital tries in those seasons, Wales would never have gained the Five Nations championship's ultimate prize. He scored four tries in 1950 when Wales achieved the Grand Slam for the first time for thirty-nine years, and another four tries two years later included a couple that demonstrated his real pace and natural talent.

His match-winning try against England in 1952 was the result of an overlap created by Lewis Jones. Ken was on the end of the ensuing passing movement and streamed past two defenders to score near the corner. Then, in the Triple Crown match in Dublin, he again scored the crucial try of the game. Wales were leading narrowly when Cliff Morgan initiated a raid from his own half. Moving inside from his outpost on the wing, Ken took a short pass and embarked on a thrilling fifty-yard run to the Irish line. It was an act that showed the instinctive genius of a player who knew the right move to make and chose the right moment to make it.

Ken Jones was a right wing who played at a time when defences engaged in man-for-man marking, wingers rarely received more than a pass a match, and there was a predilection in threequarters for moving the ball to the left wing. Ken proved that he had no equal for speed and finish, but he frequently needed to create his own chances to collect the tries which set Wales on course for famous wins in the 1950s.

Ken Jones was revered as the ultimate hero by Welsh schoolboys.

Allan MARTIN

(Aberavon)

Not many lock forwards kick long-range penalties or conversions for their country, and not many lock forwards survive the slings and arrows of international combat to play in eight successive Five Nations championships.

Allan Martin did. The Aberavon wizard who ruled the Welsh line-out after the retirement of Delme Thomas was an accurate place-kicker who used an orthodox front-on method to land important goals in Wales's Five Nations successes of 1975 and 1976. Altogether he played in two Grand Slams, four Triple Crown sides, and helped Wales to win the Five Nations title outright four times. At the end of his career, he went into retirement as his country's most-capped second -row forward.

An easy-going character, Allan was a convert from soccer who quickly matured into a line-out expert at Sandfields Comprehensive in Port Talbot, where he won a record number of Welsh School caps. His calm temperament was ideally suited to the role he performed for Wales between 1974 and 1981. All line-out jumpers have had to contend with jabs to the ribs, jersey-tugging and numerous other obstructions to their freedom at rugby's vital set-piece. Yet Allan, the gentlest of giants, was unfazed by such nonsense. He always met the nefarious tricks of opponents with an aloofness which had a reassuring effect on the rest of his pack and which allowed him to concentrate fully on his own act. He was always in just the right frame of mind to pounce on line-out ball like an uncaged panther. For internationals he invariably managed to lift his game - and himself - to new heights, both metaphorically and physically.

For twenty-three of his

'Big Al', the Aberavon wizard, was a line-out specialist for Wales and the Lions.

Five Nations matches he was partnered in Wales's engine-room by Swansea's Geoff Wheel. Wheel was the conscientious artisan who endlessly ripped balls out of line-out mauls set up by the man they called 'Big Al', and the pair complemented each other as effectively as did Phil Bennett and Gareth Edwards. Admittedly, the second row does not carry the same high profile which surrounds the half-back positions; but make no mistake, without Wheel and Martin's possession, Wales would have struggled to achieve the forward dominance so crucial to any successful team. Together, they subdued the best England, Scotland, Ireland and France had to offer.

During the second half of his international career, Allan stoically battled against the invisible nuisance of tendonitis in his shoulder. Cortisone injections kept the pain at bay, but at times he compared playing with the affliction to having one arm strapped behind his back. Welsh supporters accordingly boasted that, even with one arm tied behind his back, he was better than anyone England could pit against him.

He finished his middle-of-the-line-out duties for Wales in 1981 and was eventually replaced by Bob Norster. These days, Allan organises the Welsh Classicals - the golden oldies (some of whom are fast becoming silver seniors) from the crowning years reunited to play in veterans' tournaments. Twenty years on, he looks almost as fit and certainly as dark and placid as the panther of old.

Cliff MORGAN
(Cardiff, Bective Rangers)

There used to be a theory that potential international fly-halves born in the Rhondda Valley had a head start on their rivals in other parts of Wales. Young boys stepping from the front doors of the terraced houses which lined the valley's towns learned to become natural jinkers and side-steppers to evade the speeding lorries carrying the Rhondda's coal along the narrow streets.

Cliff Morgan followed a distinguished line of Rhondda sons who played for Wales: Cliff Jones, Billy Cleaver and Glyn Davies. All showed abilities as escapologists which made Harry Houdini look like a novice, and the quartet monopolised the Welsh fly-half position for a quarter of a century.

Cliff Morgan was the last and most notable of the famous four. He succeeded Glyn Davies as Wales's No. 6 (the fly-half's label in the days when sides were numbered from backs to forwards) for the match against Ireland in 1951. For the next seven years, Cliff was the automatic choice of the Welsh selectors, creating a Welsh record (which still stands) for most international appearances by a fly-half.

He was at his best on the attack. Habitually, he carried the ball low in two hands, head tilted forward as if sniffing out a gap. Then, when he sensed an opening, his head was tossed back and his short bow-legs switched gear to transport him outside opponents in a wide arc. That sharp change of pace - the result of all those years spent dodging traffic at home in Trebanog - was his biggest asset, enabling Cliff to set up countless tries for the threequarters who played alongside him.

As a schoolboy at Tonyrefail, he developed his skills under the watchful eye of Ned Gribble, a coach who instilled in Cliff Morgan an everlasting love of rugby football. The young Cliff graduated from the front row of the scrum via the centre to fly-half. Once he won a school match with a dropped goal, only to be admonished by a stern Mr Gribble for neglecting his threequarters. As a result, Cliff never attempted to drop a goal throughout his senior career - a rare abstinence in a fly-half.

A dark, keen-eyed player standing 5ft 7in, Cliff first took control of the Welsh midfield in the 1952 Grand Slam season. Early in his tenure, there was a weakness in his kicking, but he more than made up for that deficiency with his quick-wittedness as a runner. He was a shrewd tactician who was an accomplished option-taker, whether gliding over the billiard-table surface of Twickenham or skating on the primordial slime of Cardiff Arms Park. And with maturity came sound cover defence and deftness to his tactical punting.

Throughout his career, he was a huge box-office attraction. Apart from guiding Wales to four championship titles, he was the spark that ignited the 1955 Lions in South Africa. There he sent spectators into raptures with his electric display on the firm grounds of the veldt.

Then, to his fans' astonishment, he retired young at the age of twenty-seven. He realised that some of the sting had gone from his tail and chose to quit while still in his prime. It was a decision he never regretted and, though the public pined for his extraordinary rugby talents, Cliff was soon back doing what he did best: entertaining rugby followers, first as an astute journalist, and eventually as the broadcaster with the lyrical voice whose commentaries exuded his passion for the game.

Cliff Morgan, one of a long line of distinguished Rhondda 'sons' to have played for Wales.

Robert NORSTER (Cardiff)

One of the unkindest comments made about Welsh rugby's hierarchy in the unhappy 1980s was that their style of management, and in particular the use of squad sessions, drove ambitious internationals to sign professional rugby league forms. Certainly, many of Wales's leading players during a decade of disappointment turned to the paid ranks, while others, in much-publicised autobiographies, voiced their disapproval of the unreasonable demands that were being made on individuals by boring, time-consuming squad practices. On top of all the resentment being expressed off the field, unimaginative man-management led to a string of indifferent displays by Wales on the field.

Yet one man managed to rise above all the bickering. He was Bob Norster, the big middle-of-the-line jumper from Cardiff who succeeded Allan Martin as Wales's primary source of line-out possession.

When he was fit - he was often sidelined with painful back problems - Bob's athleticism and application stood out like a beacon among candles. There was a dearth of international-class locks to partner him for Wales, yet he soldiered on single-handed to span eight seasons which brought him few rewards. Most of his illustrious predecessors for Wales - Roy John, Rhys Williams, Brian Price, Delme Thomas and Allan Martin - benefited from playing with strong consorts whom they could rely on for protection and support. But Bob had no companion to supply a regular physical presence in the way that Brian Thomas did for Brian Price, or Geoff Wheel did for Allan Martin.

Wales enjoyed one rare and conspicuous success in 1988, when a side which had finished third in the inaugural World Cup won the Triple Crown and shared the Five Nations championship with France. Bob was instrumental

Bob Norster.

in helping his country to those honours. A supple, wiry lock, he scaled the heights which other British jumpers could not reach at the line-out. His clean two-handed catches were perfectly timed and, for once, Wales's back division, spearheaded by Jonathan Davies, put to good use the possession coming from Bob's aerial work.

Injury forced him to pack up first-class rugby in 1990. He finished his international career on thirty-four caps - a Welsh record for a lock that he shares with Allan Martin. Yet within months of announcing his retirement, his advice was being sought by the selectors after Welsh rugby had fallen into its deepest recession. More recently, as manager working in tandem with coach Alan Davies, he has taken Wales back to rugby's equivalent of the early learning centre and, although he hasn't yet presided over a Grand Slam side, at least Bob can take consolation in the knowledge that he has contributed off the field to the greatest international recovery in Welsh history.

Alun PASK (Abertillery)

Alun Pask was the player of the 1960s who did for rugby headgear what the Beatles did for teenage hair-styles: he set a trend. The traditional scrum-cap was discarded in favour of a tight white band, although some cheeky Welshmen, jealous perhaps that the Abertillery forward occupied an international shirt for which there were several promising challengers, said that the band was simply a sartorial frill designed to get him noticed by the selectors.

Yet from 1961, when he scored a try as a blind-side flanker on his debut in Paris, Alun enjoyed an unbroken run of five seasons in Wales's scrum. Immediately, he impressed as a forward capable of sound defence, although he tended to have a *dégagé* view of the rucks and mauls. Mobile for a big man - he was 6ft 3in - and a good handler, he certainly needed no accessories to his intelligent rugby brain to persuade the Welsh selectors of his indispensability.

He settled in his favourite position, No. 8, in 1962 and quickly set about redefining his role in the Welsh side. He was the first Welshman to appreciate the attacking potential of the back row in the modern game, and he easily slipped into the high-gear style which was already a feature of French loose play. During his formative years as a Loughborough student he had been an expert Sevens player, so he was well equipped to practise the handling game at speed.

Crowds enjoyed the idiosyncratic bits of his play, too. Apart from performing the basic skills proficiently, Alun sold a credible dummy, put up chip-kicks from the back of the scrum for his wingers to follow up, and he made a habit of carrying the ball in one hand. Spectators loved all this - they left matches disappointed if he had not completed at least one run with the ball clasped in his right claw.

Two Five Nations incidents stand out from a distinguished career. Neither

Alun Pask, without his headband.

demonstrates his total command of modern back-row play; instead, these moments are chosen to support the contention that he was one of the most complete players to represent Wales since the war.

In 1962, France were favourites to beat Wales and wrap up their fourth consecutive championship title. Yet at Cardiff, an unfancied home XV achieved a 3-0 win, and Alun pulled off a match-saving tackle from behind on Rancoule, the flying French winger. All No. 8s are expected to cover, but the one from the rear is the most difficult of the tackles to execute; when a forward effects such a move on a threequarter in full flight, that is a feat worth commending.

The other Alun Pask memory to treasure is of the 1965 Triple Crown win against Ireland. In the first half of a muddy match, he was withdrawn from the scrum to play full-back when the Welsh backs had to be rearranged owing to an injury to John Dawes. Big Alun was the model of security: he kicked, tackled and fielded with textbook rectitude, helping Wales through a tricky spell when they were under intense pressure before Dawes returned.

Alun captained Wales to the championship in 1966, but it was felt that the narrow failure in Dublin that season exposed tactical flaws in his leadership. The Lions' selectors possibly subscribed to this theory, for Alun was pipped to the captaincy of that summer's party by the Scot, Mike Campbell-Lamerton. The Welshman had a good tour in New Zealand and gave the captain his full support. He then retired suddenly, midway through the 1967 Five Nations campaign.

Brian PRICE
(Newport)

Wales were well served by athletic line-out technicians in the 1950s. Roy John and Rhys Williams between them claimed sufficient possession to help their country to win the Five Nations title five times. The hopes for maintaining Welsh dominance in this department in the 1960s were then pinned on Brian Price, the Bargoed beanpole.

Brian honourably extended Wales's proud line-out pedigree with his effortless jumping and clean catching. He was a natural ball player who honed his handling skills at basketball - a game he advocated for all rugby forwards - and he was agile enough to play international soccer in goal for British North Borneo during his National Service.

Brian broke into rugby's big time in 1960-61. After performing with some style for Newport against the Springboks, he was selected as the Barbarians' uncapped player in the team that won a famous victory over South Africa. The Welsh selectors, suitably impressed by his abilities, called him into their side for the last two internationals of the season.

That was the beginning of a distinguished career for the Welshman. During the decade, Brian cleaned out all his northern hemisphere line-out rivals and shrugged off a series of injuries suffered at the hands of clumsy adversaries who sometimes resorted to foul means to counter his aerial expertise. Punches to his ribs as he went up for the ball were common - though once, when playing the Scots in the days before replacements were allowed, even brave Brian needed a little encouragement after sustaining a hamstring injury. He was told by a medical officer after receiving pain-killing injections: 'You can't do any more damage to the hamstring; it's completely ruptured, so you may as well go back on.' Typically, Brian returned to the fray to do his duty on one good leg!

Despite being the target of such rough treatment, his double-act with Neath's Brian Thomas was good news for Wales in their Five Nations triumphs between 1964 and 1966. The two Brians were the brains of the effective Welsh packs which laid the foundations of those championship-winning seasons. But, after a disappointing Lions tour to New Zealand in 1966, a slight loss of form and a couple of operations seemed to put paid to Brian Price's international career.

Brian Price, another great Welsh line-out specialist and captain of Wales's Triple Crown side of 1969.

His club persuaded him to make a comeback in 1968-69, a season that became his Indian summer. The national selectors nominated him captain of the newly-formed Welsh squad, and he performed marvels in blending youthful but talented backs and wizened, wily forwards into an irresistible force that tossed aside the threats from their Five Nations challengers.

Wales won the Triple Crown and championship in style, although controversy surrounded the skipper's part in the home win against Ireland. Early in the match, Price lashed out with his fist after an opponent had allegedly held him back. His haymaker laid flat the Irish captain, and a hush descended on Cardiff. Brian received a stern lecture from the referee, who sensed that there had been some provocation. But even his best friends thought he was lucky to stay on the field.

In the summer, New Zealand proved to be the graveyard for his hopes of bowing out of Test rugby with wins against the mighty All Blacks. A year later, he was professionalised by the Welsh Rugby Union for receiving payment for a newspaper article. Thus a forward with an unsurpassed technical knowledge of the game was barred from coaching and making what would surely have been a telling contribution to senior Welsh rugby.

Graham PRICE
(Pontypool)

Just as Cambridge University is the magnet for the bright young things who seek the glittering prizes of the academic world, so Pontypool Rugby Football Club was the draw for ambitious young Welsh forwards of the 1970s and 1980s. The club acquired a reputation for producing consummate scrummagers and maulers, and the far-sighted methods of its famous professor, Ray Prosser (the former Wales and Lions prop who was the club's coach), were acclaimed world wide.

One of the most distinguished of the Pontypool graduates was Graham Price, a tight-head prop whose strength and mobility first impressed the Welsh selectors in 1972, when he played in a national trial as a twenty-year-old. No callow youth, Graham gave as good as he got and continued knocking on the door of the Wales XV for two more years before breaking into the first side coached by John Dawes in 1975.

That Welsh side included six new caps but, with Gareth Edwards, Mervyn Davies, Gerald Davies and JPR Williams present to inspire the beginners, Wales romped to an astonishing 25-10 win in Paris - their first (and, to date, last) victory at the modern Parc des Princes. There were promising debuts by all the newcomers, but Graham capped his first international appearance with a fairy-tale flourish. He galloped seventy yards in support of a kick ahead to score the final try of a match which marked Wales's transition from the successful Clive Rowlands era into the equally successful John Dawes age.

Pontypool supplied the entire Welsh front row against France, and the trio were picked *en bloc* for fifteen Five Nations matches between 1975 and 1979, helping Wales to collect honours in each of their seasons together. Nicknamed the 'Viet Gwent' by Max Boyce, the Pontypool front row sucked the energy out of their adversaries. Their club's pattern - which fast became the Welsh pattern - was to subdue and control up front in the early stages of matches, establishing a sound forward platform; then, as the opposition wilted in the last quarter, the pack would release the ball for the backs to open up and score tries. A flurry of points in the last twenty minutes of games regularly set the seal on convincing Welsh triumphs during the crowning years between 1976 and 1979.

Graham stayed in the international side for nine seasons, a record which speaks volumes for his dedication. His upper-body strength he put down to a strict diet of chips with everything. He was also one of the cleanest forwards of his day.

Even when the winning stopped in the early 1980s, Graham continued to ply his front-row trade for his country. He was the master craftsman - no one gained the upper hand when scrummaging against him - and the Welsh forwards never budged when Graham was propping up his corner of the scrum. Where Welsh rugby was now left wanting was behind its packs: suddenly, the rich seam of try-scoring backs had dried up. But there was never any shortage of good possession to use.

During his long career, Graham saw Welsh forward play adapt itself to several new laws. Every alteration in the rules called for higher levels of fitness, particularly from front-row players, but Graham was more than ready to meet the fresh challenges with enthusiasm. Since he retired in 1983 as his country's most-capped prop, Welsh rugby has longed for another golden prospect with Graham Price's conspicuous skills.

Graham Price, the most distinguished of the Pontypool forwards to play for Wales and the Lions in the 1970s and early 1980s.

Clive ROWLANDS (Pontypool)

If ever a Welshman deserved a knighthood for his services to rugby football, then few would argue that there is anyone with a superior claim to the title 'Sir' than Clive Rowlands. He has devoted a lifetime, as player, captain, coach, selector, manager, and president of the Union - you name it, he has done it - to Welsh rugby.

Clive is a son of 'God's Country', the fertile rugby crescent that bows its way through the Tawe valley to Swansea Bay. He learned the game at Ystradgynlais GS, where he was primarily a flanker, and developed his strong tactical sense as a fly-half in the tough West Wales leagues playing for Cwmtwrch and Abercrave. He had a brief spell at Llanelli as understudy to Onllwyn Brace, who was an important mentor to the developing scrum-half, and then joined Pontypool in 1962 after qualifying as a teacher at Cardiff Training College.

His selection for Wales the next season came as a surprise to many pundits. He was criticised in some quarters for the slowness of his service, and he never claimed to be the sharpest scrum-half around the field. However, for sturdiness on his legs and standing his ground in front of advancing 16st opponents, he was in a class of his own. Furthermore, he possessed a convincing dummy which created the chances for rare breaks from scrummages. Yet it was as a kicking scrum-half that he entered the Welsh side against England in 1963. Already Pontypool skipper, he was invested as Wales's captain on his debut and went on to set a unique international record, leading his country throughout his fourteen-cap career.

In charge of an inexperienced team containing six new caps, he had to swallow his pride and face the brickbats after piloting Wales to defeat in that first match. Yet both his determination to turn his fledgelings into winners and his ability to take a firm tactical hold on a game shone through one month later, when he directed Wales to their first win at Murrayfield for ten years.

The match will be forever remembered as the 'touchline Test'. Clive's apprenticeship in West Wales rugby had equipped him with an effective hook-kick - a punt over his shoulder back towards the touchline. The Scotland match contained more than one hundred line-outs, and Welsh wags celebrating their 6-0 victory rumbled the captain's strategy. 'He has six variations which are signalled to the backs, and every one means the ball will be kicked into touch!'

There was never any doubt about who was captain on the field during Clive's reign. Forget democracy; reject consultation. He ruled the Welsh XV with an iron fist - not a velvet glove in sight. Yet, for sheer drive, he has had no post-war equal. With other teams, his enthusiasm, patriotism and force of character might have been unsuitable, but he imbued his Wales sides with a mighty corporate spirit. When a largely unchanged selection returned for the 1964 Five Nations campaign, Clive was the master tactician who led his limited charges to a share of the championship.

Undoubtedly, Wales's best season under Clive Rowlands was 1965. Although the side, toiling under new laws designed to encourage more expansive back play, had been thumped 3-24 by South Africa in May 1964, Clive, with typical vibrancy, bounced back to lead them to their first Triple Crown for thirteen years. Needless to say, the old grip - tactically and morally - was as tight as ever.

Clive Rowlands: player, captain, coach, selector, manager and president of the WRU.

He was dropped in 1966, retired in 1968, and immediately began his long and varied administrative association with the WRU.

Brian THOMAS (Cambridge U, Neath)

Uncompromising, hard, vigorous, robust, 'man of iron' . . . these were the battered clichés used by the popular press when describing the forward play of big Brian Thomas, the Cambridge University, Neath and Wales lock of the 1960s. On the field, Brian was the player who protected his colleagues from attempted interference by opponents. Every successful team needs its minder, and Brian Thomas admirably filled that post in the triumphant Welsh XVs of 1964, 1965, 1966 and 1969.

Rugby has featured prominently in the life of Brian since he was first enthralled by the game as a five-year-old. He is now best-known as the Neath supremo who has employed the highest-quality management to propel his club to the top of the Heineken Welsh Leagues.

He possessed tremendous physical presence as a youth and won Welsh schoolboy caps before serving three years in the Cambridge packs of the early 1960s. Even as an undergraduate, he was acknowledged as a hard diamond among gems. A student who demonstrated his practicality by studying metallurgy, he was on the victorious side in all his Varsity matches, showing a resolute will to win that was rare among college players and which made him a folk hero with his university's supporters.

It was while he was in his final year at Cambridge that the call to represent his country first came. In January 1963, he combined with Brian Price - a happy partnership that was to bolster Wales in fourteen Five Nations matches - in a side which was beaten 6-13 by England. But that inauspicious start merely strengthened his determination to succeed, especially against the English. In his next international, against Scotland, he toiled in the dimly-lit nether regions of a Welsh pack that won the lion's share of possession from a game which yielded the staggering total of 111 line-outs. And, by the end of his first season, he had drawn a learning curve to be proud of: decidedly concave upwards.

As the Welsh claimed championship honours for three successive seasons, between 1964-66, Brian's reputation in South Wales soared sky-high. At the same time he put the fear of God into international opponents, only meeting his match in the forest of arms and legs at scrums, mauls and rucks when he came up against the New Zealand pine tree, Colin Meads.

Brian was a no-frills forward whose work rate and controlled aggression were invaluable to Wales. His specialist skill was mauling. Perfectly equipped with well-developed forearms, he was able to wrestle the ball free from mêlées and was invariably the invisible agent whose skilful smuggling transferred vital second-phase possession to his scrum-half. He was no slouch at the line-out either, despite operating in the shadow of Brian Price.

His career was touched by controversy. After Wales defeated England in a rough match in 1965, he was dropped from a side which went on to win the Triple Crown. No reason was ever given, but the word was that Brian was neglected by the selectors because of his over-robust play. (An interesting fact worth quoting here is that he was never sent off until 1970, more than a year after his last international comeback.)

But probably the biggest injustice meted out to Brian was his omission from the 1966 Lions party on the ridiculous grounds that he was too hard for New Zealand. He had the last laugh when the tourists were skinned 0-4 in the Test series.

Delme THOMAS
(Llanelli)

If the chances for a last-minute victory depended on one forward winning a line-out, who would be your jumper? Ask that question of any Welshman in the early half of the second Welsh golden era (1969-74), and the unanimous reply would be Delme Thomas, the one-man tower-block from Bancyfelin. Delme was an electricity linesman with the South Wales Electricity Board but, on the rugby field, he reached such lofty heights with his leaping at the line-outs that opponents wondered whether the entire National Grid was wired to his heels.

Ironically, at a time when the number of line-outs in matches was being reduced (after the introduction of the law restricting touch-kicking in the 1968-69 season), the clean ball won by Delme became very important to the Welsh style of play. Apart from the obvious necessity for good possession in order to score tries, the line-out was a useful platform for launching drives to set up rucks or mauls. These sucked in defenders and yielded the precious possession which enabled the Welsh backs to make structured second-phase attacks.

Whether jumping at two or four in the line-out, Delme won a wealth of good ball for the exciting Welsh backs of his day; for example, five of his country's scores in the 1969 Triple Crown win against England stemmed from the work of the big lock. He depended heavily on the technique of palming - tapping the ball with one hand to his scrum-half - and having such an acrobatic man as Gareth Edwards to pick up the rare misdirected deflections meant that Wales could have plenty of confidence in a method that few others dared to copy.

Delme was a one-club man. He joined his beloved Llanelli in the early 1960s, and he practised assiduously to improve his skills. Weight training helped him to develop his physique and, in 1966, he was a shock choice for the Lions tour to Australia and New Zealand. He won his first cap for Wales later the same year, but, for the next three seasons, he made only intermittent appearances as a reserve for Brian Price. When Price was injured before that 1969 Triple Crown match, Delme stepped in to make his massive contribution to a grand win. After that, he was recognised as the leading line-out ace in British rugby.

Those present at Murrayfield on 6 February 1971 witnessed Delme's finest hour for Wales. With Scotland leading 18-14, Barry John opened the doors of the last-chance saloon by scrambling into touch in the home 22 with time running out. At the ensuing set-piece, with all Wales willing Delme to lift his tired body for one last leap, the lock did his stuff admirably to intercept the Scottish throw - 'Delme Thomas palming,' ran Bill McLaren's commentary as the match reached its climax. True, in the reviews of the game, Gerald Davies (who scored the try created by Delme's efforts at the front of the line-out) and John Taylor (who made the most famous conversion since St Paul's Damascus roadshow) won the Oscars for their lead parts in the winning score. But both men and the rest of the Welsh side would be quick to acknowledge the best supporting role played by Delme Thomas in that classic sequence.

The proudest moment of this unassuming gentle giant's career came twenty months later, when he captained Llanelli to their 9-3 win over

the All Blacks. Recurring knee trouble was a factor in his retirement at the end of that season but, ever ready to serve his country, he recharged his batteries to return to the Wales side which was beaten by England at Twickenham in 1974.

The Welsh forwards establish control at the line-out: Delme Thomas palms, Denzil Williams protects and Dai Morris provides. Gareth Edwards is the Welsh scrum-half.

David WATKINS
(Newport)

Look at black and white films of Wales matches played in the mid-1960s and your attention will be attracted to a neat No. 10. His hair is closely cropped, and he flits hither and thither, leaving a trail of would-be tacklers in his wake. He is so small that in his Welsh jersey he looks as lost as a pygmy in a spacesuit. David Watkins is the player and, thirty years ago, he was the hottest property in Welsh rugby.

The miner's son from Blaina rocketed into the Wales team in 1963, carrying with him a glowing reputation as a mesmeric runner and drop-goal expert gained during his period with Cwmcelyn Youth. He had few opportunities to excel in his first season but, after helping Brian Price to inspire the black and amber army on parade for Newport in their famous win against the fifth All Blacks, he proved the natural successor to Cliff Morgan as the Wales fly-half in 1964.

His delicate grubber-kicks caused havoc in the Scottish, Irish and French defences that season, while he demonstrated his searing pace off the mark when he scored a vital solo try in Dublin. The criticism that he was too much of an individualist and that he failed to engage his backs effectively in attack was often levelled at him in those early days for Wales, but the significant event which really flagged his coming of age was his appointment as captain of Newport in 1964-65.

Suddenly, there appeared a new maturity to David's play. Of course, he still thrilled crowds with those twinkle-toes of his, crammed into size $5^1/_2$ boots which had to be specially cobbled for him. But overnight he became more confident, tactically more aware, and the mark of the expert was stamped on his line-kicking. When Wales and Ireland met in the Triple Crown showdown in March 1965, David's kick from deep inside his own half lifted a long first-half siege and led to the try that broke the deadlock in an explosive championship decider.

Then, with the sudden rejection of scrum-half Clive Rowlands in 1966, David became his country's kingpin behind the scrum, calling the shots remarkably well in support of Alun Pask, his captain, as Wales won the championship title for the second season running. Later the same year, he captained the Lions in two Tests against New Zealand.

Strongly challenged by Barry John, the rising star in the West, for the fly-half berth in 1966-67, David was typically among the first to send a congratulatory telegram to his young rival when John replaced him in the Welsh side. David did return to captain Wales later that season but, alas, his career in rugby union was all too brief: in October 1967, after barely five years at the top, he turned professional with Salford, collecting a record five-figure signing-on fee. He was twenty-five, at his peak, and went on to become the most successful Rugby League convert ever to have left South Wales.

Who knows what David Watkins, a talented player who was in the fine tradition of Welsh fly-halves, might have achieved had he stayed in the national XV to help usher in the second golden era?

David Watkins was one of a line of great Welsh fly-halves.

JPR WILLIAMS
(London Welsh, Bridgend)

Pity today's schoolboys, weighed down by the endless acronyms - ATs, NATs, SATs, KS, GCSE - which confuse the education process. It was all so very different twenty-five years ago, when everyone knew precisely what O level meant. Those were the days when simple sporting souls loaded their uncluttered memories with just two sets of initials, one for each half of the year: LBW in the cricket season and JPR during the rugby months.

JPR (John Peter Rhys) Williams was the full-back who arrived as a callow youth of nineteen in the first senior Wales team to be coached by Clive Rowlands. More than a decade later, he finally hung up his international boots, having been the highest common factor running almost continuously through an era of unparalleled success for Welsh rugby. At the final count, his Triple Crown involvement ran to a record six wins - one more than Gareth Edwards - and his unique achievement of eleven wins in eleven matches against England is never likely to be equalled.

His single most striking characteristic was his competitiveness. Whether playing in front of two men and a dog on a windswept Welsh quagmire, or performing before 65,000 on the green sward of Twickenham, JPR Williams was the man who always gave 100 per cent.

Full-backs are expected to tackle, but JPR was more than just a one-man ringfence to opponents. He relished the physical contact of the confrontation, and vividly verified Sir Isaac Newton's maxim that the rate of change of momentum is directly proportional to the applied force. Forget being struck on the head by an apple; if you were in collision with this apple of every Welshman's eye, you were lucky to get off lightly.

JPR was a London medical student when Clive Rowlands called him up from the London Welsh staff college set up at Old Deer Park by John Dawes. Apart from his tackling, the other basic requirement of the last line's art mastered by JPR was fielding the high ball. As a line-kicker he was only moderate, but it was his ability to exploit the Australian dispensation concerned with restricting kicking to touch which elevated him to the status of superstar in the Wales team.

The new law gave vent to a running style of full-back play which suited his adventurous spirit. His well-timed interventions into the back line began creating tries for Wales in his first season in the side and, during his career, he went on to score six tries himself - an international record for a full-back for Wales. His thirst for action was so unquenchable early on that spectators at the Stade Colombes watching Wales play France in 1969 could hear the Welsh captain, Brian Price, instructing his full-back to stay back behind his threequarters while the red shirts were playing into a stiff wind.

Another crucial (yet unexpected) gift which JPR possessed was for mauling. Clive Rowlands encouraged all of his team - not only the forwards - to ruck and maul vigorously. As coach, Rowlands had realised that backs were just as likely as forwards to arrive first at the breakdown; to keep play moving, therefore, the backs needed to become proficient at going in to set up second-phase possession. JPR was as useful as a ninth forward in the loose, and once, in Australia in 1978, he actually won a Welsh cap as a flanker.

Retirement in 1979 was temporary. He made a comeback in Wales's centenary season, 1980-81, showing England that there was life still in the old dog, but he was finally dropped later that year after a poor Welsh performance at Murrayfield. JPR has since proved an impossible act to follow.

JPR Williams, captain of the last Wales side to win the championship title outright, in 1979.

Rhys WILLIAMS
(Llanelli)

There is no new thing under the sun, according to the Good Book. As controversy rages worldwide over recent law changes in rugby's good book, particularly the new legislation relating to rucks and mauls, it is true to say that feelings ran just as high forty years ago,when radical alterations to the rules governing the line-out were first introduced.

The result of the changes in 1954 was to nullify the effective technique of Neath's salmon-leaping line-out ace, Roy John, whose *modus operandi* depended for its success on the patterned blocking of his props and second-row partners. When the International Board outlawed this so-called wedge method, a new breed of line-out expert who could hold his own in the absence of protectors was sought.

Rhys Williams was the player who admirably filled the part for Wales between 1954 and 1960. A beefy forward from Cwmllynfell, who graduated with a science degree from Cardiff University, big Rhys brought the systematic, intellectual approach of the research chemist to his tight-forward work. At the height of his career for Wales and the Lions, he was the master of all the forward arts: line-out catching, scrummaging and mauling, even the ancient skill of dribbling. He was the real pack professor in Welsh rugby and, at a time when line-outs had a tendency to develop into standing mauls, his middle-of-the-line strength was priceless.

Wales prospered when Rhys entered their side midway through the 1954 campaign. He helped them to wins against Ireland, France and Scotland, and Wales finished the season joint champions with France and England. He was at the heart of his country's effort again in 1955, another championship-sharing season, and his line-out prowess for the Lions in South Africa that year was a vital ingredient of the tourists' winning recipe in the third Test.

In 1956, a fresh challenge to Welsh supremacy was launched by a new-look England pack which included the young second-row pairing of the Harlequins giants, John Currie and David Marques. Rhys, showing no signs of fatigue after the long tour of South Africa, stoked the engine-room of a Wales pack which, although struggling to hold its own against the coltish exuberance of the English, managed to set up a narrow 8-3 victory at Twickenham and proceeded to win the Five Nations title outright.

Several barren seasons followed for Wales, but there were plenty of rugby honours still to be collected by Rhys Williams. He captained his club, was greeted as a 'blood-brother' by the magnificent All Black forwards against whom he toiled for the 1959 Lions, and he came home from New Zealand to captain Wales in their bid for the 1960 championship title. Indeed, the Welsh team was packed with returning Lions for the opening match at Twickenham. But sadly Rhys, the fair-haired colossus who always played fair, found his side beaten 6-14, a whipping compared with the low-scoring norms of the day. He was dropped for Wales's remaining matches and retired at the end of the season.

FRANCE PLAYER PROFILES

Serge Blanco.

Pierre ALBALADEJO
(Dax)

The rugby career of Pierre Albaladejo falls into two separate halves. First, there was a period as an honest journeyman as a full-back with Dax. This included a sudden call-up for France's win against England on the occasion of the Tricolours' first shared championship title in 1954 and an equally sudden return to relative obscurity.

Then, in his mid-twenties, his club converted him into an outside-half, a move which caused considerable controversy at Dax. Albaladejo was not a showy performer by nature, although he was a deadly kicker who had once propelled the club to the Yves du Manoir Challenge Trophy with four drop-goals in the final. Now he was to discover a new lease of life in an unaccustomed role.

Smooth and efficient at setting the Dax threequarters moving, the player who was known as the forgotten man of French rugby was remembered by his country in 1960, soon after undergoing his positional transformation. After a disappointing draw in Paris with England, the ever-conservative French selectors made only five changes for their next match, although Albaladejo became the sixth when Roger Martine withdrew injured.

Forming an effective unit in tandem with the distinctive Mont-de-Marsan scrum-half, Pierre Lacroix, the man from Dax took his recall phlegmatically. Yes, he flourished on the end of Lacroix's extra-long pass; yes, he got his line going for both French wingers to score tries; and yes, France convincingly beat Wales in the mud, four tries to one. But no rave reviews were filed for Albaladejo. However, he did keep his place for the final match of the season, against Ireland, where victory for France would yield a share of the championship with England.

That match made him. Seldom has one player shot so unexpectedly to fame as a result of one game as Albaladejo did that sunny early-spring afternoon in Paris. He set a world record by dropping three goals - two off his left foot - and the bags of confidence he brought, particularly to the first-phase attacks of the backs, were vital ingredients in a heady French mix of dashing open play and spectacular scores. The upshot was a then record total of points for France in a Five Nations match, 23-6.

It is always a sure sign of a sportsman's arrival on the world scene when followers refer to him by a pet name. Albaladejo was immediately christened 'Monsieur Drop' for his achievements against Ireland, and the name stuck - a blessing for British commentators who found the challenge of his syllables almost insurmountable. The long-legged fly-half was then a fixture in the French sides which won the Five Nations championship in 1961 and 1962, playing throughout with Lacroix as his half-back partner. Place-kicker, drop-kicker and tactical kicker, Albaladejo was also indispensable as a playmaker for the French backs.

Weaknesses? There were a few. He wasn't the first (nor last) class outside-half who didn't relish tackling, and he didn't enjoy the close attention of opposing back rows either, especially later in his career when he missed the quick service of Lacroix. But for his exquisite kicking - twelve drop-goals and more than 100 points in thirty Tests for France - he will never again be the forgotten man.

Pierre BERBIZIER
(Lourdes, Agen)

Pierre Berbizier was the type of scrum-half whom French forwards and backs alike welcomed with open arms. He wasn't the world's finest passer of a rugby football, nor was he the hardest tackler ever to represent his country. Instead, his special aptitude was his uncanny tactical reading of a game. Possessed of a sixth sense when it came to anticipating how a match would evolve, he put himself about the pitch in an unobtrusive manner that disguised his high work rate, but which certainly helped to conserve the energy of his *confrères*.

Berbizier emerged as the new French playmaker in the 1981 Grand Slam season and went on to become a key element in the successes of the 1980s. Whenever his forwards were held up at ruck or maul, the little scrum-half was at hand to direct operations. A flicked pass to a loose forward or an orthodox link with his fly-half to set the back line moving - kicking was anathema to him - would follow with the inevitability that night follows day. Then he would scuttle off to chivvy his pack into winning more second-phase possession. Eventually, either a scoring opportunity presented itself or the referee intervened.

Berbizier was tireless in his endeavours, and the nickname given to him by his team-mates - *'le patron'* - was a measure of the esteem in

Pierre Berbizier sets his backs moving against Wales at Cardiff in 1988.

which he was held. He was France's facilitator - the spiritual leader of the pack and the man who called the shots in the backs.

Internal wrangles in the French set-up interrupted his run in the national side during the early 1980s, and Berbizier vied with four other scrum-halves for the No. 9 shirt before establishing his place in the prelude to the 1987 World Cup. Adapting to coach Jacques Fouroux's favoured pressure game, Berbizier was *le petit général* on the field and directed a team nominally captained by Daniel Dubroca, first to a famous win against New Zealand, then to a Grand Slam, and eventually into the World Cup final. His displays in the inaugural tournament held in Australia and New Zealand were so impressive that he was bracketed with John Kirwan as player-of-the-competition.

On paper, France were at their zenith: joint champions with Wales in 1988, they became outright title winners again in 1989 with Berbizier as captain. Two years later, when French tactics reverted to fluid football, Berbizier was still viewed as the scrum-half best equipped to oversee activities on the field, and he shrewdly marshalled the rejuvenated Tricolours through the campaign, despite carrying a leg injury. The race for the Grand Slam went to a photo-finish and, in an epic decider with England, the French were pipped by only a couple of points.

The match was Berbizier's fifty-sixth and final Test. With the long-knife sharpeners going on to double time in France, the half-back was incomprehensibly dropped from the squad for the 1991 Rugby World Cup. Then, following another shake-out, he returned as France's coach within twelve months of his last international.

Roland BERTRANNE
(Bagnères, Toulon)

Roland Bertranne was the French threequarter who managed to keep his place when all about him were losing theirs. He entered the national side in 1971, at a time when France were desperately seeking to play the dashing rugby their followers craved. He survived the French revolution of the 1970s when the hierarchy demanded a forward-orientated game. And he was still there to make a contribution when the tactical pendulum swayed back to an expansive fifteen-man approach under Jean-Pierre Rives. He was able to conform to whatever style of rugby was required.

Bertranne's early mentor was Jean Gachassin, the jack-in-the-box French utility back of the 1960s who played out the twilight years of his career with Bagnères, one of the less fashionable village clubs in the vicinity of the rugby strongholds of Lourdes, Tarbes and Dax. Gachassin imbued the club with a love for the classic flowing game, and Bertranne, with his page-boy haircut and dark features, quickly developed into an adroit exponent of open, attacking rugby. The panache of youth and the coolness of the supremely confident sportsman were embodied in his stocky frame and he immediately impressed Englishmen with his all-round ability when he made his international debut at Twickenham in 1971, scoring a try. On the strength of his performance that day, he was honoured with an invitation to participate in the centenary celebrations of the Rugby Football Union. Injury, alas, prevented him from taking part, but he compensated for that misfortune by going on to play sixty-nine times for his country, the French record until eclipsed by Serge Blanco in 1989.

Sometimes Bertranne played in the centre, sometimes on the wing. There was agreement among those who felt he expressed himself

 Roland Bertranne.

better as a wing that his acceleration was virtually superhuman. Yet others believed that his natural aptitude for giving a well-timed pass - constructive qualities which he absorbed from Gachassin - made him a must for the centre spot. Curiously, however, none of these talents were judged important to the grim method adopted by France in 1977. That year Bertranne was chosen for his honest defence in midfield, and he did his job well: France won the Grand Slam without conceding a try.

By the time Bertranne's last Five Nations campaign came round in 1981, the fickle French had ditched their negative tactics. Now Rives was at the helm and hell-bent on his commitment to attacking football. France were left wielding the wooden spoon in 1980, but the spirit prevailed the following season when there was more tenacity in evidence throughout the side. As a result, Bertranne was able to add another Grand Slam to his record of achievement, getting France off to a happy start with a try in the opening match against Scotland.

Sadly, he found himself cast as the villain of two French defeats by the All Blacks and was forced to contend with criticisms of his attitude and age. Fed up, he retired from rugby and took up rally-driving instead as a new sporting interest.

Serge BLANCO
(Biarritz)

Serge Blanco was the dominant personality in the Five Nations throughout the 1980s, taking France to the edge of greatness. His country won the Grand Slam twice, took or shared the championship title six times, and reached the final of the World Cup in 1987. Above all, he typified the *joie-de-vivre* style of rugby.

Blanco was without doubt a class player whose commitment to adventure and enjoyment was unshakeable. On his own admission, traditional defensive duties was the area of his game which appealed to him the least. The Blanco philosophy was: tries conceded, nine; tries scored, ten; end result, happiness. His maxim was that attack is the best form of defence, and the sight of Blanco ghosting out of his own half to initiate another move was an image that cheered not only dyed-in-the-wool rugby-lovers, but sports-worshippers of all denominations.

In a career spanning a dozen seasons, Blanco became the world's most-capped player, making ninety-three Test appearances. Some of his early experiences were on the wing, where his speed off the mark made audiences sit up and realise that here was one of the fastest men ever to don kit. That remarkable pace of his was the vehicle that took him to thirty-eight tries in internationals, a figure which includes a world-record number of touchdowns for a full-back and places him second on the all-time list of

The incomparable Serge Blanco, in his last Five Nations match, against England, 1991, which England won 21-19.

Test try-scorers.

Year in year out, Blanco's enthusiasm for running rugby never waned. His exciting counter-attacks from apparently impossible situations were regarded as delightful titbits when he came into Rives's Grand Slam team in 1981 but, six years later, they had become meat and drink to a French side that achieved another clean sweep in the inaugural World Cup year. Blanco's sparks of genius shone like a beacon in a French XV coached by Jacques Fouroux, who seemed to concentrate on tactics which militated against the enterprising rugby of his most irresistible force.

Right up to his last Five Nations match, Blanco's love of the unexpected was passionate. Who will ever forget the champagne moment at Twickenham in the 1991 Grand Slam decider, when Blanco launched a movement from his own in-goal area? The attack developed along the French right wing and culminated in a vintage try under the English posts. By his role as the originator of such a marvellous score, Blanco confirmed his standing as one of rugby's leading legends.

The only flaw related to his temperament. He wasn't above occasionally acting the old soldier after a heavy tackle, and his general tendency to over-react was a trait that, when captain of his country, did him no good at all. When France fell to England in a foul-strewn quarter-final in the 1991 World Cup, Blanco lost his decorum early in the game: in an undignified release of his tension, he laid into the England winger, Nigel Heslop, and was fortunate not to be dismissed from the field. As captain of a fancied team up against strong opposition, he needed to set a disciplined example to his colleagues. His failure to do so tainted his exit from Test rugby.

An unusual action shot of Serge Blanco, hungry as always for possession.

14

André BONIFACE
(Mont-de-Marsan)

In the country where the vine flourishes, a gifted threequarter whets the neutral enthusiast's appetite for rugby like the sparkle of a vintage champagne. The player who carried the *appellation contrôlée* designation during the rise of the French game was André Boniface.

His initial experience of international rugby was as an exceptionally fast winger. Capped as a teenager in 1954, he quickly impressed critics with his balanced running and grace, and a sign of his precocious commitment to open back play was his penchant for tossing a reverse pass at speed back to his centres when he was hemmed in by the touchline. Such an action was highly unorthodox in the French game of the mid-1950s, but Boniface believed in continuity, and the spirited threequarter style which was to set the rugby world alight years later clearly found its first expression through the figure of the young flyer.

However, the successful France teams of Jean Prat and Lucien Mias thrived on a disciplined diet of patterned forward play, while their threequarters were selected primarily to bear the brunt of the defensive duties and score the tries created by the attacking ploys of the pack. Boniface obediently toed the line early in his career, but found himself in and out of the French XV until united at national level as a centre with his younger brother, Guy, during the Tricolours' tour of

André Boniface in France's team of 1954 which shared the championship honours with Wales and England. R Brejassou, R Bienes, J Prat, P Labadie. Crouching: A Boniface, M Prat, G Dufau, M Vannier, A Haget, R Marti

New Zealand in 1961.

That trip caused the French to pause for thought and adapt their game. After three years of continuous glory, their forwards met their match in New Zealand, losing the Test series 0-3. Virtually the only redeeming feature of the visit for the French was the emergence of the Boniface brothers as a pair of brilliant centres. They were a fun-loving duo, on and off the field, and both found authority tiresome. But their temperaments were ideal to give fresh hope to a team whose self-esteem was badly undermined by the All Blacks, and they brought a new dimension to French rugby with their confidence and mastery of the basic skills of giving and taking a pass. After New Zealand had carefully undone the much-vaunted teamwork of the French forwards early in the series, the creativity of the 'Boni' brothers became the principal strike weapon of the hard-pressed tourists.

André Boniface's deceptive acceleration took him sailing through countless gaps when he played in the 1962 team which won the Five Nations championship, but illness affected the form of his sibling and, sadly, the pair never played together that season. The pride of French rugby was nevertheless sustained by the brothers throughout the mid-1960s when the national side, recoiling from a rash of retirements, went through a rebuilding stage. In total, Guy and André played centre eighteen times together, a French record which stood for twenty-six years. But, more important, their selfless play in forging opportunities for their wingers to run in tries originated a distinctive French style which became an inspiration to succeeding generations of threequarters.

nding: B Chevallier, L Mias, M Celaya, H Domec, enave.

Christian CARRERE
(Toulon)

Le Grand Chelem eluded France until 1968 when the Holy Grail of the knights in blue was finally achieved under the captaincy of Christian Carrère, the youngest man to lead France in a Test since the war.

Ironically, the team which claimed the Five Nations' supreme prize was a long way short of being the best that France ever produced. Luck played its part in the opening win of the season against Scotland, and five changes were made for the 16-6 defeat of Ireland. The French selectors then underlined their lack of confidence in the side by going for an astonishing nine changes for the match with England and, by the end of the campaign, the remarkable total of thirty-one players had appeared in the Grand Slam team.

Consequently, the success of Carrère as captain was extraordinary. He had under him experienced players of the calibre of Dauga and Spanghero; the blue-eyed boys, Maso, Gachassin and Lux in midfield; and the Camberabero brothers at half-back who were capable of exercising a strong tactical grip on a match . Any one of these could reasonably have expected to get the job as skipper ahead of the back-row man, but the sure touch Carrère used in calmly handling his colleagues was a style of man-management that worked wonders on the illustrious - and not so illustrious - names in his charge. France has never yet found another leader with the *sang-froid* of Carrère.

The details of his brief career are interesting. Brought up in Morocco, where his father was stationed with the French Armed Forces, the young Carrère showed expertise as a handball player before returning to the Bigorre in his teens. At Tarbes he took quickly to rugby, the proficiency of his handling owing much to his earlier sporting experiences in North Africa. A later move to the Côte d'Azure led to a place at flanker in the Toulon side before he was plucked from the leading pack of Crauste-pretenders to demonstrate that he was the natural heir to the open-side throne vacated by the former French captain.

He marked his Five Nations debut against Scotland in 1967 with a try. France won the Five Nations championship that year, and Carrère carried the heavy mantle as Crauste's replacement with surprising ease. There was an incisiveness to his work in attack and, although he showed less enthusiasm for defensive duties, his adroit positional sense made up for any shortcomings of technique in his tackling.

Injuries dogged him after the Grand Slam triumph, but he was back in 1970 to lead France to a share of the Five Nations title. In 1971 his side was unbeaten until the last match of the season - the championship showdown with Wales. France lost the game 5-9 and, at twenty-seven, Carrère's Test days were over.

Michel CELAYA
(Biarritz)

If Jean Prat was the first French captain to achieve greatness, Michel Celaya was the first skipper upon whom the selectors tried to thrust it. Prat had pointed the French in the direction of rugby's promised land. A year after his international retirement, the job of delivering France to that land of milk and honey was given to Celaya.

Michel Celaya's debut for France was in 1953, against England at Twickenham. He served a tough apprenticeship but came through with flying colours in Prat's teams of 1954 and 1955, showing grace and impressing with his high work rate.

But his reign as captain turned out to be an utter disaster. France's first full Five Nations season under Celaya was 1957. All four matches were lost for the first time since 1929, and it was clear that the additional responsibility of leadership lay awkwardly on the ample shoulders of the handsome Basque. The losing run continued the next season and, when Celaya's XV succumbed 0-14 to England at the Stade Colombes, matters were brought to a head. The French rugby hierarchy suffered the humiliating experience of a mass demonstration of disapproval. *'Démission, démission,'* ('resign, resign') demanded the angry French crowd, the object of their wrath being Roger Lerou, the chairman of the selectors.

The guillotine fell in typical Gallic fashion for the next international. Out went eight players, and in came an all-Lourdes threequarter line. Curiously, Celaya retained the captaincy - he was a forward who was too skilful and dedicated to omit, and there was then no obvious candidate to succeed him at the helm.

Altogether, Lourdes provided seven players to a French XV which trounced Australia 19-0. The Tricolours went on to record their first-ever win at Cardiff and finished the season with a victory against Ireland.

Celaya was then nominated captain again for France's first tour of South Africa, although his misfortune with injury on that trip proved a happy accident for his country. Unable to play in the Tests, he handed the skipper's armband to Lucien Mias. France won the series and looked forward eagerly to the 1959 Five Nations championship.

Celaya returned to the French team as a flanker - he was normally a lock or No. 8 in internationals - for the opening match of the new season against Scotland. Relieved of the burden of captaincy - 'I'm no gendarme', he reflected - he once again enjoyed having to drive just himself instead of fourteen others.

He was a regular in the French sides which dominated the Five Nations championship in the years that followed, playing a major role in the development of back-row tactics. Celaya was typical of the new breed of dynamic French pack-man: highly mobile with safe hands, and conspicuous in a white headband, he relished the fast interpassing game of the French loose forwards. Ploys, the collective name for attacking forward moves, brought a fresh dimension to rugby, and none was more adept at the execution of the ploy than Michel Celaya.

From left to right: Michel Crauste, François Moncla and Michel Celaya, three important members of the French team which drew with England 3-3 in 1960.

Michel CRAUSTE
(Racing Club of France, Lourdes)

If you were playing international rugby against France between 1958 and 1966, two things were certain. One, Michel Crauste would be in the back row facing you, and two, the Frenchman would leave his mark on both your body and your mind with his daredevil tackling and his ubiquitous loose play. For his whiter-than-white complexion and archetypal drooping French moustache he took the sobriquet 'Attila', and the devastation he caused in his thirty-five Five Nations appearances for his country would have done the Hunnish king proud. Michel Crauste's courage and ruthlessness on the rugby field made him the scourge of England, Scotland, Ireland and Wales.

He arrived in the France side with propitious timing in 1958. That was the year of French rugby's 'big bang', and Crauste was quickly recognised as the prototype loose forward needed to practise a rapidly expanding game based on back-row attack. Crauste missed out on South Africa in 1958, but he did enjoy some memorable successes at club and national level in the following seasons. Though a native of the rugby-mad south-west, his job as a technician with the French electricity concern EDF took him first to Paris, where he helped Racing Club to become champions of France in 1959, and then to the Bigorre, where he was hailed as the natural heir to Jean Prat and featured in Lourdes's victorious team of 1960.

Crauste never had a bad game for France and was acknowledged worldwide as the complete flanker. An outstanding member of the Five Nations team that won or shared the championship every season between 1959 and 1962, probably his finest hour came on a cold, crisp Paris afternoon in February 1962, facing England. With all the French forwards throwing the ball about accurately, Crauste showed the speed, directness and determination that were his hallmarks and scored a hat-trick of tries. It was the performance of a true virtuoso. When he cut loose, he picked his way through the England defence with the polished finesse of a threequarter. When he didn't have the ball, you could bet your final franc that he would pop up at a colleague's elbow to collect a pass and keep alive the attack.

Crauste was given the captaincy of France late in his career, and somewhat begrudgingly, it was felt. The trouble was that he was sometimes in trouble for his roughness; there were doubts about his ability to read the game; and his critics believed that he was better being led than leading. Nevertheless, in 1966, he skippered France literally to within a centimetre of the Five Nations title when he took an unbeaten team to Cardiff for the crunch match of the season against Wales. Leading 8-6 with time running out, France conceded a famous try to Stuart Watkins but, even then, all was not lost. Wales gave away a kickable penalty in the dying moments, but Lacaze's attempt was cruelly and narrowly blown off course, and Crauste's championship challenge fell at the last hurdle.

The captain declared that he was through with international rugby after a then record sixty-three Test appearances. He found a new lease of life playing at No. 8 for Lourdes, and he lifted the club championship shield in 1968. But he steadfastly refused all invitations to make a comeback with France.

Christian DARROUY
(Mont-de-Marsan)

Christian Darrouy, a soccer player as a teenager, took to rugby like a bird to the air. He was a winger with the sheer pace to fly round most of his opponents in French club rugby, seldom needing any guile to beat them. Poor defence was a weakness early in his career, however; after five consecutive Tests for France in 1957, when he was only twenty, Darrouy made only intermittent appearances in the five years that followed.

During that time he worked carefully at his game, toughening his tackling while retaining his cutting edge as a try-scorer, and developing a clever ruse to outwit the best of defences. Approaching a would-be tackler, he adopted a habit of slowing down before rapidly accelerating away, leaving his nonplussed opponent flat-footed. The trick brought Darrouy many tries, most of which were finished off with elegant arcing runs to the posts, while others were the product of his opportunism. Opposing full-backs, about to clear their lines, were sometimes lulled into a false sense of security by his apparent dawdling. But their kicks were charged down as the winger put in a final burst to smother the clearance and, in a flash, Darrouy would gather the rebound and hare over for an unexpected try.

Probably the most significant factor in his international rehabilitation in 1963 was the successful run his club made for the French championship. Darrouy, with his keen anticipatory instincts, could hardly fail to benefit from playing outside the creative Boniface brothers. The Mont-de-Marsan trio were selected *en bloc* for that year's Five Nations matches, and Darrouy blossomed as a seasoned winger well served by his club centres. He also guaranteed an extended international run for himself by scoring a hat-trick of tries against Ireland in Dublin.

Although the French sides of 1963-66 won no honours, plaudits were heaped on them for their commitment to fluid rugby. The contributions made by the mercurial men from Mont-de-Marsan were considerable. Darrouy went on to become France's most prolific try-scorer and was a real crowd-puller at all Five Nations venues. There was something of a greyhound in his smooth running action, and certainly those who backed him to score tries made the odd franc or three. In the 1964 *tournoi* he collected three touchdowns; there were four to his name in the 1965 competition, and two more followed in the strong French challenge for the title in 1966. Nearly all his forty Tests and his record twenty-three tries for France were as a left wing, though Darrouy was equally at home on the right where he scored countless times for his club.

In 1967, Christian Darrouy became the first wing threequarter to captain France in the Five Nations championship since Adolphe Jauréguy, thirty-eight years earlier. As Michel Crauste and the Boniface brothers had recently retired from international rugby, Darrouy was the senior player and natural leader of the French squad. He took his duties seriously and finished his last season in the Five Nations championship as the proud skipper of the first French side to win the title for five years.

Benoit DAUGA
(Mont-de-Marsan)

Big Benoit Dauga was the French forward who became a legend in his own line-out. When he was discovered playing for the French Armed Forces against the Combined Services in 1963, observers were confident that here was a man destined for greatness. For a start, French rugby had never possessed a forward as tall as Dauga (6ft 4in), he showed the agility, pace and adroitness of a top-class basketball player, and he was eager to learn the game.

Within a year of his breakthrough into first-class rugby, he was in the French side at Murrayfield facing Scotland. Yet it is possible that he might never have had the chance to perform at the highest level. Critics argued that he was too lean, too stringy, to take the knocks of international rugby, particularly in the free-for-all of the line-out. Had he not been selected so young - he was only twenty-one when he made his Five Nations debut in 1964 - he would almost certainly have become a basketball international instead of, in the words of Jean Prat, 'the greatest forward ever produced by France'.

In 1964, the French XV was in a transitional stage: the backs were experienced enough, but the front five of the pack, including Dauga, were rookies. The lofty lad proved to be the find of the season. In a demanding Test against the New Zealand tourists, which he passed with distinction, his vigour in the line-out quashed once and for all the gibe that he wasn't tough enough for international rugby. His mobility was an added bonus to the athleticism and clean catching he displayed at the set-piece; against Ireland, in the last match of his first season, Dauga was here, there and everywhere in a record win for France in the Five Nations tournament.

'Benoit Dauga needs to curb his tendency to go buccaneering away from the pack' was a fair criticism of the tall man's solo raids in the loose during that first season. But what France really needed were two or three more giants to complement Dauga in the line-out and to give his runs support. And two were found in Walter Spanghero and André Herrero. Spanghero partnered Dauga at lock with Herrero at No. 8 in South Africa in July 1964, when France followed on from 1958 by beating the Springboks again. As an effective second row coupling, Dauga and Spanghero went on to play fifteen times for their country and were together until the former moved back to No. 8 half-way through France's championship title win in 1967. Both men were in the side again in 1968 - France's first Grand Slam - but Spanghero was at No. 8 this time with Dauga at lock.

From left to right: Carrère, Spanghero, Cester and Dauga, important members of France's team in 1968.

A difficulty was beginning to confront the French selectors. The problem was that these two important players both wanted to show their prowess at No. 8. Rumours spread that the one would not play for France if the other were chosen and, sadly, there was no administrator or captain with the strength of character to persuade the big men to act in the best interests of French rugby. Although their last appearance together was in South Africa in 1971, either Dauga or Spanghero played for France in the following seventeen Tests - but not one of those games saw the two men take the field together.

The last of Dauga's sixty-three caps was in 1972, but the final seasons of sporadic appearances robbed him of the accolade of being France's most-capped player in Five Nations matches. That would have been a richly deserved honour for a forward who was always a delight to watch.

Amédée DOMENECH
(Vichy, Brive)

A chronic weakness of the four Home Unions in the past thirty years has been their failure to develop athletic forwards. Australia and France, by contrast, have consistently nurtured big, agile men whose running and handling skills would have impressed basketball coaches. Among the early generation of talented French ball players was Amédée Domenech, a colourful character who won his first cap as a twenty-year-old prop in 1954.

As the cornerstone of the French packs which made history by winning shares of the Five Nations championship in 1954 and 1955, young Amédée looked set for a long tenure as first-choice loose-head in his country's front row. Immensely strong for his age, he gave early warning of his speed during the 1955 international against Ireland, when he followed up a break by the French forwards to finish the move by outpacing the Irish backs for the only try of the match. That incident was typical of his try-hungry appetite: he relished the individual foray, and his bulldozing style made him difficult to block.

He was ever-present in the national sides of 1956 and 1957, being ranked top prop in both seasons by the French Rugby Union writers. Then, in 1958, his world fell apart, and the intoxicating Lucien Mias era of champagne rugby passed him by. Domenech was made a scapegoat for the dreadful 0-14 drubbing by England that year. As deliberate measures were taken to improve the cohesion of the side, his approach was considered unsuited to Mias's experiments, and out of the blue, Aldo Quaglio, who was a flanker for Mias's club Mazamet, moved into Domenech's spot. France then began winning after a miserable run of defeats.

Domenech declared himself unavailable for the successful tour of South Africa that summer, so the French selection committee found themselves in a quandary when they convened to choose the team to open the 1959 *tournoi* against Scotland. Their initial inclination was to restore him to their side. But Mias was not convinced that Domenech was ready to embrace the role envisaged for him, and it was Quaglio, a hero of the South African exercise, who appeared in all the Five Nations matches. Domenech's supporters made accusations that a 'mafia' of those involved in the South Africa tour was operating, an allegation totally rejected by Mias who believed that the prop could easily adapt his game to fit the new French method if he so desired.

By the start of the next season Mias had retired, Quaglio turned professional and Domenech was recalled to play the best rugby of his career. Now a committed convert to Mias's tenets, his dexterity and pace were put to good use in the forwards' ploys. Invariably, it was Domenech who was deputed to peel off and gather the tap-down from the back of the line-out. Certainly, no one was better equipped to form the vertex of the wedge-shaped attack which followed the peel, and he became a pivotal figure in France's championship wins of 1960, 1961 and 1962.

Off the field, the man who raised the peel to a rugby art form was a larger-than-life personality nicknamed 'the duke'. The origins of the sobriquet are cloudy, but a clearer insight into the character of this happy-go-lucky restaurateur-turned-successful politician was rather nicely reflected by a slogan he once displayed in his bistro in Brive: 'Love and wine speed the hours.'

Patrice LAGISQUET
(Bayonne)

Forget *le piat d'or:* the discerning French public adore rugby played *au grand large* - what the British call an expansive game. Sadly, between 1984 and 1990, France did not employ the full width of the field after Jean-Pierre Rives passed from the scene, and the irony was that, in Patrice Lagisquet, they had lurking on the touchline a man who was the deadliest finisher in international rugby, the best-equipped winger in Europe to capitalise on the overlaps and half-chances frequently created by open play.

Once in possession, Lagisquet needed only to edge his neck and shoulders past an opponent to manoeuvre himself clear. Then, moving with the grace of a thoroughbred, he left his chasers lying several lengths behind as he crossed the line, usually untouched, for a try. By comparison, British and Irish defenders in the Five Nations tournament were cart-horses.

Established sprinters - Lagisquet had clocked 10.6 sec over 100 metres - do not generally become effective wingers on the rugby field. But Lagisquet was the exception to the rule. His natural running talent was honed in the testing cauldron of the French club championship where, known as 'the Bayonne express', he was a prolific try-scorer who developed into an intelligent rugby player well able to create his own chances out of nothing. He wasn't just a speed merchant waiting to be worked clear - far from it; Lagisquet's panoply of skills included swerves, jinks and deft changes of pace.

First capped on the right wing in 1983-84, he spent much of his time during the mid-1980s in reserve. It was at the 1987 Rugby World Cup, where he was introduced for the quarter-final against Fiji, that he began his fruitful spell on France's left wing. He collected tries avidly, helping his country to honours against their Five Nations neighbours in 1988 and 1989 before joining the select band of scorers who have completed twenty touchdowns in Tests.

Two tries recorded against Ireland were among the most important of his tally. France are notoriously poor starters to the season and can usually be written off when trailing 0-15 away from home. But when they found themselves in just such a position in Dublin in January 1989, it was Lagisquet who extricated them from impending defeat with tries which were the products of wonderful attacking rugby. France won 26-21 and went on to be champions that year.

Patrice Lagisquet.

Performances like this left neutral observers wondering what France might have achieved had they abandoned the colourless rugby of the previous few years. Who knows how many tries Lagisquet might have conjured up playing in a team permanently committed to fifteen-man rugby?

Sadly, the Bayonne express broke down early in 1991 with cartilage problems and failed to restart properly during that year's World Cup or the following championship season. No doubt his absence from rugby allowed more time for the admirable work he did off the field raising money for deprived children, but opponents to whom he had shown no charity on the field will have heaved a sigh of relief.

Lucien MIAS (Mazamet)

Although only fifty-seventh on the list of French caps, Lucien Mias deserves selection in any top ten of his country's leading players for his achievements and radical thinking on rugby.

First capped at lock in 1951 as a young schoolmaster, the metamorphosis of Mias began the following season when he was in a losing side torn apart by the visiting Springboks. He was absorbed by the way the South African pack operated as a unit both in defence and attack. For forwards to be used offensively was unheard of in France, and Mias began reassessing his individual game and considering how he might transform forward play at club and national level.

In the mid-1950s, Mias took an extended break from the game while he retrained as a doctor. He returned in 1957-58 fitter, faster, a stone lighter, and with a miracle cure for French rugby, which was then suffering from a severe bout of depression brought on by a complete breakdown in the previous Five Nations championship.

His home club Mazamet was the guinea pig in his experiment, and France were the control group. Mias explored the idea of forward collectivism, bringing the pack together to work as a unit and, while France continued losing, the plan yielded fascinating results at club level, Mazamet reaching the final of the French championship for the first time. The thrust of their forward game was formation attack: a player shedding himself from a line-out would make a beeline for an opponent, committing the defender to a tackle; next, Mias and others would churn the move onwards and suck more and more defenders into the maul; finally, the ball was released, and a second phase of attack was launched at a disorganised defence. Mazamet perfected the strategy, their forwards becoming expert at a technique which became known as the peel and was eventually extensively copied.

France's defeat by England in 1958 was the watershed for the Tricolours. For the next match, wholesale changes were made behind the scrum but, in the pack, where Mias was now commanding respect for what he had achieved at club level, there was only one new face.

The reprieved forwards warmed to Mias and his theories and forged an effective bond. Mias's suggestion that they vary positions at line-outs in order to compete for possession was adopted, and Australia, Wales and Ireland were dispatched with ease. When Michel Celaya was plagued by injury on the South African tour later that year, Mias was the natural heir to the captaincy. Now he was able to give the French side the full works.

With the timely advent of Bernard Mommejat, at 6ft 3in the tallest French lock of his generation, Mias had a partner capable of winning his fair share of line-out ball, a facet of the game where French sides had struggled for years. The last weapon needed to establish Mias's attacking ploys at international level was in place and, after winning the series in South Africa, *'le docteur Rugby'*, as the medic from Mazamet was christened in France, went on to direct his country to their first Five Nations title in 1959.

His job done, Mias retired to concentrate on his professional career. Getting the French packs of the 1950s to convert from 'trench rugby' to 'champagne rugby' had been a daunting task, but Lucien Mias possessed the stentorian authority to force his colleagues to embrace change. His perception in challenging the accepted tenets of forward play revolutionised the game. Mias's immediate legacy was that France were the kings of European rugby for four seasons between 1958 and 1962, and the sport was elevated to the status of a serious national pastime in the eyes of the French public.

Robert PAPAREMBORDE
(Pau)

Props are not generally expected to collect tries, but Robert Paparemborde, France's tight-head between 1975 and 1983, turned crossing the whitewash into an art form. To show that the try he scored on his debut was not beginner's luck, he dotted down another in his second Test and finished with eight in his fifty-five internationals - a French record for a prop.

But try-scoring was nothing more than a useful by-product of Paparemborde's work as far as the French were concerned. He was an outstanding graduate of the hard school of tight forwards which his country has nurtured for the past thirty years. Nicknamed 'Patou', Paparemborde was brilliant in the covert operations of the dimly-lit underworld of front-row play. But that was not all. Early in his career he had played in the threequarter line and, during his many Tests, the legacy of that experience was clear: he was a fine handler who ran with the speed and purpose of an intelligent centre.

Paparemborde served his representative apprenticeship in the France B team before making his full debut in South Africa in 1975. The visit was a crossroads for France. Many of the players originally chosen had declined their invitations to tour, and an inexperienced pack of forwards, including 'Patou' underwent a baptism of fire, losing both Tests heavily. Yet the team spirit which had been developed on that trip sustained France in the Five Nations tournament as they vied with Wales for honours in the following four seasons. Paparemborde was just one of several players discovered in South Africa who went on to form the backbone of the successful French sides of the late 1970s.

Robert Paparemborde, a try-scoring tight-head, playing here for France against England.

He was described as the team's anchor-man. Physically strong, his sagging shoulders seemed to slope down to his midriff, causing any number of problems for opposing loose-heads. When scrummaging, he tended to brace his free right hand on his outside knee, thus adopting an unusual stance which merely compounded the troubles of his adversaries. This was perfectly legal and was a means to the end of disrupting the shoves attempted against the French scrum.

With two redoubtable compatriots, Alain Paco and Gerard Cholley, Paparemborde comprised a formidable French front row which played in twenty-one Tests - a world record for a partnership that stood for a dozen years. Their effective crabbing of the scrummage was a crucial ingredient of France's forward domination in the 1977 championship; it wasn't pretty to watch but it took the wind out of the sails of their challengers. That year, France played controlled rugby that was more akin to the power-based Springbok game than to the traditional flamboyant French style, and Robert Paparemborde was an integral part of the side as it progressed unchanged to France's second-ever Grand Slam.

In another four years he was on the Grand Slam trail again, one of only four surrivors of the 1977 squad - Bertranne, Rives and Imbernon were the others.

During 1980-81, Paparemborde was elected to the steering committee of the FFR (French Rugby Union), thus becoming the first player in the Five Nations to feature in a Grand Slam win while serving his union as an administrator.

Jean PRAT (Lourdes)

Following French international rugby before the 1939-45 war was an unrewarding experience. France's teams often resembled headless chickens: the players showed little or no tactical sense and had only marginally more stamina and discipline. Enthusiasm and skill there were in plenty, but no pre-war French captain had either the wit or the generalship required to transform his side into potential champions.

Then, in the early 1950s, Jean Prat of Lourdes was promoted to lead France following the retirement of the much-respected Agen forward, Guy Basquet. Prat had already served France loyally, missing only one international between 1945 and 1952 before becoming skipper in 1953.

His credentials for the captaincy were impeccable. He was a distinguished Lourdes back-rower who had performed miracles by leading the club to the French championship in 1948 and 1952. Determination and tenacity, legacies of his prowess as a cross-country champion, were features of his own game, and he had played prominent roles in dramatic French successes at Swansea in 1948 (their first win in Wales), at Twickenham in 1951 (their first win in England), and at Murrayfield in 1952 (their first win in Scotland).

Within a year, Jean Prat's strong personality had taken a grip on the French side. In 1954, leading a young and inexperienced XV with an iron fist, he instigated a tight-marking strategy which immediately paid dividends. The campaign began with resounding wins against Scotland, Ireland and New Zealand in which no points were conceded. But Cardiff proved to be Prat's Waterloo. Against a Welsh side well-used to the pressures of tight marking, Prat's troops, including six of his Lourdes cadets, scored try for try but lost on penalties.

Prat shrewdly stuck by his tactics for the last battle of the season, against England. The English had already won the Triple Crown, but the mathematics of the championship indicated that Prat could win for France a share of the title by conquering the old enemy. He did: a snap drop-goal, one of his specialities, and his conversion of a try scored by his brother Maurice, inscribed Jean Prat's name as the first on the tablet of French championship-winning captains.

Jean Prat, the first of France's championship winning captains.

His name was there again the following season. In his ninth year in the *tournoi des Cinq Nations,* he took France to the brink of a Grand Slam. Good wins against Scotland and Ireland were followed by one of Prat's best individual performances, against England at Twickenham. At the Mecca of the game, he so dominated proceedings that even his own pack were in awe of him. Amédée Domenech, a young prop, found Prat's exhortations to do this, do that and do everything so overbearing that once, finding himself unexpectedly in possession, he tossed the ball like a hot potato to his captain. But, before Domenech could mutter, 'See what you can do with it,' Prat had dropped his second goal of the match.

Interest surrounding the Grand Slam match against Wales was unprecedented. A record Paris crowd saw the pesky Welsh take advantage of a poor first-half showing by the French and, although Prat stirred his men to perform brilliantly in the second half, the damage was done. 'Monsieur Rugby', as the French skipper was known in Britain, bowed out of international rugby with the consolation of a second shared championship title, and his world records of most points and most drop-goals by a forward at Test level still stand.

Jean Prat took Lourdes to three more French club championships before retiring in 1958. However, his influence as mentor to his beloved Lourdes and to the French game in general was an important factor in the rise of his nation's rugby fortune

Jean-Pierre RIVES
(Toulouse, Racing Club of France)

The newcomer who erupted on to world rugby in 1975 with all the energy of a supernova was Jean-Pierre Rives. The flaxen-haired Frenchman made his international debut on a cold, dry February afternoon at Twickenham, stamping his strong personality on the game with a performance packed with natural talent. A flanker, he demonstrated the ability to crop up in the right place at the right time to use his intelligence either to save his side from a threatening situation or to set up scoring opportunities.

In the years that followed, the boundless enthusiasm of the blond bombshell was channelled into winning. Ever-present in Five Nations matches between 1976-78, which included a French Grand Slam under Jacques Fouroux in 1977, Rives railed against French tactics which brought ten wins in twelve championship matches. He disliked the emphasis on organisation and found the tight discipline of the squad oppressive, even though it was fruitful. It was no surprise therefore that, when he succeeded Jean-Pierre Bastiat as France's captain for the 1979 season, Rives preferred to commit his charges to an expansive, fifteen-man approach.

His first triumph as captain was with an experimental French team in New Zealand the following summer. He instilled in his tourists a spirit of adventure, shunning the 1977 attitude of victory at all costs. After defeat in the first Test, Rives inspired his side with his own courageous, non-stop action in the second Test at Auckland and, in a coruscating display of running rugby, France notched up four tries and recorded their first win in an international in New Zealand.

Rives's faith in open, attacking football was evident once more in the 1980 Five Nations championship. France suffered a severe drought that season. Through lack of a competent line-out jumper and mauling deficiencies, the sources of French possession ran dry. Poor results left the side holders of the wooden spoon for the first time since 1969. Still the pundits appreciated Rives's refreshing outlook on the game. There was fulsome praise for his style and Peter West represented the views of many when he proposed in *The Times:* 'Rives surely embodies the old chivalrous Corinthian spirit which exuded fun and panache.'

France introduced heavier equipment up front the following season to shovel the ball out for the backs. Rives and his back row were irresistible and, with typical Gallic unpredictability, the

French rose from wooden-spoonists to Grand Slammers. His finest performance was at Twickenham on the final Saturday of the campaign. Rives tackled the English out of the game with the force of a bulldozer, and he was active in making both French tries.

Rives led three more Grand Slam challenges before standing down in 1984 after thirty-four Tests in charge of his country. To the end, he practised his philosophy of enterprising, direct rugby and, arguably, the team which came closest to his ideal was the one he led in his last season. France were masters of the creative arts that year, and only lapses of discipline in the decider with Scotland deprived Rives of the honour of captaining two Grand Slam sides.

Jean-Pierre Rives passes out to Philippe Sella in a France v Wales match.

Philippe SELLA
(Agen)

He could win matches with wonderfully creative football, scoring near-impossible tries or giving exquisitely-weighted passes for colleagues to score; and he could save apparently certain tries by firm tackles delivered with all the power and efficiency of a bulldozer clearing a building site.

The gallery of great French centres is adorned with the portraits of men who were touched by genius: the Boniface brothers, Jo Maso, Denis Charvet and Didier Codorniou all ran with the grace of balanced athletes to thrill crowds in the Five Nations although, above all, it was their commitment to total rugby which singles them out as worthy entrants to any hall of fame. Sella, too, richly deserves his place among the old masters and, indeed, his battery of skills have led his followers to propose that Sella, more phlegmatic and certainly more prominent in defence than many bygone French threequarters, should be rated best of them all.

Blessed with the natural hardness and easy fitness which result from a rural upbringing, Sella first entered France's Test side in 1982. He had the rare distinction of winning school, junior and student caps for France before opening the eyes of the senior selectors to his talents. Immediately, he impressed with his enthusiasm for the game. To those watching him in his first season as a senior international, it was clear that the young man possessed a real zest for rugby and, throughout a long career, he never lost that starry-eyed outlook on his sport. By his own admission, the joy of making a crunching tackle gave him as much satisfaction as any of the Test tries he scored.

Without doubt, his versatility was the secret to his long tenure in the French side. Even at a time when France placed a greater emphasis on forward play, Sella's indispensable qualities were recognised by his country. A remarkable run of forty-five consecutive caps included a bumper bundle of tries in 1986, when he became only the fourth player in the history of the Five Nations to touch down in each match of the championship.

Another Sella try, at Twickenham in 1987 on the way to the Grand Slam, bore all the hallmarks of his genuine class. With the scores level midway through the second half, he latched on to a loose English pass near his own ten-metre line. Thereafter he made a teasing run of sixty-five metres, playing cat and mouse with the English defenders before beating them by a whisker for the try that decided the match.

Sella was the automatic choice to succeed Serge Blanco as France's skipper after the 1991 World Cup, although his captaincy had its ups and downs. An impressive match as the side's tactical fountainhead against Wales was followed by a *débâcle* in Paris, where France lost more than just the match against England. However, such recent events did nothing to dim the view that Sella has been the world's best all-round centre for the past decade. His retirement will leave a huge vacuum in the Tricolours' threequarter line.

Philippe Sella (left and below), usually associated with flowing rugby, is equally skilled in defence.

Walter SPANGHERO
(Narbonne)

Walter Spanghero's progress from farmer's son to national institution was the rags-to-riches story of French rugby. His family was devoted to the game, and Spanghero became one of the best-loved and most sporting forwards at a time when the distinctive approach of the French was respected everywhere.

His long list of achievements began in 1964, when he was a last-minute inclusion in the French party to tour South Africa. At that juncture, French rugby was yearning for heavy, fast lock forwards, and Spanghero, at around 15st, was exactly the rare, mobile specimen needed to give steel to the scrummage. Indeed, after his Test debut in the second row of France's famous 8-6 win against the Springboks, South Africans referred to him as the world's quickest 15st player.

He walked into the French team for the Five Nations matches of 1965 and, for four seasons, he was the player his country could not drop. His broad shoulders, narrow waist and powerful legs gave him the classical silhouette of a body-builder. But British and Irish packs discovered that Spanghero had none of the mirror-posing vanity of the iron-pumpers: here was a dynamic team-man with a lust for the ball. His style of play in the second phase fitted perfectly the tactical plans which carried France to both the Five Nations title in 1967 and their first Grand Slam the following year.

Quite early in his Test career, it was put to Spanghero that he should move to prop. With more and more 6ft-3in-plus French forwards coming through, Spanghero was slightly on the small side to be effective as a line-out jumper. But at Narbonne, where he played with three of his brothers, there was no need for such a conversion. Instead, Spanghero graduated to the back row where he felt he could make the most of his pace. The switch caused problems: his former lock partner for France, Benoit Dauga, had made the same decision, and what had been a great second-row union now became a rivalry which, to outsiders, appeared at times to be excessively bitter.

Spanghero found himself at odds with his colleagues in the French squad. His Five Nations appearances were restricted to two matches from April 1969 until April 1972, when Dauga was dropped and Spanghero returned as captain against England. The man they called 'The Colossus of Narbonne' inspired France to play the open rugby for which his countrymen are admired and, in the last match staged at the Stades Colombes, his team trounced England 37-12. Spanghero was warmly applauded for knitting his charges together, and the prodigal son was welcomed back as a national hero.

After 1973, when Jean-Pierre Romeu narrowly failed with a late conversion attempt and robbed his captain of the honour of leading France to the Five Nations championship, Spanghero retired from Tests to expand his business operations in Toulouse and Narbonne. Thus passed the player who believed: 'Rugby is nothing without heart.' Surely no motto could better sum up the character of a forward who frequently appeared with a broken nose, suffered sundry other facial injuries, and fractured virtually every part of his anatomy there is to fracture.

Walter Spanghero seen here in the first French side to win the Grand Slam: 1968. Back: J-M Cabanier, A Abadie, J-P Salut, A Gruarin, C Carrère, W Spanghero, E Cester, B Dauga, Air Commodore GC Lamb. Crouching: B Duprat, J-P Lux, J Gachassin, P Villepreux, J-H Mir, J Trillo, A Campaes.

Michel VANNIER
(Racing Club of France, Châlon)

Raise the subject of French full-back play with any rugby follower under the age of thirty and the only name to spring to mind will be Serge Blanco. But, during the 1950s, there was another great French full-back who was every inch as extraordinary as Monsieur Blanco. He was Michel Vannier, and he performed at a time when the laws of rugby made last-line play an entirely different kettle of fish from the expansive game expected of modern backs.

Arguably, no station on the field had its role as fundamentally altered by the 1968-69 dispensation law restricting direct kicking to touch as did the full-back. Prior to the change, the requisites for the position were courage in the tackle, accurate line-kicking, and safety under the high ball. Michel Vannier demonstrated all these attributes playing for Racing Club in Paris, where he was a draughtsman, and quickly found himself promoted to the national team in 1953 at the age of twenty-one.

Vannier remained France's first-choice full-back for the next five years. The most elegant French back of his generation, what set him apart from his predecessors behind the line was his unflappability. Great sportsmen share the common quality of appearing to have oceans of time in which to perform their skills. Vannier never panicked and he never played himself into difficulties. These characteristics were a particular advantage in the high-pressure duties of place-kicking and, altogether, Vannier landed 180 points in forty-three Tests for France, a national record that stood for fifteen years. More consistent as a kicker from awkward angles than from short range, he was also a lethal exponent of the drop-goal; among his haul of points, the most valuable were the two left-footed drop goals which sealed France's maiden Test win at Cardiff in 1958.

Naturally, Vannier was an automatic selection for his country's tour to South Africa in 1958. But playing against a Combined XV at Springs in the third game of the visit, he tore knee ligaments so badly that it was predicted that his rugby days were finished. But thanks to skilful surgery and his own determination, he overcame the injury and forced his way back into France's side in 1960. In addition to retaining all his former expertise, he now boldly pioneered attacking full-back play. A good sprinter in his youth, he still possessed the necessary pace to make telling breaks from deep defence.

Vannier played in the French sides which won the championship (with England) in 1960 and (outright) in 1961, but the most majestic display of his career was against South Africa in Paris in 1961. In a match advertised as a world championship decider, his technical ability and tactical sense were important features of a famous draw.

Vannier had begun his international tenure to the unwelcome sound of jeers from the partisan supporters of the rugby-mad south of France - he was one of the handful of leading players who was born and played his rugby north of the Loire. True, there were occasions when his defence against foot rushes was suspect. But, by the end of his Test career, the jeers had turned to cheers, and the *'brin d'osier'* - a nickname derived from his surname - is remembered as one of the best of France's internationals.

Michel Vannier suffered a fatal brain clot in 1991, aged fifty-nine, and was mourned worldwide by former players and followers of the game who had had the privilege of seeing him perform in his prime.

Pierre VILLEPREUX
(Toulouse)

From time to time, French rugby produces players who set the world alight with an incandescent glow. Conversely, it seems, the French authorities are equally adept at turning a blind eye to genius when it lies under their own noses. The unusual case of Pierre Villepreux illustrates both sides of this Gallic enigma.

Villepreux the player began his senior career with Brive before joining Toulouse in his student days. First picked for France in 1967, he made one appearance in the side which won the Five Nations title that year, and had one game for the 1968 champions.

It was on tour in New Zealand and Australia following the Grand Slam season that Villepreux really made his mark. He first gave notice of his power as a positive thinker half-way through the visit, when his spirit of adventure in launching effective attacks out of defence filled his team-mates with a similar desire to run the ball in the style cherished by the French public. That was the beginning of what turned out to be a crusade by Villepreux on behalf of all-out attacking rugby, and it was a campaign he led by example in his playing days. For his flair he was adored in France and very highly respected worldwide.

The introduction of the laws restricting direct kicking to touch in 1968-69 suited Villepreux's game to a T. He exercised all the classical skills of full-back play: he was cool, calm and collected under pressure, he tackled courageously, and he kicked well. But it was for his ability to read a game, and especially for the perfect timing of his intrusions into the threequarter line in attack, that Villepreux was hailed the world's best full-back. That honour, it should be added, was conferred at a time when JPR Williams, the Wales full-back, was also building a considerable reputation.

But for all the pleasure French rugby gave during the Villepreux years, there were no championship titles to savour. Pierre retired from international rugby in 1972, but continued to captain Toulouse before concentrating on coaching. Villepreux the coach, like Villepreux the player, became revered everywhere for his talent - well, almost everywhere. He won fresh converts to his tactical religion, preaching the same gospel of fifteen-man rugby he had practised as a player. He proved himself as coach to the French Universities, made Toulouse France's premier club, and his technical expertise was sought by both the Italian and English national sides. Only the myopic French rugby authorities failed to recognise his gifts.

Throughout the 1980s, France had the players to win the Grand Slam every season. Instead, the Tricolours, misguided by the muddled thinking of coach Jacques Fouroux (and later Daniel Dubroca), restrained their natural tendency to play genuine running rugby and ended up expounding a stodgy form of forward-dominated football, only occasionally reverting to their instincts to produce something that would live in the memory.

How a country which consistently produces rugby footballers who are complete athletes can ignore Villepreux's credentials as a coach is the greatest conundrum of the modern French game. Now that France has a new regime in the corridors of its rugby power, perhaps Pierre Villepreux's ambition to coach the national XV will finally be fulfilled.

Pierre Villepreux sells a dummy at Twickenham in 1971. Nigel Horton and Keith Fairbrother trail in his wake.

INDEX OF FIVE NATIONS PLAYERS 1947-1993

Bill Beaumont commiserates with Jean-Pierre Rives after England had beaten France 17-13, in 1980.

ENGLAND

Throughout this section of the book, the number of caps shown are those won in the Five Nations championship.

Ackford, P J (Harlequins)
Born 26 February 1958
12 caps 1989-91 (lock)

Adey, G J (Leicester)
Born 13 June 1945
2 caps 1976 (No 8)

Adkins, S J (Coventry)
Born 2 June 1922;
died 2 January 1992
7 caps 1950-53 (No 8, lock)

Agar, A E (Harlequins)
Born 12 November 1923
6 caps 1952-53 (centre)

Allison, D F (Coventry)
Born 20 April 1931
7 caps 1956-58 (full-back)

Andrew, C R
(Cambridge U, Nottingham, Wasps, Toulouse)
Born 18 February 1963
31 caps 1985-93 (stand-off)

Arthur, T G (Wasps)
Born 5 September 1940
2 caps 1966 (centre)

Ashby, R C (Wasps)
Born 24 January 1937
2 caps 1966 (scrum-half)

Ashcroft, A (Waterloo)
Born 21 August 1930
15 caps 1956-59 (No 8)

Bailey, M D
(Cambridge U, Wasps)
Born 21 November 1960
3 caps 1990 (wing)

Bainbridge, S
(Gosforth, Fylde)
Born 7 October 1956
13 caps 1982-87 (lock)

Baker, D G S
(Old Merchant Taylors)
Born 29 November 1929
4 caps 1955 (stand-off)

Bance, J F (Bedford)
Born 15 January 1925
1 cap 1954 (lock)

Barley, B (Wakefield)
Born 4 January 1960
3 caps 1984 (centre)

Barnes, S (Bristol, Bath)
Born 22 November 1962
5 caps 1986-93
(full-back, stand-off)

Bartlett, J T (Waterloo)
Born 17 October 1924;
died 16 January 1969
1 cap 1951 (lock)

Bartlett, R M (Harlequins)
Born 13 February 1929;
died 5 March 1984
7 caps 1957-58 (stand-off)

Barton, J (Coventry)
Born 19 March 1943
4 caps 1967-72 (lock)

Baume, J L (Northern)
Born 18 July 1920
1 cap 1950 (prop)

Bayfield, M C (Northampton)
Born 21 December 1966
8 caps 1992-93 (lock)

Bazley, R C (Waterloo)
Born 15 December 1929
10 caps 1952-55 (wing)

Beaumont, W B (Fylde)
Born 9 March 1952
26 caps 1975-82 (lock)

Beer, I D S (Harlequins)
Born 28 April 1931
2 caps 1955 (No 8)

Beese, M C (Liverpool)
Born 8 October 1948
3 caps 1972 (centre)

Bell, P J (Blackheath)
Born 28 April 1937
4 caps 1968 (flanker)

Bendon, G J (Wasps)
Born 9 April 1929
4 caps 1959 (prop)

Bennett, N O (St Mary's Hospital, Waterloo)
Born 21 September 1922
6 caps 1947-48 (centre)

Bennett, W N
(Bedford, London Welsh)
Born 20 April 1951
6 caps 1975-79 (stand-off)

Berridge, M J (Northampton)
Born 28 February 1923;
died 2 October 1973
2 caps 1949 (prop)

Blakeway, P J (Gloucester)
Born 31 December 1950
17 caps 1980-85 (prop)

Bond, A M (Sale)
Born 3 August 1953
4 caps 1979-82 (centre)

Boobbyer, B (Rosslyn Park)
Born 25 February 1928
9 caps 1950-52 (centre)

Botting, I J (Oxford U)
Born 18 May 1922;
died 9 July 1980
2 caps 1950 (wing)

Boyle, S B (Gloucester)
Born 9 August 1953
3 caps 1983 (lock)

Brain, S E (Coventry)
Born 11 November 1954
8 caps 1985-86 (hooker)

Braithwaite-Exley, B
(Headingley)
Born 30 November 1927
1 cap 1949 (No 8)

Brinn, A (Gloucester)
Born 21 July 1940
3 caps 1972 (lock)

Brooke, T J (Richmond)
Born 8 October 1940
2 caps 1968 (centre)

Brophy, T (Liverpool)
Born 8 July 1941
8 caps 1964-66 (stand-off)

Bucknall, A L (Richmond)
Born 7 June 1945
8 caps 1970-71 (flanker)

Bulpitt, M P (Blackheath)
Born 12 April 1944
1 cap 1970 (wing)

Burton, M A (Gloucester)
Born 18 December 1945
13 caps 1972-78 (prop)

Butler, P E (Gloucester)
Born 23 June 1951
1 cap 1976 (full-back)

Butterfield, J (Northampton)
Born 9 August 1929
26 caps 1953-59 (centre)

Cain, J J (Waterloo)
Born 12 June 1920
1 cap 1950 (flanker)

Cannell, L B (Oxford U, St Mary's Hospital)
Born 10 June 1926
18 caps 1948-57 (centre)

Caplan, D W N (Headingley)
Born 5 April 1954
2 caps 1978 (full-back)

Cardus, R M (Roundhay)
Born 23 May 1956
2 caps 1979 (centre)

Carleton, J (Orrell)
Born 24 November 1955
20 caps 1980-84 (wing)

Carling, W D C
(Durham U, Harlequins)
Born 12 December 1965
24 caps 1988-93 (centre)

Challis, R (Bristol)
Born 9 March 1932
3 caps 1957 (full-back)

Chilcott, G J (Bath)
Born 20 November 1956
7 caps 1986-89 (prop)

Clarke, B B (Bath)
Born 15 April 1968
4 caps 1993 (No 8)

Clarke, S J S
(Cambridge U, Blackheath)
Born 2 April 1938
9 caps 1963-65 (scrum-half)

Clements, J E W
(Old Cranleighans)
Born 18 August 1932;
died 4 October 1986
3 caps 1959 (flanker)

Clough, F J
(Cambridge U, Orrell)
Born 1 November 1962
2 caps 1986 (centre)

Colclough, M J (Angoulême, Wasps, Swansea)
Born 2 September 1953
22 caps 1978-86 (lock)

Collins, P J (Camborne)
Born 4 November 1928
3 caps 1952 (full-back)

Cook, P W (Richmond)
Born 8 January 1943
2 caps 1965 (wing)

Cooke, D A (Harlequins)
Born 10 February 1949
4 caps 1976 (centre)

Cooke, D H (Harlequins)
Born 19 November 1955
9 caps 1981-85 (flanker)

Cooper, M J (Moseley)
Born 23 April 1948
9 caps 1973-77 (stand-off)

Corless, B J
(Coventry, Moseley)
Born 7 November 1945
9 caps 1976-78 (centre)

Cotton, F E (Loughborough Colleges, Coventry, Sale)
Born 3 January 1947
25 caps 1971-81 (prop)

Coulman, M J (Moseley)
Born 6 May 1944
8 caps 1967-68 (prop)

Cowling, R J (Leicester)
Born 24 March 1944
7 caps 1977-79 (prop)

Cowman, A R
(Loughborough Colleges, Coventry)
Born 18 March 1949
3 caps 1971-73 (stand-off)

Currie, J D (Oxford U, Harlequins, Bristol)
Born 3 May 1932;
died 8 December 1990
23 caps 1956-62 (lock)

Cusani, D A (Orrell)
Born 16 July 1959
1 cap 1987 (lock)

Cusworth, L (Leicester)
Born 3 July 1954
10 caps 1982-88 (stand-off)

Dalton, T J (Coventry)
Born 2 September 1940
1 cap 1969 (wing)

Danby, T (Harlequins)
Born 10 August 1926
1 cap 1949 (wing)

Davies, G H (Cambridge U, Coventry, Wasps)
Born 18 February 1959
13 caps 1981-86
(stand-off, centre, full-back)

Davies, W P C (Harlequins)
Born 6 August 1928
10 caps 1953-58 (centre)

Davis, A M (Harlequins)
Born 23 January 1942
11 caps 1963-70 (lock)

Dawe, R G R (Bath)
Born 4 September 1959
3 caps 1987 (hooker)

Dee, J M
(Hartlepool Rovers)
Born 22 October 1938
1 cap 1962 (centre)

De Glanville, P R (Bath)
Born 1 October 1968
1 cap 1993 (wing)

Dixon, P J
(Harlequins, Gosforth)
Born 30 April 1944
20 caps 1972-78 (flanker)

Doble, S A (Moseley)
Born 9 March 1944;
died 17 September 1977
1 cap 1973 (full-back)

Dodge, P W (Leicester)
Born 22 February 1958
24 caps 1978-85 (centre)

Donnelly, M P (Oxford U)
Born 17 October 1917
1 cap 1947 (centre)

Dooley, W A (Preston Grasshoppers, Fylde)
Born 2 October 1957
33 caps 1985-93 (lock)

Dovey, B A (Rosslyn Park)
Born 24 October 1938
2 caps 1963 (prop)

Drake-Lee, N J
(Cambridge U, Leicester)
Born 7 April 1942
7 caps 1963-65 (prop)

Duckham, D J (Coventry)
Born 28 June 1946
29 caps 1969-76
(centre, wing)

Dun, A F (Wasps)
Born 26 November 1960
1 cap 1984 (flanker)

Egerton, D W (Bath)
Born 19 October 1961
1 cap 1990 (flanker)

Estcourt, N S D (Blackheath)
Born 7 January 1929
1 cap 1955 (full-back)

Evans, E (Sale)
Born 1 February 1921;
died 12 January 1991
26 caps 1950-58 (hooker)

Evans, G W (Coventry)
Born 10 December 1950
8 caps 1972-74 (centre)

Fairbrother, K E (Coventry)
Born 8 May 1944
11 caps 1969-71 (prop)

Fielding, K J (Loughborough Colleges, Moseley)
Born 8 July 1949
9 caps 1969-72 (wing)

Finlan, J F (Moseley)
Born 9 September 1941
11 caps 1967-73 (stand-off)

Ford, P J (Gloucester)
Born 2 May 1932
4 caps 1964 (flanker)

Frankcom, G P
(Cambridge U, Bedford)
Born 5 April 1942
4 caps 1965 (centre)

French, R J (St Helens)
Born 23 December 1939
4 caps 1961 (lock)

Gavins, M N (Leicester)
Born 14 October 1934
1 cap 1961 (full-back)

Gay, D J (Bath)
Born 10 March 1948
4 caps 1968 (No 8)

George, J T (Falmouth)
Born 24 August 1918
3 caps 1947-49 (lock)

Gibbs, G A (Bristol)
Born 31 March 1920
2 caps 1947-48 (prop)

Gibbs, N (Harlequins)
Born 24 September 1922
2 caps 1954 (full-back)

Glover, P B (Bath)
Born 25 September 1945
1 cap 1971 (wing)

Godwin, H (Coventry)
Born 21 December 1935
6 caps 1959-64 (hooker)

Gray, A (Otley)
Born 4 September 1917;
died 25 August 1991
3 caps 1947 (full-back)

Greenwood, J R H (Waterloo)
Born 11 September 1940
4 caps 1966-69 (flanker)

Gregory, J A (Blackheath)
Born 22 June 1923
1 cap 1949 (wing)

Guest, R H (Waterloo)
Born 12 March 1918
9 caps 1947-49 (wing)

Guscott, J C (Bath)
Born 7 July 1965
16 caps 1990-93 (centre)

Hale, P M (Moseley)
Born 12 August 1943
2 caps 1970 (wing)

Hall, J P (Bath)
Born 15 March 1962
13 caps 1984-87 (flanker)

Hall, N M (Richmond)
Born 2 August 1925;
died 26 June 1972
16 caps 1947-55
(stand-off, full-back)

Halliday, S J
(Bath, Harlequins)
Born 13 July 1960
15 caps 1986-92
(centre, wing)

Hancock, A W
(Northampton)
Born 19 June 1939
3 caps 1965-66 (wing)

Hancock, W J H (Newport)
Born 26 September 1932
2 caps 1955 (lock)

Hannaford, R C (Bristol)
Born 19 October 1944
3 caps 1971 (No 8)

Harding, R M (Bristol)
Born 29 August 1953
4 caps 1985-88 (scrum-half)

Harding, V S J (Saracens)
Born 18 June 1932
6 caps 1961-62 (lock)

Hardy, E M P (Blackheath)
Born 3 November 1927
3 caps 1951 (stand-off)

Hare, W H
(Nottingham, Leicester)
Born 29 November 1952
18 caps 1974-84 (full-back)

Harrison, M E (Wakefield)
Born 19 April 1956
9 caps 1986-88 (wing)

Hastings, G W (Gloucester)
Born 7 November 1924
12 caps 1955-58 (prop)

Hazell, D St G (Leicester)
Born 23 April 1931
4 caps 1955 (prop)

Hearn, R D (Bedford)
Born 12 August 1940
6 caps 1966-67 (centre)

Heaton, J (Waterloo)
Born 30 August 1912
3 caps 1947 (centre)

Henderson, A P
(Edinburgh Wanderers)
Born 26 May 1920
9 caps 1947-49 (hooker)

Herbert, A J (Wasps)
Born 1 January 1933
6 caps 1958-59 (flanker)

Hesford, R (Bristol)
Born 26 March 1951
8 caps 1981-85
(flanker, No 8, lock)

Heslop, N J (Orrell)
Born 4 December 1963
5 caps 1991-92 (wing)

Hetherington, J G G
(Northampton)
Born 3 March 1932
5 caps 1958-59 (full-back)

Hewitt, E N (Coventry)
Born 22 April 1924
3 caps 1951 (full-back)

Higgins, R (Liverpool)
Born 11 July 1930;
died 29 December 1979
12 caps 1954-59 (flanker)

Hignell, A J
(Cambridge U, Bristol)
Born 4 September 1955
12 caps 1976-79 (full-back)

Hill, R J (Bath)
Born 4 May 1961
13 caps 1985-91 (scrum-half)

Hiller, R (Harlequins)
Born 14 October 1942
16 caps 1968-72 (full-back)

Hodgkinson, S D
(Nottingham)
Born 15 December 1962
8 caps 1990-91 (full-back)

Hodgson, S A M
(Durham City)
Born 14 May 1928
10 caps 1960-64 (hooker)

Hofmeyr, M B (Oxford U)
Born 9 December 1925;
died 26 June 1990
3 caps 1950 (full-back)

Holmes, C B (Manchester)
Born 11 January 1915
3 caps 1947-48 (wing)

Holmes, W (Nuneaton)
Born 10 September 1925
15 caps 1950-53 (prop)

Holmes, W B (Cambridge U)
Born 6 January 1928;
died 10 November 1949
4 caps 1949 (full-back)

Hook, W G (Gloucester)
Born 21 December 1920
2 caps 1951-52 (full-back)

Horrocks-Taylor, J P
(Cambridge U, Leicester, Middlesbrough)
Born 27 October 1934
4 caps 1958-64 (stand-off)

Horsfall, E L (Harlequins)
Born 11 August 1917;
died 1 June 1981
1 cap 1949 (flanker)

Horton, A L (Blackheath)
Born 13 July 1938
6 caps 1965-66 (prop)

Horton, J P (Bath)
Born 11 April 1951
10 caps 1978-83 (stand-off)

Horton, N E
(Moseley, Toulouse)
Born 13 April 1948
20 caps 1969-80 (lock)

Hosen, R W
(Bristol, Northampton)
Born 12 June 1933
6 caps 1964-67
(wing, full-back)

Hosking, G R D' A
(Devonport Services)
Born 11 March 1922
5 caps 1949-50 (lock)

Hunter, I (Northampton)
Born 15 February 1969
2 caps 1993 (wing)

Hurst, A C B (Wasps)
Born 1 October 1935
1 cap 1962 (wing)

Hyde, J P (Northampton)
Born 8 June 1930
2 caps 1950 (wing)

Jackson, B K
(Broughton Park)
Born 9 August 1937
2 caps 1970 (flanker, prop)

Jackson, P B (Coventry)
Born 22 September 1930
19 caps 1956-63 (wing)

Jacobs, C R (Northampton)
Born 28 October 1928
24 caps 1956-64 (prop)

Janion, J P A (Bedford)
Born 25 September 1946
6 caps 1971-72 (wing, centre)

Jeavons, N C (Moseley)
Born 12 November 1957
11 caps 1981-83 (flanker)

Jeeps, R E G (Northampton)
Born 25 November 1931
22 caps 1956-62 (scrum-half)

Jennins, C R (Waterloo)
Born 5 February 1942
2 caps 1967 (centre)

Johnson, M O (Leicester)
Born 9 March 1970
1 cap 1993 (lock)

Jones, H A (Barnstaple)
Born 22 August 1918
3 caps 1950 (lock)

Jorden, A M (Cambridge U, Blackheath, Bedford)
Born 28 January 1947
7 caps 1970-75 (full-back)

Judd, P E (Coventry)
Born 8 April 1934
16 caps 1962-67 (prop)

Keeling, J H
(Guy's Hospital)
Born 28 October 1925
1 cap 1948 (hooker)

Keen, B W (Newcastle U)
Born 1 June 1944
4 caps 1968 (prop)

Kelly, G A (Bedford)
Born 9 February 1914
4 caps 1947-48 (prop)

Kemp, T A (Richmond)
Born 12 August 1915
1 cap 1948 (stand-off)

Kendall-Carpenter, J M
(Oxford U, Bath)
Born 25 September 1925; died 24 May 1990
21 caps 1949-54 (No 8, prop)

Kennedy, R D
(Camborne School of Mines)
Born 14 August 1925;
died May 1979
3 caps 1949 (wing)

Kent, C P (Rosslyn Park)
Born 4 August 1953
5 caps 1977-78 (centre)

Keyworth, M (Swansea)
Born 19 February 1948
3 caps 1976 (flanker)

King, I (Harrogate)
Born 5 May 1923
2 caps 1954 (full-back)

Kingston, P (Gloucester)
Born 24 July 1951
3 caps 1979 (scrum-half)

Knight, P M (Bristol)
Born 7 October 1947
2 caps 1972 (full-back)

Labuschagne, N A
(Harlequins, Guy's Hospital)
Born 26 May 1931
5 caps 1953-55 (hooker)

Lampkowski, M S
(Headingley)
Born 4 January 1953
3 caps 1976 (scrum-half)

Larter, P J
(Northampton, RAF)
Born 7 September 1944
17 caps 1968-73 (lock)

Leadbetter, M M
(Broughton Park)
Born 25 July 1946
1 cap 1970 (lock)

Leadbetter, V H
(Edinburgh Wanderers)
Born September 1929
2 caps 1954 (No 8, lock)

Leonard, J P
(Saracens, Harlequins)
Born 14 August 1967
12 caps 1991-93 (prop)

Lewis, A O (Bath)
Born 20 August 1920
9 caps 1952-54 (flanker)

Lloyd, R H (Harlequins)
Born 3 March 1943
4 caps 1968 (centre)

Luya, H F
(Waterloo, Headingley)
Born 3 February 1918
5 caps 1948-49 (lock)

Madge, R J P (Exeter)
Born 19 December 1914
3 caps 1948 (scrum-half)

Manley, D C (Exeter)
Born 17 February 1932
4 caps 1963 (flanker)

Marques, R W D
(Cambridge U, Harlequins)
Born 9 December 1932
21 caps 1956-61 (lock)

Martin, C R (Bath)
Born 27 June 1961
4 caps 1985 (full-back)

Martin, N O (Harlequins)
Born 26 June 1946
1 cap 1972 (flanker)

Matthews, J R C (Harlequins)
Born 14 June 1920
9 caps 1949-52 (lock)

Maxwell, A W
(New Brighton, Headingley)
Born 3 March 1951
5 caps 1976-78 (centre)

McFadyean, C W (Moseley)
Born 11 March 1943
9 caps 1966-68 (centre, wing)

Melville, N D (Wasps)
Born 6 January 1961
10 caps 1985-88 (scrum-half)

Mills, S G F (Gloucester)
Born 25 February 1951
1 cap 1983 (hooker)

Moore, B C
(Nottingham, Harlequins)
Born 11 January 1962
25 caps 1987-93 (hooker)

Moore, P B C (Blackheath)
Born 6 April 1921
1 cap 1951 (No 8)

Moore, W K T (Leicester)
Born 24 February 1921
7 caps 1947-50 (scrum-half)

Mordell, R J (Rosslyn Park)
Born 2 July 1950
1 cap 1978 (flanker)

Morgan, W G D
(Medicals, Newcastle)
Born 30 November 1935
8 caps 1960-61 (No 8)

Morley, A J (Bristol)
Born 25 June 1950
3 caps 1973-75 (wing)

Morris, C D
(Liverpool St Helens, Orrell)
Born 9 February 1964
12 caps 1989-93 (scrum-half)

Mycock, J S (Sale)
Born 17 January 1916
4 caps 1947 (lock)

Neale, B A (Rosslyn Park)
Born 15 September 1923
3 caps 1951 (lock)

Neary, A (Broughton Park)
Born 25 November 1948
34 caps 1971-80 (flanker)

Nelmes, B G (Cardiff)
Born 17 April 1948
3 caps 1978 (prop)

Newman, S C (Oxford U)
Born 27 July 1919
2 caps 1947-48 (full-back)

Newton-Thompson, J O
(Oxford U)
Born 2 December 1920;
died 3 March 1974
2 caps 1947 (scrum-half)

Ninnes, B F (Coventry)
Born 23 March 1948
1 cap 1971 (lock)

Novak, M J (Harlequins)
Born 27 September 1947
3 caps 1970 (wing)

Oakley, L F L (Bedford)
Born 24 January 1926;
died November 1981
1 cap 1951 (centre)

Old, A G B (Middlesbrough, Leicester, Sheffield)
Born 23 September 1945
12 caps 1972-78 (stand-off)

Orwin, J (Gloucester, RAF, Bedford)
Born 20 March 1954
8 caps 1985-88 (lock)

Oti, C C (Cambridge U, Nottingham, Wasps)
Born 16 June 1965
6 caps 1988-89 (wing)

Owen, J E (Coventry)
Born 21 September 1939
11 caps 1963-66 (lock)

Page, J J
(Bedford, Northampton)
Born 16 April 1947
5 caps 1971-75 (scrum-half)

Pallant, J N (Nottingham)
Born 24 December 1944
3 caps 1967 (No 8, lock)

Palmer, J A (Bath)
Born 13 February 1957
1 cap 1986 (centre)

Pargetter, T A (Coventry)
Born 21 July 1932
2 caps 1962-63 (lock)

Parsons, M J (Northampton)
Born 13 March 1943
4 caps 1968 (lock)

Patterson, W M (Sale)
Born 11 April 1936
1 cap 1961 (centre)

Payne, C M (Harlequins)
Born 19 May 1937
10 caps 1964-66 (lock)

Pearce, G S (Northampton)
Born 2 March 1956
22 caps 1979-87 (prop)

Pears, D (Harlequins)
Born 6 December 1962
1 cap 1992 (stand-off)

Peart, T G A H
(Hartlepool Rovers)
Born 10 September 1936;
died 3 August 1988
2 caps 1964 (No 8)

Perry, D G (Bedford)
Born 26 December 1937
11 caps 1963-66 (No 8)

Perry, S V
(Cambridge U, Waterloo)
Born 16 July 1918
6 caps 1947-48 (lock)

Phillips, M S (Fylde)
Born 3 March 1935
20 caps 1958-64
(centre, wing)

Pickering, R D A (Bradford)

Born 15 June 1943
6 caps 1967-68 (scrum-half)

Plummer, K C (Bristol)
Born 17 January 1947
4 caps 1969-76 (wing)

Powell, D L (Northampton)
Born 17 May 1942
10 caps 1966-71 (prop)

Preece, I (Coventry)
Born 15 December 1920; died 14 March 1987
12 caps 1948-51
(stand-off, centre)

Preece, P S (Coventry)
Born 15 November 1949
8 caps 1973-76 (centre, wing)

Preston, N J (Richmond)
Born 5 April 1958
2 caps 1980 (centre)

Price, J (Coventry)
Born 1938
1 cap 1961 (lock)

Price, T W (Cheltenham)
Born 26 July 1914; died 11 July 1991
6 caps 1948-49 (prop)

Probyn, J A (Wasps)
Born 27 April 1956
22 caps 1988-93 (prop)

Prout, D H (Northampton)
Born 10 November 1942
2 caps 1968 (wing)

Pullin, J V (Bristol)
Born 1 November 1941
33 caps 1966-76 (hooker)

Purdy, S J (Rugby)
Born 6 February 1936
1 cap 1962 (flanker)

Quinn, J P (New Brighton)
Born 19 February 1930; died 18 January 1986
4 caps 1954 (centre)

Rafter, M (Bristol)
Born 31 March 1952
13 caps 1977-81 (flanker)

Ralston, C W (Richmond)
Born 25 May 1944
16 caps 1972-75 (lock)

Ranson, J M (Rosslyn Park)
Born 26 July 1938
4 caps 1964 (wing)

Redfern, S P (Leicester)
Born 26 October 1957
1 cap 1984 (prop)

Redman, N C (Bath)
Born 16 August 1964
3 caps 1986-87 (lock)

Redmond, G F
(Cambridge U)
Born 23 March 1943
1 cap 1970 (No 8)

Redwood, B W (Bristol)
Born 6 February 1939
2 caps 1968 (scrum-half)

Rees, G W (Nottingham)
Born 2 May 1960
8 caps 1986-89 (flanker)

Regan, M (Liverpool)
Born 24 September 1929
11 caps 1953-56 (stand-off)

Rendall, P A G (Wasps)
Born 18 February 1954
18 caps 1984-90 (prop)

Richards, D (Leicester)
Born 11 July 1963
18 caps 1986-92 (No 8)

Richards, S B (Richmond)
Born 28 August 1941
8 caps 1965-67 (hooker)

Rimmer, G (Waterloo)
Born 28 February 1925
10 caps 1949-54 (scrum-half)

Rimmer, L I (Bath)
Born 31 May 1935
4 caps 1961 (flanker)

Ripley, A G (Rosslyn Park)
Born 1 December 1947
17 caps 1972-76 (No 8)

Risman, A B W (Manchester U, Loughborough Colleges)
Born 23 November 1937
7 caps 1959-61
(stand-off, centre)

Rittson-Thomas, G C
(Oxford U)
Born 18 December 1926
3 caps 1951 (flanker)

Robbins, G L (Coventry)
Born 24 September 1956
2 caps 1986 (No 8)

Robbins, P G D (Oxford U, Moseley, Coventry)
Born 21 September 1933; died 25 March 1987
17 caps 1956-62 (flanker)

Roberts, J (Sale)
Born 25 June 1932
16 caps 1960-63 (wing)

Roberts, V G
(Penryn, Harlequins)
Born 6 August 1924
16 caps 1947-56 (flanker)

Robinson, E F (Coventry)
Born 17 January 1929; died 2 July 1993
4 caps 1954-61 (hooker)

Robinson, R A (Bath)
Born 3 April 1964
4 caps 1989 (flanker)

Rodber, T A K
(Army, Northampton)
Born 2 July 1969
2 caps 1992 (No 8)

Rogers, D P (Bedford)
Born 20 June 1935
28 caps 1961-69 (flanker)

Rollitt, D M (Bristol)
Born 24 March 1943
9 caps 1967-75
(flanker, No 8)

Rose, W M H (Cambridge U, Coventry, Harlequins)
Born 12 January 1957
8 caps 1981-87 (full-back)

Rossborough, P A (Coventry)
Born 30 June 1948
5 caps 1971-75 (full-back)

Rosser, D W A (Wasps)
Born 27 March 1938
5 caps 1965-66 (centre)

Roughley, D (Liverpool)
Born 10 December 1946
2 caps 1974 (centre)

Rowell, R E (Leicester)
Born 29 August 1939
2 caps 1964-65 (lock)

Rudd, E L (Liverpool)
Born 28 September 1944
6 caps 1965-66 (wing)

Rutherford, D
(Percy Park, Gloucester)
Born 22 September 1937
12 caps 1960-66 (full-back)

Ryan, P H (Richmond)
Born 1 October 1930
2 caps 1955 (flanker)

Salmon, J L B (Harlequins)
Born 16 October 1959
6 caps 1986-87 (centre)

Sanders, D L (Harlequins)
Born 6 September 1924
8 caps 1954-56 (prop)

Sangwin, R D
(Hull and East Riding)
Born 2 December 1937
1 cap 1964 (centre)

Sargent, G A F (Gloucester)
Born 18 October 1949
1 cap 1981 (prop)

Savage, K F (Northampton)
Born 24 August 1940
11 caps 1966-68 (wing)

Scott, E K (St Mary's Hospital, Redruth)
Born 14 June 1918
4 caps 1947-48 (centre)

Scott, H (Manchester)
Born 7 November 1926
1 cap 1955 (full-back)

Scott, J P
(Rosslyn Park, Cardiff)
Born 28 September 1954
27 caps 1978-84 (No 8)

Scott, J S M (Oxford U)
Born 23 January 1935
1 cap 1958 (full-back)

Shackleton, I R
(Cambridge U)
Born 17 June 1948
3 caps 1970 (stand-off)

Sharp, R A W (Oxford U, Wasps, Redruth)
Born 9 September 1938
13 caps 1960-63 (stand-off)

Sheppard, A (Bristol)
Born 1 May 1950
2 caps 1981-85 (prop)

Sherriff, G A (Saracens)
Born 29 May 1937
1 cap 1966 (No 8)

Shuttleworth, D W
(Headingley)
Born 22 July 1928
2 caps 1951-53 (scrum-half)

Silk, N (Harlequins)
Born 26 May 1941
4 caps 1965 (flanker)

Simms, K G (Cambridge U, Liverpool, Wasps)
Born 25 December 1964
11 caps 1985-88 (centre)

Simpson, C P (Harlequins)

Bev Risman

Born 21 September 1942
1 cap 1965 (wing)

Simpson, P D (Bath)
Born 7 June 1958
2 caps 1984-87
(flanker, No 8)

Skinner, M G (Harlequins)
Born 26 November 1958
12 caps 1988-92 (flanker)

Slemen, M A C (Liverpool)
Born 11 May 1951
27 caps 1976-84 (wing)

Small, H D (Oxford U)
Born 7 January 1922
4 caps 1950 (flanker)

Smart, C E (Newport)
Born 5 March 1950
13 caps 1979-83 (prop)

Smith, J V
(Cambridge U, Rosslyn Park)
Born 23 May 1926
4 caps 1950 (wing)

Smith, K (Roundhay)
Born 19 November 1952
4 caps 1974-75 (centre)

Smith, M J K (Oxford U)
Born 30 June 1933
1 cap 1956 (stand-off)

Smith, S J (Sale)
Born 22 July 1951
23 caps 1973-83 (scrum-half)

Smith, S R (Richmond)
Born 21 October 1934
5 caps 1959-64 (scrum-half)

Smith, S T (Wasps)
Born 29 April 1960
6 caps 1985-86 (wing)

Smith, T H (Northampton)
Born 3 April 1920
1 cap 1951 (hooker)

Spencer, J (Harlequins)
Born 27 June 1939
1 cap 1966 (scrum-half)

Spencer, J S
(Cambridge U, Headingley)
Born 10 August 1947
11 caps 1969-71 (centre)

Squires, P J (Harrogate)
Born 4 August 1951
23 caps 1973-79 (wing)

Starmer-Smith, N C
(Harlequins)
Born 25 December 1944
4 caps 1970 (scrum-half)

Steeds, J H (Saracens)
Born 27 September 1916
5 caps 1949-50 (hooker)

Steele-Bodger, M R
(Cambridge U)
Born 4 September 1925
8 caps 1947-48 (flanker)

Stevens, C B (Penzance-Newlyn, Harlequins)
Born 2 June 1940
19 caps 1970-75 (prop)

Stirling, R V
(Leicester, RAF, Wasps)
Born 4 September 1919;
died 15 January 1991
16 caps 1951-54 (prop)

Swarbrick, D W (Oxford U)
Born 17 January 1927
5 caps 1947-49 (wing)

Swift, A H (Swansea)
Born 24 May 1959
3 caps 1983 (wing)

Syddall, J P (Waterloo)
Born 7 March 1956
1 cap 1982 (lock)

Sykes, F D (Northampton)
Born 9 December 1927
2 caps 1955 (wing)

Sykes, P W (Wasps)
Born 3 March 1925
7 caps 1948-53 (scrum-half)

Syrett, R E (Wasps)
Born 5 January 1931
10 caps 1958-62 (flanker)

Taylor, P J (Northampton)
Born 6 June 1931
6 caps 1955-62 (No 8)

Taylor, R B (Northampton)
Born 30 April 1942
13 caps 1966-71
(flanker, No 8)

Teague, M C
(Gloucester, Moseley)
Born 8 October 1959
16 caps 1985-93
(flanker, No 8)

Thompson, P H
(Headingley, Waterloo)
Born 18 January 1929
16 caps 1956-59 (wing)

Thorne, J D (Bristol)
Born 1 January 1934
3 caps 1963 (hooker)

Tindall, V R (Liverpool U)
Born 1 August 1928
4 caps 1951 (wing)

The England team against France in 1980. England went on to win the Grand JP Scott, NJ Preston, A Neary, PJ Wheeler. Front: WH Hare, CR Woodward, JP Horton, AGB Old (replacement).

Towell, A C (Bedford)
Born 1925
2 caps 1948-51 (centre)

Travers, B H (Harlequins)
Born 7 July 1919
6 caps 1947-49
(No 8, flanker)

Treadwell, W T (Wasps)
Born 13 March 1939
3 caps 1966 (hooker)

Trick, D M (Bath)
Born 26 October 1960
1 cap 1983 (wing)

Turner, M F (Blackheath)
Born 1 August 1921
2 caps 1948 (wing)

Underwood, A M (Exeter)
Born 19 July 1940
5 caps 1962-64 (wing, centre)

Underwood, R
(Leicester, RAF)
Born 19 June 1963
38 caps 1984-93 (wing)

Underwood, T (Leicester)
Born 17 February 1969
2 caps 1993 (wing)

Uren, R (Waterloo)
Born 26 February 1926
4 caps 1948-50 (full-back)

Uttley, R M (Gosforth)
Born 11 September 1949
18 caps 1973-80
(lock, No 8, flanker)

Van Ryneveld, C B
(Oxford U)
Born 19 March 1928
4 caps 1949 (centre)

Vaughan, D B (Headingley)
Born 15 July 1925;
died 19 April 1977
7 caps 1948-50
(No 8, flanker)

Wackett, J A S
(Rosslyn Park)
Born 27 September 1930
2 caps 1959 (hooker)

Wade, M R (Cambridge U)
Born 13 September 1937
3 caps 1962 (centre)

Walker, H W (Coventry)
Born 11 February 1915
8 caps 1947-48 (prop)

Wardlow, C S (Northampton)
Born 12 July 1942
4 caps 1971 (centre)

Warfield, P J
(Rosslyn Park, Durham U)
Born 1 April 1951
5 caps 1973-75 (centre)

Watkins, J A (Gloucester)
Born 28 November 1945
3 caps 1973-75 (flanker)

Watt, D E J (Bristol)
Born 5 July 1938
4 caps 1967 (lock)

Webb, J M (Bristol, Bath)
Born 24 August 1963
16 caps 1988-93 (full-back)

Webb, R E (Coventry)
Born 18 August 1943
11 caps 1967-72 (wing)

Webb, St L H (Bedford)
Born 17 March 1931;
died 30 May 1978
4 caps 1959 (prop)

Webster, J G (Moseley)
Born 24 August 1946
8 caps 1972-75 (scrum-half)

Weighill, R H G
(RAF, Harlequins)
Born 9 September 1920
4 caps 1947-48 (No 8)

West, B R (Loughborough
Colleges, Northampton)
Born 7 June 1948
7 caps 1968-70 (flanker)

Weston, L E
(West of Scotland)
Born 22 February 1947
2 caps 1972 (scrum-half)

Weston, M P
(Richmond, Durham City)
Born 21 August 1938
24 caps 1960-68
(centre, stand-off)

Wheeler, P J (Leicester)
Born 26 November 1948
36 caps 1975-84 (hooker)

White, C (Gosforth)
Born 31 March 1948
3 caps 1984 (prop)

White, D F (Northampton)
Born 16 January 1926
13 caps 1947-53 (flanker)

Wightman, B J
(Moseley, Coventry)
Born 23 September 1936
3 caps 1959-63 (No 8)

Wilkins, D T (United
Services, RN, Roundhay)
Born 26 December 1924
12 caps 1951-53 (lock)

: Mr C Norling (referee), PJ Blakeway, FE Cotton, RM Uttley, MJ Colcough,
en, WB Beaumont (captain), SJ Smith, J Carleton,

Wilkinson, R M (Bedford)
Born 25 July 1951
4 caps 1976 (lock)

Willcox, J G
(Oxford U, Harlequins)
Born 16 February 1937
15 caps 1961-64 (full-back)

Williams, C G
(Gloucester, RAF)
Born 21 December 1950
1 cap 1976 (stand-off)

Williams, J E
(Old Millhillians, Sale)
Born 31 January 1932
9 caps 1954-65 (scrum-half)

Williams, J M
(Penzance-Newlyn)
Born 24 August 1927
2 caps 1951 (centre)

Williams, P N (Orrell)
Born 14 December 1958
1 cap 1987 (stand-off)

Wilson, D S (Metropolitan Police, Harlequins)
Born 7 October 1926
7 caps 1953-55 (flanker)

Wilson K J (Gloucester)
Born 25 November 1938
1 cap 1963 (prop)

Winn, C E (Rosslyn Park)
Born 13 November 1926
7 caps 1952-54 (wing)

Winterbottom, P J
(Headingley, Harlequins)
Born 31 May 1960
37 caps 1982-93 (flanker)

Wintle, T C (Northampton)
Born 10 January 1940
5 caps 1966-69 (scrum-half)

Woodgate, E E (Paignton)
Born 21 January 1922
1 cap 1952 (prop)

Woodruff, C G (Harlequins)
Born 30 October 1920
4 caps 1951 (wing)

Woodward, C R (Leicester)
Born 6 January 1956
17 caps 1980-84 (centre)

Woodward, J E (Wasps)
Born 17 April 1931
13 caps 1952-56 (wing)

Wrench, F D B (Harlequins)
Born 27 November 1936
2 caps 1964 (prop)

Wright, I D (Northampton)
Born 24 December 1945
4 caps 1971
(stand-off, centre)

Wright, T P (Blackheath)
Born 28 February 1931
12 caps 1960-62 (prop)

Wyatt, D M (Bedford)
Born 4 December 1949
1 cap 1976 (wing)

Yarranton, P G
(RAF, Wasps)
Born 30 September 1924
4 caps 1954-55 (lock)

Young, J R C
(Oxford U, Harlequins)
Born 6 September 1937
8 caps 1958-61 (wing)

Young, M (Gosforth)
Born 4 January 1946
9 caps 1977-79 (scrum-half)

Young, P D
(Dublin Wanderers)
Born 9 November 1927
8 caps 1954-55 (lock)

Youngs, N G (Leicester)
Born 15 December 1959
5 caps 1983-84 (scrum-half)

Peter Winterbottom gets a hand from Mike Teague and Dean Richards against France, 1991.

SCOTLAND

Abercrombie, J G
(Edinburgh U)
Born 9 May 1928;
died 23 August 1992
7 caps 1949-50 (hooker)

Aitken, J (Gala)
Born 22 November 1947
18 caps 1977-84 (prop)

Aitken, R (London Scottish)
Born 29 June 1914
1 cap 1947 (prop)

Allan, J
(Edinburgh Academicals)
Born 25 November 1963
2 caps 1991 (hooker)

Allan, J L (Melrose)
Born 4 March 1927
4 caps 1952-53 (centre)

Allan, J L F (Cambridge U)
Born 20 August 1934
2 caps 1957 (wing)

Allan, R C
(Hutchesons' GSFP)
Born 16 March 1939
1 cap 1969 (scrum-half)

Allardice, W D
(Aberdeen GSFP)
Born 4 November 1919
7 caps 1948-49 (scrum-half)

Anderson, E
(Stewart's College FP)
Born 20 October 1918
2 caps 1947 (scrum-half)

Armstrong, G (Jedforest)
Born 30 September 1966
16 caps 1989-93 (scrum-half)

Arneil, R J
(Edinburgh Academicals,
Leicester, Northampton)
Born 1 May 1944
17 caps 1968-72 (flanker)

Baird, G R T (Kelso)
Born 12 April 1960
21 caps 1982-88 (wing)

Barnes, I A (Hawick)
Born 19 April 1948
6 caps 1972-77 (lock, flanker)

Bearne, K R F (Cambridge U,
London Scottish)
Born 11 March 1937
2 caps 1960 (No 8)

Beattie, J R
(Glasgow Academicals)
Born 27 November 1957
21 caps 1980-87 (No 8, lock)

Bell, D L (Watsonians)
Born 28 April 1949
4 caps 1975 (centre)

Biggar, A G
(London Scottish)
Born 4 August 1946
9 caps 1970-72 (wing, centre)

Biggar, M A
(London Scottish)
Born 20 November 1949
22 caps 1975-80 (flanker)

Black, A W (Edinburgh U)
Born 6 May 1925
6 caps 1947-50 (scrum-half)

Black, W P (Glasgow HSFP)
Born 27 November 1921
5 caps 1948-51
(prop, lock, No 8)

Blaikie, C F (Heriot's FP)
Born 21 November 1941
7 caps 1963-69 (full-back)

Bos, F H ten
(Oxford U, London Scottish)
Born 21 April 1937
15 caps 1959-63 (lock)

Boyle, A C W
(London Scottish)
Born 11 November 1937
3 caps 1963 (prop)

Boyle, A H W (St Thomas's
Hospital, London Scottish)
Born 30 September 1945
4 caps 1967-68 (No 8)

Brash, J C (Cambridge U)
Born May 1939
1 cap 1961 (flanker)

Breakey, R W (Gosforth)
Born 14 November 1956
1 cap 1978 (stand-off)

Brewster, A K
(Stewart's-Melville FP)
Born 3 May 1954
5 caps 1977-86 (flanker, prop)

Brown, A R (Gala)
Born 10 December 1949
4 caps 1971-72 (full-back)

Brown, G L
(West of Scotland)
Born 1 November 1947
24 caps 1970-76
(lock, flanker)

Brown, P C
(West of Scotland, Gala)
Born 16 December 1941
21 caps 1964-73 (lock, No 8)

Bruce, C R
(Glasgow Academicals)
Born 25 April 1918
8 caps 1947-49
(centre, stand-off)

Bruce, N S (Blackheath,
Army, London Scottish)
Born 24 June 1932;
died 28 March 1992
27 caps 1958-64 (hooker)

Bruce, R M (Gordonians)
Born 19 June 1922
3 caps 1948 (prop, flanker)

Bruce-Lockhart, L
(London Scottish)
Born 12 October 1921
5 caps 1948-53
(centre, stand-off)

Bryce, R D H
(West of Scotland)
Born 12 November 1941
1 cap 1973 (prop)

Budge, G M
(Edinburgh Wanderers)
Born 7 November 1920;
died 14 November 1979
4 caps 1950 (prop)

Burnell, A P
(London Scottish)
Born 29 September 1965
19 caps 1989-93 (prop)

Burnett, J N (Heriot's FP)
Born 12 July 1947
4 caps 1980 (prop)

Burrell, G (Gala)
Born 21 January 1921
3 caps 1950 (full-back)

Calder, F
(Stewart's-Melville FP)
Born 20 August 1957
20 caps 1986-90 (flanker)

Calder, J H
(Stewart's-Melville FP)
Born 20 August 1957
19 caps 1981-85 (flanker)

Callander, G J (Kelso)
Born 5 July 1959
4 caps 1988 (hooker)

Cameron, A (Glasgow HSFP)
Born 24 June 1929;
died 1 April 1991
16 caps 1948-56
(centre, stand-off, full-back)

Cameron, A D
(Hillhead HSFP)
Born 4 March 1924
3 caps 1951-54 (wing, centre)

Cameron, D (Glasgow HSFP)
Born 25 December 1927
5 caps 1953-54 (centre)

Cameron, N W (Glasgow U)
Born 2 September 1925;
died August 1978
3 caps 1952-53 (full-back)

Campbell, A J (Hawick)
Born 1 January 1959
12 caps 1984-88 (lock)

Campbell, H H (Cambridge
U, London Scottish)
Born 10 November 1921
4 caps 1947-48 (prop, lock)

Campbell, N M
(London Scottish)
Born 23 September 1929
2 caps 1956 (scrum-half)

Campbell-Lamerton, J R E
(London Scottish)
Born 21 February 1959
1 cap 1986 (lock)

Campbell-Lamerton, M J
(Halifax, Army, London
Scottish)
Born 1 August 1933
21 caps 1961-66 (lock)

Carmichael, A B
(West of Scotland)
Born 2 February 1944
41 caps 1967-78 (prop)

Cawkwell, G L (Oxford U)
Born 25 October 1919
1 cap 1947 (lock)

Chalmers, C M (Melrose)
Born 15 October 1968
20 caps 1989-93 (stand-off)

Charters, R G (Hawick)
Born 29 October 1930
3 caps 1955 (centre)

Chisholm, D H (Melrose)
Born 23 January 1937
11 caps 1964-68 (stand-off)

Chisholm, R W T (Melrose)
Born 16 October 1929;
died 2 November 1991
9 caps 1955-58 (full-back)

Clark, R L (Edinburgh
Wanderers, Royal Navy)
Born 27 January 1944
7 caps 1972-73 (hooker)

Coltman, S (Hawick)
Born 27 March 1920
5 caps 1948-49 (prop)

Connell, G C
(Trinity Academicals,
London Scottish)
Born 3 October 1944
4 caps 1968-70 (stand-off)

Cordial, I F
(Edinburgh Wanderers)
Born 1928
4 caps 1952 (centre)

Coughtrie, S
(Edinburgh Academicals)
Born 19 July 1935
11 caps 1959-63 (scrum-half)

Coutts, F H (Melrose, Army)
Born 8 July 1918
3 caps 1947 (lock)

Coutts, I D F
(Old Alleynians)
Born 27 April 1928
2 caps 1951-52 (centre)

Cowan, R C (Selkirk)
Born 26 November 1941
5 caps 1961-62 (centre, wing)

Cowie, W L K
(Edinburgh Wanderers)
Born 1 June 1926
1 cap 1953 (No 8)

Cramb, R I (Harlequins)
Born 7 September 1963
2 caps 1988 (stand-off)

Cranston, A G (Hawick)
Born 11 December 1949
8 caps 1976-78 (centre, wing)

Cronin, D F
(Bath, London Scottish)
Born 17 April 1963
20 caps 1988-93 (lock)

Cunningham, R F (Gala)
Born 4 January 1953
2 caps 1979 (prop)

Currie, L R (Dunfermline)
Born 1921;
died 1983
7 caps 1948-49 (lock, prop)

Cuthbertson, W
(Kilmarnock, Harlequins)
Born 6 December 1949
13 caps 1980-84 (lock)

Dalgleish, K J (Edinburgh Wanderers, Cambridge U)
Born 7 June 1931;
died 1974
4 caps 1951-53 (wing, centre)

Davidson, J A
(London Scottish, Edinburgh Wanderers)
Born 6 August 1932
3 caps 1959-60 (No 8)

Davidson, J N G
(Edinburgh U)
Born 28 January 1931
7 caps 1952-54 (stand-off)

Dawson, J C
(Glasgow Academicals)
Born 29 October 1925
18 caps 1948-53 (lock, prop)

Deans, C T (Hawick)
Born 3 May 1955
37 caps 1978-87 (hooker)

Deans, D T (Hawick)
Born 30 April 1945
1 cap 1968 (hooker)

Deas, D W (Heriot's FP)
Born 30 March 1919
2 caps 1947 (No 8, lock)

Dick, L G
(Loughborough Colleges, Jordanhill, Swansea)
Born 20 December 1950
12 caps 1972-77 (wing)

Dickson, G (Gala)
Born 10 December 1954
7 caps 1979-82
(flanker, No 8)

Docherty, J T
(Glasgow HSFP)
Born 5 June 1931
7 caps 1955-58
(stand-off, centre)

Dods, P W (Gala)
Born 6 January 1958
17 caps 1983-91 (full-back)

Dorward, A F
(Cambridge U, Gala)
Born 3 March 1925
14 caps 1950-57 (scrum-half)

Douglas, J
(Stewart's College FP)
Born 18 December 1934
11 caps 1961-63 (No 8, lock)

Drummond, C W (Melrose)
Born 26 May 1923;
died 9 June 1985
11 caps 1947-50
(centre, wing)

Duffy, H (Jedforest)
Born 1 April 1934
1 cap 1955 (flanker)

Duncan, M D F
(West of Scotland)
Born 29 August 1959
12 caps 1986-89 (wing)

Dunlop, Q (West of Scotland)
Born 9 March 1943
1 cap 1971 (hooker)

Edwards, D B
(Heriot's FP)
Born 19 March 1930
2 caps 1960 (flanker)

Edwards, N G B
(Harlequins)
Born 20 August 1964
4 caps 1992 (lock)

Elgie, M K
(London Scottish)
Born 6 March 1933
7 caps 1954-55 (centre)

Elliot, C (Langholm)
Born 24 February 1933
11 caps 1958-65 (wing)

Elliot, T (Gala)
Born 6 April 1926
13 caps 1955-58 (prop)

Elliot, T G (Langholm)
Born 1 March 1941
4 caps 1968-70 (flanker)

Elliot, W I D
(Edinburgh Academicals)
Born 18 April 1923
26 caps 1947-54 (flanker)

Fergusson, E A J
(Oxford U)
Born 28 October 1932
4 caps 1954 (lock)

Finlay, R (Watsonians)
Born 9 April 1923
1 cap 1948 (lock)

Fisher, A T
(Waterloo, Watsonians)
Born 3 September 1916;
died 26 January 1983
2 caps 1947 (hooker)

Fisher, C D (Waterloo)
Born 27 December 1949
3 caps 1976 (hooker)

Fisher, J P (Royal HSFP, London Scottish)
Born 17 March 1939
21 caps 1963-68
(No 8, flanker)

Forsyth, I W
(Stewart's College FP)
Born 4 July 1946
4 caps 1973 (centre)

Fox, J (Gala)
Born 30 August 1921
4 caps 1952 (prop, hooker)

Frame, J N M
(Edinburgh U, Gala)
Born 8 October 1946
18 caps 1968-72 (centre)

Friebe, J P (Glasgow HSFP)
Born 9 May 1931
1 cap 1952 (No 8)

Fulton, A K (Edinburgh U, Dollar Academicals)
Born 10 April 1929
2 caps 1952-54 (scrum-half)

Gammell, W B B
(Edinburgh Wanderers)
Born 29 December 1952
5 caps 1977-78 (wing)

Geddes, K I
(London Scottish)
Born 23 October 1918;
died 30 March 1991
4 caps 1947 (full-back)

Gemmill, R (Glasgow HSFP)
Born 20 February 1930
7 caps 1950-51 (lock)

Gilbert-Smith, D S
(London Scottish)
Born 3 December 1931
1 cap 1952 (flanker)

Gill, A D (Gala)
Born 30 August 1949
4 caps 1974 (wing)

Glasgow, R J C
(Dunfermline)
Born 5 November 1930
10 caps 1962-65 (flanker)

Glen, W S
(Edinburgh Wanderers)
Born 13 March 1932
1 cap 1955 (flanker)

Gloag, L G (Cambridge U)
Born 30 October 1925;
died 28 February 1984
4 caps 1949 (centre)

Gordon, R
(Edinburgh Wanderers)
Born 25 July 1930
6 caps 1951-53 (wing)

Gossman, B M
(West of Scotland)
Born 5 May 1951
3 caps 1980-83 (stand-off)

Gossman, J S
(West of Scotland)
1 cap 1980 (wing)

Grant, D (Hawick)
Born 19 April 1938
11 caps 1965-68 (flanker)

Grant, M L (Harlequins)
Born 8 November 1927;
died 29 October 1992
4 caps 1955-57
(centre, stand-off)

Grant, T O (Hawick)
Born 5 September 1932
4 caps 1960-64 (lock, No 8)

Gray, C A (Nottingham)
Born 11 July 1960
12 caps 1989-91 (lock)

Gray, D (West of Scotland)
Born 28 March 1953
8 caps 1978-81 (lock)

Gray, T
(Northampton, Heriot's FP)
Born 20 January 1917
3 caps 1950-51 (full-back)

Greenwood, J T
(Dunfermline, Perthshire Academicals)
Born 1929
19 caps 1952-59
(flanker, No 8)

Hannah, R S M
(West of Scotland)
Born 15 December 1945
1 cap 1971 (wing)

Hastie, A J (Melrose)
Born 29 July 1935
15 caps 1961-68 (scrum-half)

Hastie, I R (Kelso)
Born 7 September 1929
6 caps 1955-59 (prop)

Hastings, A G
(Cambridge U, Watsonians, London Scottish)
Born 3 January 1962
28 caps 1986-93 (full-back)

Hastings, S (Watsonians)
Born 4 December 1964
30 caps 1986-93 (centre)

Hay, B H (Boroughmuir)
Born 23 May 1950
17 caps 1976-81
(full-back, wing)

Hegarty, C B (Hawick)
Born 29 November 1950
4 caps 1978 (flanker)

Hegarty, J J (Hawick)
Born 13 April 1925
6 caps 1951-55 (flanker, lock)

Henderson, B C
(Edinburgh Wanderers)
Born 1940
12 caps 1963-66 (centre)

Henderson, I C
(Edinburgh Academicals)
Born 31 October 1918
5 caps 1947-48 (hooker, prop, lock)

Henderson, J H
(Oxford U, Richmond)
Born 9 February 1930
8 caps 1953-54 (lock, flanker)

Henriksen, E H
(Royal HSFP)
1 cap 1953 (No 8)

Hepburn, D P (Woodford)
Born 15 March 1920
8 caps 1948-49
(stand-off, centre)

Hinshelwood, A J W
(London Scottish)
Born 23 March 1942
17 caps 1966-70 (wing)

Hodgson, C G
(London Scottish)
Born 11 May 1938
2 caps 1968 (wing)

Hogg, C G (Boroughmuir)
Born 2 March 1948
2 caps 1978 (wing)

Hoyer-Millar, G C
(Oxford U)
Born 13 December 1929
1 cap 1953 (hooker)

Hunter, I G (Selkirk)
Born 7 August 1958
4 caps 1984-85 (scrum-half)

Hunter, J M (Cambridge U)
Born 12 November 1920
1 cap 1947 (lock)

Hunter, M D (Glasgow High)
Born 24 April 1945
1 cap 1974 (centre)

Hunter, W J (Hawick)
Born 5 June 1934
6 caps 1964-67 (lock)

Inglis, H M
(Edinburgh Academicals)
Born 3 August 1931
6 caps 1951-52 (lock, No 8)

Inglis, J M (Selkirk)
Born 20 March 1928
1 cap 1952 (prop)

Innes, J R S
(Aberdeen GSFP)
Born 16 September 1917
4 caps 1948 (centre)

Irvine, A R (Heriot's FP)
born 16 September 1951
39 caps 1973-82
(full-back, wing)

Jackson, T G H (Army)
Born 15 October 1921
11 caps 1947-49 (wing)

Jackson, W D (Hawick)
Born 5 December 1941
6 caps 1964-69 (wing)

Jeffrey, J (Kelso)
Born 25 March 1959
24 caps 1985-91 (flanker)

Johnston, D I (Watsonians)
Born 20 October 1958
19 caps 1980-86 (centre)

Johnston, J (Melrose)
Born 17 September 1925
4 caps 1952 (lock)

Jones, P M (Gloucester)
Born 28 December 1963
1 cap 1992 (prop)

Keith, G J (Wasps)
Born 1941
2 caps 1968 (wing)

Keller, D H
(London Scottish)
Born 18 June 1922
7 caps 1949-50 (flanker)

Kemp, J W Y
(Glasgow HSFP)
Born 13 February 1933
25 caps 1954-60 (lock)

Kennedy, A E (Watsonians)
Born 30 July 1954
2 caps 1984 (centre)

Ker, A B M (Kelso)
Born 19 October 1954
2 caps 1988 (stand-off)

Kerr, W (London Scottish)
Born 14 September 1930
1 cap 1953 (flanker)

King, J H F (Selkirk)
Born 10 April 1925;
died 8 September 1982
4 caps 1953-54 (hooker)

Kininmonth, P W
(Oxford U, Richmond)
Born 23 June 1924
19 caps 1949-54
(No 8, flanker)

Laidlaw, F A L (Melrose)
Born 20 September 1940
26 caps 1965-71 (hooker)

Laidlaw, R J (Jedforest)
Born 5 October 1953
34 caps 1980-88 (scrum-half)

Lambie, I K (Watsonians)
Born 13 April 1954
2 caps 1979 (No 8)

Lauder, W (Neath)
Born 4 November 1948
14 caps 1969-77 (flanker)

Laughland, I H P
(London Scottish)
Born 29 October 1935
28 caps 1959-67
(centre, stand-off)

Lawrie, K G (Gala)
Born 31 July 1951
3 caps 1980 (hooker)

Lawson, A J M (Edinburgh Wanderers, London Scottish)
Born 19 May 1948
13 caps 1972-80 (scrum-half)

Lees, J B (Gala)
Born 11 August 1919
4 caps 1947-48
(No 8, flanker)

Leslie, D G (Dundee HSFP, West of Scotland, Gala)
Born 14 April 1952
24 caps 1975-85
(No 8, flanker)

Lineen, S R P (Boroughmuir)
Born 25 December 1961
16 caps 1989-92 (centre)

Logan, K M (Stirling Co)
Born 3 April 1972
1 cap 1993 (centre)

Lumsden, I J M
(Bath, Watsonians)
Born 6 April 1923
6 caps 1947-49
(stand-off, full-back)

Lyall, G G (Gala)
Born 23 May 1921
4 caps 1948 (hooker)

Macdonald, D C
(Edinburgh U)
Born 1931
4 caps 1953-58 (No 8)

Macdonald, D S M
(Oxford U, London Scottish, West of Scotland)
Born 25 September 1951
7 caps 1977-78 (No 8)

Macdonald, J D
(London Scottish, Army)
Born 5 April 1938
8 caps 1966-67 (prop)

Macdonald, K R
(Stewart's College FP)
Born 13 May 1933
6 caps 1956-57 (centre)

Macdonald, R (Edinburgh U)
Born 18 January 1928
4 caps 1950 (centre)

Macdonald, W G
(London Scottish)
Born 30 December 1938
1 cap 1969 (centre)

MacEwan, N A
(Gala, Highland)
Born 12 December 1941
17 caps 1971-75 (flanker)

MacEwen, R K G (Cambridge U, London Scottish)
Born 25 February 1928
12 caps 1954-58 (hooker)

MacGregor, I A A
(Hillhead HSFP, Llanelli)
Born 9 August 1931
9 caps 1955-57 (flanker)

Mackenzie, D D
(Edinburgh U)
Born 28 December 1921
6 caps 1947-48 (wing)

Mackie, G Y (Highland)
Born 19 April 1949
3 caps 1976-78 (No 8)

MacLachlan, L P
(Oxford U, London Scottish)
Born 16 March 1928
3 caps 1954 (scrum-half)

Maclennan, W D
(Watsonians)
Born 4 April 1921
2 caps 1947 (wing)

Macphail, J A R
(Edinburgh Academicals)
14 October 1923
1 cap 1949 (hooker)

Madsen, D F (Gosforth)
Born 16 April 1947
14 caps 1974-78 (hooker)

Mair, N G R (Edinburgh U)
Born 7 October 1928
4 caps 1951 (hooker)

Marshall, J C
(London Scottish)
Born 30 January 1929
4 caps 1954 (full-back)

Maxwell, J M (Langholm)
Born 30 April 1932
1 cap 1957 (stand-off)

McClung, T
(Edinburgh Academicals)
Born 14 February 1933
9 caps 1956-60
(centre, stand-off)

McCrae, I G (Gordonians)
Born 19 May 1941
5 caps 1967-72 (scrum-half)

McGeechan, I R (Headingley)
Born 30 October 1946
27 caps 1973-79
(stand-off, centre)

McGlashan, T P L
(Royal HSFP)
Born 29 December 1925
7 caps 1947-54 (prop)

McGuinness, G M
(West of Scotland)
Born 14 September 1953
5 caps 1983-85 (prop)

McHarg, A F (West of Scotland, London Scottish)
Born 17 June 1944
37 caps 1968-79 (lock, No 8)

McIvor, D J
(Edinburgh Academicals)
Born 29 June 1964
4 caps 1992 (flanker)

McKeating, E (Heriot's FP)
Born 1 September 1936
5 caps 1957-61 (centre)

McLauchlan, J (Jordanhill)
Born 14 April 1942
35 caps 1969-79 (prop)

McLean, D I (Royal HSFP)
Born 1 May 1923,
died 21 March 1962
2 caps 1947 (flanker, No 8)

McLeod, H F (Hawick)
Born 8 June 1932
36 caps 1954-62 (prop)

McMillan, K H D (Sale)
Born 1926
4 caps 1953 (flanker)

McPartlin, J J
(Harlequins, Oxford U)
Born 12 June 1938
6 caps 1960-62 (centre)

Michie, E J S (Aberdeen U, Aberdeen GSFP)
Born 7 November 1933
14 caps 1954-57 (lock)

Millican, J G (Edinburgh U)
Born 21 August 1951
3 caps 1973 (flanker)

Milne, I G
(Heriot's FP, Harlequins)
Born 17 June 1958
28 caps 1979-89 (prop)

Milne, K S (Heriot's FP)
Born 1 December 1961
19 caps 1989-93 (hooker)

Mitchell, G W E
(Edinburgh Wanderers)

Born 23 November 1943
2 caps 1968 (lock)

Moore, A
(Edinburgh Academicals)
Born 19 August 1963
3 caps 1991 (wing)

Morgan, D W
(Stewart's-Melville FP)
Born 9 March 1947
18 caps 1973-78 (scrum-half)

Morrison, I R
(London Scottish)
Born 14 December 1962
4 caps 1993 (flanker)

Muir, D E (Heriot's FP)
Born 17 March 1925
7 caps 1950-52 (lock)

Munnoch, N M (Watsonians)
Born 4 January 1929
3 caps 1952 (hooker)

Munro, S
(Ayr, West of Scotland)
Born 11 June 1958
7 caps 1980-84 (wing)

Munro, W H
(Glasgow HSFP)
Born 28 September 1918;
died 12 September 1970
2 caps 1947
(stand-off, centre)

Murdoch, W C W
(Hillhead HSFP)
Born 3 October 1914;
died October 1987
4 caps 1948 (full-back)

Murray, K T (Hawick)
Born 23 March 1962
3 caps 1985 (centre)

Neill, J B
(Edinburgh Academicals)
Born 28 July 1937
6 caps 1963-65 (prop)

Nichol, J A (Royal HSFP)
Born 12 February 1932
3 caps 1955 (scrum-half)

Nicol, A D (Dundee HSFP)
Born 12 March 1971
4 caps 1992 (scrum-half)

Orr, J H
(Edinburgh City Police)
Born 13 June 1918
2 caps 1947 (flanker)

Paterson, D S (Gala)
Born 27 March 1943
7 caps 1970-72 (scrum-half)

Paxton, I A M (Selkirk)
Born 29 December 1957
23 caps 1982-88 (No 8, lock)

Paxton, R E (Kelso)
Born 4 April 1957
1 cap 1982 (flanker)

Pender, N E K (Hawick)
Born 1 February 1948
4 caps 1977-78 (prop)

Pollock, J A (Gosforth)
Born 16 November 1958
6 caps 1982-85 (wing)

Rea, C W W
(West of Scotland,
Headingley)
Born 22 October 1943
9 caps 1969-71 (centre)

Reed, A I (Bath)
Born 4 May 1969
4 caps 1993 (lock)

Relph, W K L
(Stewart's School FP)
Born 28 November 1928
4 caps 1955 (hooker)

Renwick, J M (Hawick)
Born 12 February 1952
42 caps 1972-83
(centre, wing)

Robertson, I (London Scottish, Watsonians)
Born 17 January 1945
6 caps 1968-70 (stand-off)

Robertson, K W (Melrose)
Born 5 December 1954
32 caps 1979-89
(wing, centre)

Robertson, M A (Gala)
Born 1930
1 cap 1958 (flanker)

Robson, A (Hawick)
Born 16 August 1928
21 caps 1954-60 (flanker)

Rodd, J A T
(United Services, Royal Navy, London Scottish)
Born 26 August 1935
12 caps 1958-65 (scrum-half)

Rollo, D M D (Howe of Fife)
Born 7 July 1934
34 caps 1959-68 (prop)

Rose, D M (Jedforest)
Born 20 February 1931
6 caps 1951-53 (wing)

Ross, G T (Watsonians)
Born 5 July 1928
3 caps 1954 (stand-off)

Ross, I A (Hillhead HSFP)
Born 15 December 1928
4 caps 1951 (scrum-half)

Ross, K I (Boroughmuir FP)
Born 15 March 1937
10 caps 1961-63 (flanker)

Rowan, N A (Boroughmuir)
Born 17 September 1951
11 caps 1980-88 (prop)

Rutherford, J Y (Selkirk)
Born 4 October 1955
32 caps 1979-87 (stand-off)

Sampson, R W F
(London Scottish)
Born 26 September 1913
1 cap 1947 (hooker)

Scotland, K J F (Heriot's FP, Cambridge U, Leicester)
Born 29 August 1936
26 caps 1957-65
(full-back, stand-off)

Scott, D M
(Langholm, Watsonians)
Born 15 April 1928
9 caps 1950-53 (wing, centre)

Scott, J S (St Andrews U)
Born 17 February 1924
1 cap 1950 (flanker)

Shackleton, J A P
(London Scottish)
Born 3 April 1940
5 caps 1959-65 (centre)

Sharp, G
(Stewart's FP, Army)
Born 20 April 1934
3 caps 1960-64 (stand-off)

Scotland's first post-war win at Twickenham in 1971. Alastair McHarg, Chris Rea and Quintin Dunlop look on as Billy Steele touches down for a Scottish drop-out. Fran Cotton, on his England debut, just misses scoring a try.

Shedden, D
(West of Scotland)
Born 24 May 1944
13 caps 1973-78 (wing)

Shiel, A G (Melrose)
Born 13 August 1970
4 caps 1993
(centre, stand-off)

Shillinglaw, R B
(Gala, Army)
Born 1939
3 caps 1960-61 (scrum-half)

Simmers, B M
(Glasgow Academicals)
Born 26 February 1940
6 caps 1965-71
(stand-off, centre, full-back)

Sloan, D A
(Edinburgh Academicals,
London Scottish)
Born 11 May 1926
7 caps 1950-53 (centre)

Smith, A R (Cambridge U,
Gosforth, Ebbw Vale,
Edinburgh Wanderers)
Born 23 January 1933;
died 3 February 1975
30 caps 1955-62 (wing)

Smith, D W C
(London Scottish)
Born 27 October 1924
8 caps 1949-53 (wing)

Smith, G K (Kelso)
Born 2 June 1931
16 caps 1957-61
(No 8, flanker)

Smith, I R (Gloucester)
Born 16 March 1965
3 caps 1992 (flanker)

Smith, I S G
(London Scottish)
Born 16 June 1944
7 caps 1970-71 (full-back)

Smith, M A
(London Scottish)
Born 23 November 1945
3 caps 1970 (wing)

Smith, T J (Gala)
Born 31 August 1953
3 caps 1983-85 (lock)

Sole, D M B (Bath,
Edinburgh Acads)
Born 8 May 1962
26 caps 1986-92 (prop)

Spence, K M (Oxford U)
Born 21 November 1929;
died 29 January 1989
1 cap 1953 (scrum-half)

Stagg, P K (Sale)
Born 22 November 1941
22 caps 1965-70 (lock)

Stanger, A G (Hawick)
Born 14 May 1968
16 caps 1990-93 (wing)

Stark, D A (Boroughmuir)
Born 13 April 1966
4 caps 1993 (wing)

Steele, W C C
(Langholm, Bedford, RAF,
London Scottish)
Born 18 April 1947
20 caps 1969-77 (wing)

Steven, P D (Heriot's FP)
Born 4 July 1959
3 caps 1985 (wing)

Steven, R
(Edinburgh Wanderers)
1 cap 1962 (prop)

Stevenson, G D (Hawick)
Born 30 May 1933
21 caps 1956-65
(centre, wing)

Stewart, C E B (Kelso)
Born 23 December 1936
2 caps 1960-61 (flanker)

Strachan, G M (Jordanhlll)
Born 16 November 1947
3 caps 1973 (No 8)

Suddon, N (Hawick)
Born 28 June 1943
9 caps 1965-70 (prop)

Swan, J S (Army, London
Scottish, Leicester)
Born 14 July 1930
16 caps 1953-58 (wing)

Swan, M W (Oxford U,
London Scottish)
Born 4 December 1934
7 caps 1958-59 (lock)

Tait, A V (Kelso)
Born 2 July 1964
4 caps 1988 (centre)

Taylor, R C
(Kelvinside-West)
Born 31 August 1924
3 caps 1951 (flanker)

Telfer, C M (Hawick)
Born 26 February 1947
14 caps 1969-76 (stand-off)

Telfer, J W (Melrose)
Born 17 March 1940
22 caps 1964-70
(flanker, No 8)

Thomson, A M
(St Andrews U)
Born 20 February 1921
1 cap 1949 (lock)

Thomson, B E (Oxford U)
Born 19 November 1930
3 caps 1953 (prop)

Thomson, I H M
(Heriot's FP, Army)
Born 13 April 1930
7 caps 1951-53 (full-back)

On their way to the 1984 Grand Slam: Scotland v England. Back: RF Cunnin- IAM Paxton, W Cuthbertson, JR Beattie (replacement), DS Wyllie (replacement) DI Johnston, JY Rutherford, J Aitken (captain), RJ Laidlaw, CT Deans, JH Calde

Thomson, R H
(London Scottish)
Born 12 October 1936
12 caps 1960-64 (wing)

Tomes, A J (Hawick)
Born 6 November 1951
34 caps 1976-87 (lock)

Townsend, G P J (Gala)
Born 26 April 1973
1 cap 1993 (centre)

Tukalo, I (Selkirk)
Born 5 March 1961
21 caps 1985-92 (wing)

Turk, A S (Langholm)
Born 9 January 1948
1 cap 1971 (centre)

Turnbull, D J (Hawick)
Born 2 October 1961
11 caps 1988-93 (flanker)

Turnbull, F O (Kelso)
Born 3 June 1919
1 cap 1951 (centre)

Turner, J W C (Gala)
Born 28 September 1943;
died 19 May 1992
15 caps 1966-71
(stand-off, centre)

Valentine, A R
(RNAS, Anthorn)
Born 5 February 1928
3 caps 1953 (flanker)

Valentine, D D (Hawick)
Born 12 September 1926;
died 14 August 1976
2 caps 1947 (flanker)

Waddell, G H (London
Scottish, Cambridge U)
Born 12 April 1937
16 caps 1957-62 (stand-off)

Wainwright, R I
(Edinburgh Academicals)
Born 22 March 1965
2 caps 1992 (lock, flanker)

Walker, M (Oxford U)
Born 11 March 1930
1 cap 1952 (lock)

Watherston, W R A
(London Scottish)
Born 5 March 1933
3 caps 1963 (flanker)

Watson, W S (Boroughmuir)
Born 7 January 1949
9 caps 1974-79
(No 8, flanker)

Watt, A G J
(Glasgow High-Kelvinside)
Born 10 July 1967
1 cap 1993 (prop)

lacement), JA Pollock (replacement), IG Milne, DG Leslie, AE Kennedy, AJ Tomes,
an (replacement), Mr DIH Burnett (referee). Seated: KW Robertson, GRT Baird,
s.

Watt, A G M
(Edinburgh Academicals)
Born 19 December 1916;
died 16 April 1982
5 caps 1947-48
(prop, No 8, lock)

Weatherstone, T G
(Stewart's College FP)
Born 27 June 1931
14 caps 1952-59 (wing)

Weir, G W (Melrose)
Born 4 July 1970
8 caps 1992-93 (lock, No 8)

Welsh, R B (Hawick)
Born 2 February 1943
2 caps 1967 (centre)

White, D B
(Gala, London Scottish)
Born 30 January 1958
24 caps 1982-92
(flanker, lock, No 8)

White, D M
(Kelvinside Academicals)
Born 21 November 1943
4 caps 1963 (centre)

Whyte, D J
(Edinburgh Wanderers)
Born 21 February 1940
11 caps 1965-67 (wing)

Wilson, G A (Oxford U)
Born 23 November 1922
3 caps 1949 (lock)

Wilson, J H (Watsonians)
Born 3 March 1930
1 cap 1953 (prop)

Wilson, R (London Scottish)
Born 1 July 1954
8 caps 1976-83 (stand-off)

Wilson, R L (Gala)
Born 1 July 1926
7 caps 1951-53 (prop)

Wilson, S
(Oxford U, London Scottish)
Born 22 October 1942
18 caps 1964-68 (full-back)

Wright, P H (Boroughmuir)
Born 30 December 1967
3 caps 1993 (prop)

Wright, R W J
(Edinburgh Wanderers)
Born 6 May 1949;
died 11 October 1983
1 cap 1973 (lock)

Wright, S T H
(Stewart's College FP)
1 cap 1949 (prop)

Wyllie, D S
(Stewart's-Melville FP)
Born 20 May 1963
4 caps 1985-87 (centre)

Young, R G (Watsonians)
Born 13 September 1940
1 cap 1970 (scrum-half)

Young, W B (Cambridge U,
London Scottish)
Born 7 May 1916
1 cap 1948 (flanker)

IRELAND

Agar, R D (Malone)
Born 29 March 1920
10 caps 1947-50 (No 8, lock)

Agnew, P J (CIYMS)
Born 18 March 1942
1 cap 1974 (prop)

Aherne, L F P
(Dolphin, Lansdowne)
Born 16 March 1963
11 caps 1989-92 (scrum-half)

Anderson, F E
(Queen's U Belfast, NIFC)
Born 29 August 1929
12 caps 1953-55 (prop)

Anderson, W A (Dungannon)
Born 3 April 1955
19 caps 1985-90 (lock)

Armstrong, W K (NIFC)
Born 22 October 1931
1 cap 1961 (stand-off)

Bailey, N (Northampton)
Born 20 March 1929
1 cap 1952 (wing)

Becker, V A M (Lansdowne)
Born 9 October 1947
2 caps 1974 (wing)

Bell, W E (Belfast Collegians)
Born 13 November 1924
4 caps 1953 (flanker)

Berkery, P J (Lansdowne)
Born 3 February 1929
10 caps 1954-58 (full-back)

Blake-Knox, S E F (NIFC)
Born 9 July 1948
3 caps 1976-77 (wing)

Blayney, J J (Wanderers)
Born 13 March 1925
1 cap 1950 (centre)

Bornemann, W W
(Wanderers)
Born 19 January 1936
3 caps 1960 (wing)

Bowen, D St J
(Cork Constitution)
Born 11 February 1957
3 caps 1977 (wing)

Bradley, M T (Cork
Constitution)
Born 17 November 1962
21 caps 1985-93 (scrum-half)

Brady, A M
(UC Dublin, Malone)
Born 16 October 1939
4 caps 1966-68 (hooker)

Brady, J A (Wanderers)
Born 9 April 1952
2 caps 1976 (centre)

Brady, J R (CIYMS)
Born 11 February 1931
12 caps 1951-57 (lock)

Brennan, J I (CIYMS)
Born 22 August 1934
2 caps 1957 (prop)

Bresnihan, F P K
(UC Dublin, Lansdowne,
London Irish)
Born 13 March 1944
22 caps 1966-71 (centre)

Brophy, N H
(Blackrock College, UC
Dublin, London Irish)
Born 19 November 1935
18 caps 1957-67 (wing)

Brown, E L (Instonians)
Born 6 September 1930
1 cap 1958 (flanker)

Brown, W J (Malone)
Born 19 August 1943
3 caps 1970 (wing)

Buckley, J H (Sunday's Well)
Born 1944
2 caps 1973 (flanker)

Burges, J H (Rosslyn Park)
Born 26 October 1928
2 caps 1950 (scrum-half)

Burns, I J (Wanderers)
Born 7 December 1955
1 cap 1980 (centre)

Butler, L G
(Blackrock College)
Born 9 October 1935
1 cap 1960 (hooker)

Byrne, E M J
(Blackrock College)
Born 14 September 1948
5 caps 1977-78 (prop)

Byrne, N F (UC Dublin)
Born 18 December 1938
1 cap 1962 (wing)

Byrne, S J
(UC Dublin, Lansdowne)
Born 7 June 1931
3 caps 1953-55 (wing)

Callan, C P (Lansdowne)
Born 6 January 1923
10 caps 1947-49 (lock)

Campbell, S O
(Old Belvedere)
Born 3 March 1954
18 caps 1980-84
(stand-off, centre)

Canniffe, D M (Lansdowne)
Born 14 August 1949
2 caps 1976 (scrum-half)

Cantrell, J L (UC Dublin,
Blackrock College)
Born 10 January 1954
5 caps 1976-81 (hooker)

Carr, N J (Ards)
Born 27 July 1959
10 caps 1985-87 (flanker)

Carroll, R (Lansdowne)
Born 9 February 1926
3 caps 1947-50 (scrum-half)

Casey, P J
(UC Dublin, Lansdowne)
Born 4 August 1941
11 caps 1963-65
(wing, centre)

Chambers, R R (Instonians)
Born 15 August 1927
6 caps 1951-52 (centre)

Clancy, T P J (Lansdowne)
Born 16 March 1962
6 caps 1988-89 (prop)

Clarke, C P
(Terenure College)
Born 8 March 1969
3 caps 1993 (full-back)

Clarke, D J (Dolphin)
Born 2 September 1968
1 cap 1991 (wing)

Clegg, R J (Bangor)
Born 4 December 1948
5 caps 1973-75 (prop)

Clifford, J T
(Young Munster)
Born 15 November 1923;
died 1 October 1990
13 caps 1949-52 (prop)

Clohessy, P M
(Young Munster)
Born 22 March 1966
3 caps 1993 (prop)

Collins, P C
(Lansdowne, London Irish)
Born 7 December 1959
1 cap 1990

Condon, H C (London Irish)
Born 17 February 1955
1 cap 1984 (stand-off)

Corcoran, J C (London Irish)
Born 14 July 1922
1 cap 1948 (prop)

Costello, P (Bective Rangers)
Born 18 August 1931
1 cap 1960 (lock)

Costello, R A (Garryowen)
Born 8 March 1964
1 cap 1993 (lock)

Crossan, K D (Instonians)
Born 29 December 1959
28 caps 1982-92 (wing)

Crowe, L (Old Belvedere)
Born 30 March 1928;
died 19 September 1968
3 caps 1950 (wing)

Cullen, T J (UC Dublin)
Born 5 September 1926
1 cap 1949 (scrum-half)

Culliton, M G (Wanderers)
Born 15 June 1936
18 caps 1959-64
(lock, flanker, No 8)

Cunningham, M J (UC Cork)
Born 23 June 1933
7 caps 1955-56 (flanker)

Cunningham, V J G
(St Mary's College)
Born 14 March 1967
4 caps 1993 (centre)

Curtis, A B (Oxford U)
Born 27 March 1924;
died 17 April 1989
3 caps 1950 (flanker)

Curtis, D M (London Irish)
Born 10 April 1965
7 caps 1991-92 (centre)

Daly, J C (London Irish)
Born 12 December 1916;
died 10 November 1988
7 caps 1947-48 (prop)

Danaher, P P A
(Lansdowne, Garryowen)
Born 5 October 1965
11 caps 1988-92
(full-back, centre)

Dargan, M J (Old Belvedere)
Born 9 October 1928
2 caps 1952 (flanker)

Davidson, J C (Dungannon)
Born 23 October 1942
4 caps 1969 (flanker)

Dawson, A R (Wanderers)
Born 5 June 1932
23 caps 1958-64 (hooker)

Dean, P M
(St Mary's College)
Born 28 June 1960
22 caps 1982-89
(centre, stand-off)

Deering, S M (Garryowen,
St Mary's College)
Born 5 August 1948;
died 3 November 1988
7 caps 1974-77 (flanker)

de Lacy, H (Harlequins)
Born 20 November 1919;
died 8 November 1979
2 caps 1948 (scrum-half)

Dennison, S P (Garryowen)
Born 26 January 1950
3 caps 1973-75 (wing)

Dick, C J (Ballymena)
Born 26 January 1937
7 caps 1961-63 (lock, No 8)

Dick, J S
(Queen's U Belfast)
Born 24 October 1939
1 cap 1962 (hooker)

Donaldson, J A
(Belfast Collegians)
Born 16 September 1936
3 caps 1958 (flanker)

Dooley, J F (Galwegians)
Born 10 August 1934

3 caps 1959 (centre)

Doyle, J A P (Greystones)
Born 26 April 1958
2 caps 1984 (scrum-half)

Doyle, M G
(Blackrock College,
UC Dublin, Cambridge U,
Edinburgh Wanderers)
Born 13 October 1941
16 caps 1965-68 (flanker)

Doyle, T J (Wanderers)
Born 9 June 1944
3 caps 1968 (flanker)

Duggan, A T A (Lansdowne)
Born 11 June 1942
20 caps 1964-71 (wing)

Duggan, W P
(Blackrock College)
Born 12 March 1950
33 caps 1975-84
(No 8, flanker)

Duncan, W R (Malone)
Born 14 July 1957
2 caps 1984 (flanker)

Dunlea, F J (Lansdowne)
Born 25 February 1964
3 caps 1989 (full-back)

Dwyer, P J (UC Dublin)
Born 24 May 1940
4 caps 1962-64 (prop)

Elliott, W R J (Bangor)
Born 20 November 1952
1 cap 1979 (full-back)

Elwood, E P (Lansdowne)
Born 26 February 1969
2 caps 1993 (stand-off)

English, M A F (Lansdowne,
Limerick Bohemians)
Born 2 June 1933
15 caps 1958-63 (stand-off)

Ensor, A H (Wanderers)
Born 17 August 1949
18 caps 1973-78 (full-back)

Fagan, W B C (Wanderers)
Born 23 April 1927
3 caps 1956 (prop)

Feddis, N (Lansdowne)
Born 29 December 1932
1 cap 1956 (flanker)

Feighery, C F P (Lansdowne)
Born 13 August 1946
2 caps 1972 (lock)

Feighery, T A O
(St Mary's College)
Born 16 January 1945
2 caps 1977 (prop)

Finn, M C (UC Cork, Cork
Constitution)
Born 29 March 1957
13 caps 1979-86 (wing)

Finn, R G A (UC Dublin)
Born 25 November 1953
1 cap 1977 (centre)

Fitzgerald, C F
(St Mary's College)
Born 4 June 1952
22 caps 1980-86 (hooker)

Fitzgerald, D C (Lansdowne,
De La Salle Palmerston)
Born 20 December 1957
23 caps 1984-92 (prop)

Fitzgerald, J J
(Young Munster)
Born 31 August 1961
9 caps 1988-91 (prop)

Fitzgibbon, M J J (Shannon)
Born 2 April 1965
4 caps 1992 (flanker)

Fitzpatrick, M P (Wanderers)
Born 25 November 1950
9 caps 1988-85 (prop)

Flynn, M K (Wanderers)
Born 20 March 1939
19 caps 1959-72 (centre)

Foley, B O (Shannon)
Born 6 August 1950
8 caps 1976-81 (lock)

Fortune, J J (Clontarf)
Born 1 December 1933
1 cap 1964 (wing)

Francis, N P J (Blackrock
College, London Irish)
Born 17 March 1964
10 caps 1989-93 (lock)

Galwey, M J (Shannon)
Born 8 October 1966
8 caps 1991-93 (lock)

Gaston, J T (Dublin U)
Born 28 November 1930
7 caps 1954-56 (wing)

Gavin, T J
(Moseley, London Irish)
Born 28 March 1922
2 caps 1949 (centre)

Geoghegan, S P
(London Irish)
Born 1 September 1968
11 caps 1991-93 (wing)

Gibson, C M H
(Cambridge U, NIFC)
Born 3 December 1942
56 caps 1964-79
(stand-off, centre, wing)

Gibson, M E
(Lansdowne, London Irish)
Born 3 March 1954
8 caps 1979-88 (No 8, lock)

Gilpin, F G
(Queen's U Belfast)
Born 20 October 1940
3 caps 1962
(stand-off, full-back)

Glass, D C
(Belfast Collegians)
Born 15 May 1934
3 caps 1958-61 (centre, wing)

Glennon, B T (Lansdowne)
Born 17 April 1967
1 cap 1993 (centre)

Glennon, J J (Skerries)
Born 7 July 1953
5 caps 1980-87 (lock)

Godfrey, R P (UC Dublin)
Born 16 September 1931
2 caps 1954 (centre)

Goodall, K G
(City of Derry, Newcastle U)
Born 23 February 1947
15 caps 1967-70 (No 8)

Grace, T O (UC Dublin,
St Mary's College)
Born 24 October 1948
20 caps 1972-78 (wing)

Grant, E L (CIYMS)
Born 13 April 1946
4 caps 1971 (wing)

Gregg, R J
(Queen's U Belfast)
Born 28 November 1930
7 caps 1953-54 (full-back)

Griffin, C S (London Irish)
2 caps 1951 (wing)

Griffin, J L (Wanderers)
Born 14 September 1922
2 caps 1949 (lock)

Grimshaw, C
(Queen's U Belfast)
Born 20 March 1947
1 cap 1969 (scrum-half)

Guerin, B N (Galwegians)
Born 2 January 1930
1 cap 1956 (lock)

Hakin, R F (CIYMS)
Born 3 September 1950
5 caps 1976-77 (lock)

Halpin, G F
(Wanderers, London Irish)
Born 14 February 1966
4 caps 1990-92 (prop)

Hamilton, G F (NIFC)
Born 13 May 1964
4 caps 1990-91 (flanker)

Harbison, H T
(Bective Rangers)
Born 19 August 1957
7 caps 1984-87 (hooker)

Hardy, G G
(Bective Rangers)
Born 29 March 1937;
died 27 October 1963
1 cap 1962 (stand-off)

Harper, J (Instonians)
Born 15 August 1921
3 caps 1947 (centre)

Haycock, P P
(Terenure College)
Born 19 May 1958
1 cap 1989 (wing)

Henderson, N J
(Queen's U Belfast, NIFC)
Born 10 August 1928
37 caps 1949-59
(centre, full-back)

Hewitt, D (Queen's U Belfast,
Instonians)
Born 9 September 1939
17 caps 1958-65 (centre)

Hewitt, W J (Instonians)
Born 6 June 1928
3 caps 1954-59
(stand-off, wing)

Hickie, D J
(St Mary's College)
Born 12 April 1943
6 caps 1971-72 (No 8)

Higgins, J A D (Civil Service)
Born 28 October 1920
5 caps 1947-48 (full back)

Hillary, M F (UC Dublln)
Born 6 June 1925
1 cap 1952 (wing)

Hingerty, D J (UC Dublin)
Born 11 January 1920
4 caps 1947 (flanker)

Hipwell, M L
(Terenure College)
Born 15 July 1940
10 caps 1962-71 (flanker)

Hogan, P (Garryowen)
Born 29 June 1968
1 cap 1992 (flanker)

Holland, J J (Wanderers)
Born 24 November 1955
1 cap 1986 (lock)

Hooks, K J (Queen's U
Belfast, Ards, Bangor)
Born 1 January 1960
4 caps 1981-91 (wing)

Houston, K J
(Oxford U, London Irish)
Born 20 July 1941
4 caps 1964-65 (wing, centre)

Hunter, L M (Civil Service)
Born 10 October 1943
1 cap 1968 (centre)

Hunter, W R (CIYMS)
Born 3 April 1938
10 caps 1962-66
(centre, wing)

Hutton, S A (Malone)
Born 1940
3 caps 1967 (prop)

Irwin, D G (Queen's U
Belfast, Instonians)
Born 1 February 1959
19 caps 1980-90 (centre)

Johns, P S (Dungannon)
Born 19 February 1968
4 caps 1993 (lock)

Kavanagh, J R
(UC Dublin, Wanderers)
Born 21 January 1931
31 caps 1953-62
(No 8, flanker)

Kavanagh, P J
(UC Dublin, Wanderers)
Born 2 September 1929
2 caps 1952-55 (flanker)

Keane, M I (Lansdowne)
Born 27 July 1948
44 caps 1974-84 (lock)

Kearney, R K (Wanderers)
Born 5 March 1957
3 caps 1982-86 (flanker)

Keeffe, E (Sunday's Well)
Born 16 March 1919

5 caps 1947-48 (lock)

Kelly, J C (UC Dublin)
Born 8 April 1940
10 caps 1962-64 (scrum-half)

Kelly, S (Lansdowne)
Born 15 March 1931
5 caps 1954-60 (stand-off)

Kennedy, A G
(Belfast Collegians)
Born 4 November 1932
1 cap 1956 (No 8)

Kennedy, A P (London Irish)
Born 30 January 1957
2 caps 1986 (prop)

Kennedy, K W
(Queen's U Belfast, CIYMS, London Irish)
Born 10 May 1941
36 caps 1965-75 (hooker)

Kennedy, T J (St Mary's College)
Born 19 October 1954
7 caps 1979-80 (wing)

Keogh. F S (Bective Rangers)
Born 28 June 1939
2 caps 1964 (full-back)

Keyes, R P
(Cork Constitution)
Born 1 August 1961
4 caps 1986-92 (stand-off)

Kiely, M D (Lansdowne)
Born 1934
5 caps 1962-63 (flanker)

Kiernan, M J
(Dolphin, Lansdowne)
Born 17 January 1961
35 caps 1982-91 (centre)

Kiernan, T J (UC Cork, Cork Constitution)
Born 7 January 1939
44 caps 1960-73 (full-back)

Kingston, T J (Dolphin)
Born 19 September 1963
9 caps 1988-93 (hooker)

Kyle, J W
(Queen's U Belfast, NIFC)
Born 10 January 1926
42 caps 1947-58 (stand-off)

Lamont, R A (Instonians)
Born 18 November 1941
10 caps 1965-70 (No 8)

Lane, M F (UC Cork)
Born 3 April 1926
16 caps 1947-53 (wing)

Lane, P (Old Crescent)
Born 7 September 1934
1 cap 1964 (hooker)

Lavery, P (London Irish)
Born 1949
2 caps 1974-76 (wing, centre)

Lawler, P J (Clontarf)
Born 21 March 1928
10 caps 1951-56 (lock)

Lawlor, P J
(Bective Rangers)
Born 2 July 1965
1 cap 1993 (flanker).

Leahy, M W (UC Cork)
Born 6 June 1935
1 cap 1964 (lock)

Lenihan, D G (UC Cork, Cork Constitution)
Born 12 September 1959
36 caps 1982-92 (lock)

Lydon, C T J (Galwegians)
Born 31 August 1933
1 cap 1956 (flanker)

Ireland at Twickenham in 1982. The Triple Crown winners and champions line u HP MacNeill, PA Orr, SO Campbell. Seated: RJM McGrath, PM Dean, CF Fitzge

Lynch, J F
(St Mary's College)
Born 22 September 1942
13 caps 1971-74 (prop)

Lynch, L (Lansdowne)
Born 7 May 1930
1 cap 1956 (lock)

MacHale, S (Lansdowne)
Born 6 April 1936
11 caps 1965-67 (prop)

MacNeill, H P (Dublin U,
Oxford U, Blackrock
College, London Irish)

ows. Back: JF Slattery, TM Ringland, GAJ McLoughlin, JB O'Driscoll, DG Lenihan, MI Keane, WP Duggan, ptain), Mr JJ Moore (President IRFU), MC Finn, MJ Kiernan.

Born 16 September 1958
29 caps 1981-88 (full-back)

MacSweeney, D A (Blackrock College)
Born 26 January 1936
1 cap 1955 (flanker)

Madden, M N
(Sunday's Well)
Born 24 November 1929
3 caps 1955 (lock)

Malone, N G (Oxford U)
Born 30 April 1971
2 caps 1993 (stand-off)

Mannion, N P (Corinthians, Lansdowne, Wanderers)
Born 12 January 1963
9 caps 1989-93 (No 8)

Marshall, B D E
(Queen's U Belfast)
Born 25 July 1940
1 cap 1963 (full-back)

Matthews, P M
(Ards, Wanderers)
Born 24 January 1960
25 caps 1985-92 (flanker)

Mattsson, J (Wanderers)
Born 16 July 1917
1 cap 1948 (full-back)

Mays, K M A (UC Dublin)
Born 9 August 1949
3 caps 1973 (lock)

McAleese, D R (Ballymena)
Born 14 September 1964
1 cap 1992 (stand-off)

McBride, W D (Malone)
Born 9 September 1964
9 caps 1988-93 (flanker)

McBride, W J (Ballymena)
Born 6 June 1940
53 caps 1962-75 (lock)

McCall, B W (London Irish)
Born 17 June 1959
3 caps 1985-86 (No 8, lock)

McCallan, B (Ballymena)
Born 18 July 1936
2 caps 1960 (hooker)

McCarten, R J
(London Irish)
Born 6 August 1935
3 caps 1961 (wing)

McCarthy, J S (Dolphin)
Born 30 January 1926
26 caps 1948-55 (flanker)

McCarthy P D
(Cork Constitution)
Born 27 August 1963
1 cap 1993 (prop)

McCombe, W McM
(Dublin U, Bangor)
Born 6 February 1949
5 caps 1968-75 (stand-off)

McConnell, A A McG
(Collegians)
Born 29 October 1919
6 caps 1948-49 (prop)

McCoy, J J (Dungannon, Bangor, Ballymena)
Born 28 June 1958
10 caps 1984-89 (prop)

McCracken, H L (NIFC)
Born 8 July 1927
1 cap 1954 (scrum-half)

McDermott, S J
(London Irish)
Born 28 March 1932
2 caps 1955 (scrum-half)

McDonald, J P (Malone)
Born 9 April 1960
2 caps 1990 (hooker)

McGann, B J (Lansdowne)
Born 28 May 1948
21 caps 1969-76 (stand-off)

McGrath, D G (UC Dublin, Cork Constitution)
Born 3 May 1960
1 cap 1984 (flanker)

McGrath, P J (UC Cork)
Born 20 August 1941
7 caps 1965-66 (wing)

McGrath, R J M
(Wanderers)
Born 18 July 1951
13 caps 1977-84 (scrum-half)

McGrath, T (Garryowen)
Born 3 October 1933;
died 23 September 1978
6 caps 1956-60 (No 8)

McGuire, E P (UC Galway)
Born 28 June 1939
7 caps 1963-64 (flanker)

McIlrath, J A (Ballymena)
Born 10 March 1946
3 caps 1976-77 (centre)

McKay, J W
(Queen's U, Belfast)
Born 12 July 1921
21 caps 1947-52 (flanker)

McKee, W D (NIFC)
Born 27 August 1923;
died 28 January 1982
10 caps 1948-50 (centre)

McKelvey, J M
(Queen's U, Belfast)
Born 2 April 1933
2 caps 1956 (full-back)

McKibbin, A R
(Instonians, London Irish)
Born 13 January 1958
13 caps 1977-80 (centre)

McKibbin, C H (Instonians)
Born 24 June 1948
1 cap 1976 (centre)

McKibbin, D (Instonians)
Born 6 March 1927
8 caps 1950-51 (prop, lock)

McKinney, S A (Dungannon)
Born 20 November 1946
20 caps 1972-78 (flanker)

McLennan, A C (Wanderers)
Born 8 February 1951
15 caps 1977-81 (wing)

McLoughlin, G A J
(Shannon)
Born 11 June 1952
14 caps 1979-84 (prop)

McLoughlin, R J
(UC Dublin, Blackrock College, Gosforth)
Born 24 August 1939
34 caps 1962-75 (prop)

McMaster, A W (Ballymena)
Born 2 December 1945
13 caps 1972-76 (wing)

McMorrow, A (Garryowen)
Born 6 November 1927
1 cap 1951 (full-back)

McNaughton, P P
(Greystones)
Born 18 November 1952
13 caps 1978-81 (centre)

Millar, S (Ballymena)
Born 23 May 1934
33 caps 1958-70 (prop)

Millar, W H J
(Queen's U Belfast)
Born 9 January 1924
5 caps 1951-52 (wing)

Milliken, R A (Bangor)
Born 2 September 1950
12 caps 1973-75 (centre)

Moffett, J W (Ballymena)
Born 30 April 1937
2 caps 1961 (scrum-half)

Molloy, M G
(UC Galway, London Irish)
Born 27 September 1944
23 caps 1966-73 (lock)

Moloney, J J
(St Mary's College)
Born 27 August 1949
21 caps 1972-80 (scrum-half)

Moloney, L A (Garryowen)
Born 14 June 1951
3 caps 1976-78 (full-back)

Molony, J U (UC Dublin)
Born 21 October 1924
1 cap 1950 (lock)

Monteith, J D E
(Queen's U Belfast)
Born 24 August 1922;
died 26 June 1992
3 caps 1947 (centre)

Moore, T A P (Highfield)
Born 29 April 1945
8 caps 1973-74 (No 8)

Moroney, J C M
(Garryowen)
Born 28 October 1945
5 caps 1968-69 (wing)

Moroney, R J M
(Lansdowne)
Born 3 October 1957
3 caps 1984-85 (centre)

Moroney, T A (UC Dublin)
Born 27 July 1941
2 caps 1964-67 (prop)

Morrow, R D (Bangor)
Born 24 August 1956
3 caps 1986 (flanker)

Mortell, M P
(Bective Rangers, Dolphin)
Born 13 March 1930
8 caps 1953-54 (wing)

Moylett, M M F (Shannon)
Born 29 August 1960
1 cap 1988 (lock)

Mulcahy, W A (UC Dublin, Bective Rangers, Bohemians)
Born 7 January 1935
30 caps 1958-65 (lock)

Mullan, B (Clontarf)
Died 25 September 1986
8 caps 1947-48 (wing)

Mullen, K D (Old Belvedere)
Born 26 November 1926
23 caps 1947-52 (hooker)

Mulligan, A A (Wanderers)
Born 4 February 1936
19 caps 1956-61 (scrum-half)

Mullin, B J (Dublin U, Oxford U, Blackrock College, London Irish)
Born 30 October 1963
29 caps 1985-92 (centre)

Murphy, C J (Lansdowne)
Born 19 September 1914
2 caps 1947 (full-back)

Murphy, J G M W
(London Irish)
Born 20 August 1926
4 caps 1952-58 (full-back)

Murphy, J J (Greystones)
Born 27 August 1957
2 caps 1982-84
(centre, full-back)

Murphy, K J
(Cork Constitution)
Born 21 July 1966
9 caps 1990-92 (full-back)

Murphy, N A A
(Cork Constitution)
Born 22 February 1937
36 caps 1958-69 (flanker)

Murphy-O'Connor, J C
(Bective Rangers)
Born 6 June 1925
1 cap 1954 (No 8)

Murray, J B (UC Dublin)
Born 3 April 1942
1 cap 1963 (centre)

Murtagh, C W (Portadown)
Born 30 August 1949
1 cap 1977 (lock)

Neely, M R (Collegians)
Born 24 December 1919
4 caps 1947 (prop)

Nelson, J E (Malone)
Born 16 September 1921
15 caps 1948-54 (lock)

Nesdale, T J (Garryowen)
Born 18 August 1933
1 cap 1961 (flanker)

Norton, G W
(Bective Rangers)
Born 1 April 1920
11 caps 1949-51 (full-back)

Notley, J R (Wanderers)
Born 25 June 1926
2 caps 1952

(full-back, centre)

O'Brien, B A P (Shannon)
Born 5 July 1939
3 caps 1968 (centre)

O'Brien, D J (London Irish, Cardiff, Old Belvedere)
Born 22 May 1919
19 caps 1948-52 (No 8)

O'Brien, K A (Broughton Park)
Born 5 June 1955
1 cap 1980 (full-back)

O'Callaghan, M P (Sunday's Well)
Born 1936
3 caps 1962-64 (prop)

O'Callaghan, P (Dolphin)
Born 25 March 1946
17 caps 1967-76 (prop)

O'Connell, W J (Lansdowne)
Born 22 April 1930
1 cap 1955 (lock)

O'Connor, H S (Dublin U)
Born 2 September 1933
4 caps 1957 (flanker)

O'Donnell, R C (St Mary's College)
Born 16 August 1956
3 caps 1980 (full-back)

O'Donoghue, P J (Bective Rangers)
Born 22 November 1931
10 caps 1955-58 (prop)

O'Driscoll, B J (Manchester)
Born 18 September 1943
4 caps 1971 (full-back)

O'Driscoll, J B (London Irish, Manchester)
Born 26 November 1953
21 caps 1978-84 (flanker)

O'Flanagan, M (Lansdowne)
Born 29 September 1922
1 cap 1948 (centre)

O'Hanlon, B R (Dolphin)
Born 23 October 1924
12 caps 1947-50 (wing)

O'Hara, P T (Sunday's Well, Cork Constitution)
Born 4 August 1961
10 caps 1989-93 (flanker)

O'Leary, A F (Cork Constitution)
Born 30 November 1929
3 caps 1952 (lock)

O'Meara, J A (UC Cork, Dolphin)
Born 26 June 1929
20 caps 1951-58 (scrum-half)

O'Neill, W A (UC Dublin, Wanderers)
Born 15 November 1928;
died 15 January 1985
5 caps 1952-53 (prop)

O'Reilly, A J F (Old Belvedere, Leicester)
Born 7 May 1936
27 caps 1955-70
(centre, wing)

Orr, P A (Old Wesley)
Born 14 December 1950
46 caps 1976-87 (prop)

O'Sullivan, P J A (Galwegians)
Born 2 June 1933
13 caps 1957-63 (No 8)

Patterson, C S (Instonians)
Born 3 March 1955
8 caps 1979-80 (scrum-half)

Pedlow, A C (CIYMS)
Born 20 January 1934
27 caps 1953-63
(centre, wing)

Phipps, G C (Army)
Born 2 November 1927
5 caps 1950-52
(centre, wing)

Popplewell, N J (Greystones)
Born 6 April 1964
8 caps 1992-93 (prop)

Quinlan, S V J (Blackrock College)
Born 13 October 1934
4 caps 1956-58 (wing)

Quinn, B T (Old Belvedere)
Born 1 August 1919
1 cap 1947 (wing)

Quinn, F P (Old Belvedere)
Born 5 September 1954
3 caps 1981 (wing)

Quinn, K J (Old Belvedere)
Born 14 March 1923
4 caps 1947-53 (centre)

Quinn, M A M (Lansdowne)
Born 31 May 1952
7 caps 1973-77 (stand-off)

Quirke, J M T (Blackrock College)
Born 26 June 1944
3 caps 1962-68 (scrum-half)

Rea, H H (Edinburgh U)
Born 1946
1 cap 1969 (centre)

Reid, P J (Garryowen)
Born 17 March 1924
3 caps 1948 (centre)

Reid, T E (Garryowen)
Born 3 March 1926
12 caps 1953-57 (lock)

Reidy, G F (Dolphin, Lansdowne)
Born 13 May 1926
5 caps 1953-54 (flanker)

Rigney, B J (Greystones)
Born 22 September 1963
5 caps 1991-92 (lock)

Ringland, T M (Queen's U Belfast, Ballymena)
Born 13 November 1959
27 caps 1981-88 (wing)

Ritchie, J S (London Irish)
Born 11 December 1926
2 caps 1956 (flanker)

Robbie, J C (Dublin U, Greystones)
Born 17 November 1955
7 caps 1976-81 (scrum-half)

Robinson, B F (Ballymena, London Irish)
Born 20 March 1966
10 caps 1991-93 (No 8)

Roche, R E (UC Galway)
Born 22 February 1930
4 caps 1955-57 (wing)

Roe, R (Lansdowne)
Born 11 November 1928
21 caps 1952-57 (hooker)

Ross, G R P (CIYMS)
Born 1 November 1925
1 cap 1955 (No 8)

Russell, P (Instonians)
Born 22 February 1962
1 cap 1990 (stand-off)

Saunders R (London Irish)
Born 5 August 1968
5 caps 1991-92 (scrum-half)

Scott, D (Malone)
Born 19 November 1933
2 caps 1961-62 (flanker)

Scott, R D (Queen's U Belfast)
Born 2 October 1941
5 caps 1967-68 (wing)

Sexton, J F (Dublin U, Lansdowne)
Born 27 June 1963
1 cap 1989 (wing)

Sexton, W J (Garryowen)
Born 21 July 1959
1 cap 1988 (flanker)

Sherry, B F (Terenure College)
Born 7 June 1943
4 caps 1967-68 (scrum-half)

Sherry, M J A (Lansdowne)
Born 21 June 1951
2 caps 1975 (flanker)

Slattery, J F (UC Dublin, Blackrock College)
Born 12 February 1949
49 caps 1970-84 (flanker)

Smith, B A (Oxford U, Leicester)
Born 9 September 1966
7 caps 1990-91 (stand-off)

Smith, J H (London Irish)
Born 27 July 1926
10 caps 1951-54 (prop)

Smith, S J (Ballymena)
Born 18 July 1959
14 caps 1989-93 (hooker)

Spillane, B J (Bohemians)
Born 26 January 1960
10 caps 1985-89 (No 8)

Spring, D E (Dublin U)
Born 23 August 1956
6 caps 1978-81 (lock, No 8)

Spring, R M (Lansdowne)
Born 29 August 1950
3 caps 1979 (full-back)

Staples, J E (London Irish)
Born 20 October 1965
5 caps 1991-92 (full-back)

Steele, H W (Ballymena)
Born 4 September 1948
8 caps 1976-79
(No 8, flanker, lock)

Stevenson, J B (Instonians)
Born 28 August 1929
4 caps 1958 (lock)

Strathdee, E (Queen's U Belfast)
Born 26 May 1921;
died 17 July 1971
8 caps 1947-49 (scrum-half)

Tector, W R (Wanderers)
Born 16 April 1929
3 caps 1955 (full-back)

Thompson, R H (Instonians)
Born 5 May 1931
9 caps 1952-56 (lock, No 8)

Tucker, C C (Shannon)
Born 22 September 1952
3 caps 1979-80 (flanker)

Turley, P N (Blackrock College)
Born 13 December 1936
1 cap 1962 (flanker)

Uprichard, R J H (Harlequins, RAF)
Born 31 December 1922
2 caps 1950 (centre)

Waldron, O C (Oxford U, London Irish)
Born 11 July 1943
2 caps 1966 (prop)

Wall, H (Dolphin)
Born 1 December 1935
2 caps 1965 (No 8)

Wallace, R M (Garryowen)
Born 16 January 1968
8 caps 1992-93 (wing)

Walsh, J C (UC Cork, Sunday's Well)
Born 3 November 1938;
died 28 September 1992
21 caps 1960-67 (centre)

Ward, A J P (Garryowen, St Mary's College, Greystones)
Born 8 October 1954
15 caps 1978-86 (stand-off)

Whelan, P C (Garryowen)
Born 2 May 1950
17 caps 1975-81 (hooker)

Whittle, D (Bangor)
Born 16 November 1960
1 cap 1988 (flanker)

Wilkinson, C R (Malone)
Born 4 April 1961
1 cap 1993 (full-back)

Wilson, F (CIYMS)
Born 1 September 1952
3 caps 1977 (full-back)

Wood, B G M (Garryowen)
Born 20 June 1931;
died 18 May 1982
26 caps 1954-61 (prop)

Young, R M (Collegians)
Born 29 June 1943
23 caps 1965-71 (scrum-half)

WALES

Ackerman, R A
(Newport, London Welsh)
Born 2 March 1961
17 caps 1981-85 (wing, centre)

Allen, A G (Newbridge)
Born 5 April 1967
3 caps 1990 (lock)

Anthony, L (Neath)
Born 21 November 1921
3 caps 1948 (prop)

Arnold, P (Swansea)
Born 28 April 1968
5 caps 1991-93 (lock)

Ashton, C (Aberavon)
Born 17 December 1932
7 caps 1959-61 (stand-off)

Bateman, A G (Neath)
Born 6 March 1965
2 caps 1990 (centre)

Bebb, D I E
(Carmarthen T C, Swansea)
Born 7 August 1938
30 caps 1959-67 (wing)

Beckingham, G T (Cardiff)
Born 29 July 1924
3 caps 1953-58 (hooker)

Bennett, P (Llanelli)
Born 24 October 1948
26 caps 1969-78 (wing, centre, full-back, stand-off)

Bergiers, R T E (Cardiff Coll of Ed, Llanelli)
Born 11 November 1950
9 caps 1972-75 (centre)

Bevan, G W (Llanelli)
Born 15 August 1914
1 cap 1947 (prop)

Bevan, J C
(Cardiff Coll of Ed, Cardiff)
Born 28 October 1950
9 caps 1971-73 (wing)

Bevan, J D (Aberavon)
Born 12 March 1948;
died 5 June 1986
3 caps 1975 (stand-off)

Bidgood, R A (Newport)
Born 15 September 1964
1 cap 1992 (centre)

Blackmore, S W (Cardiff)
Born 3 March 1962
1 cap 1987 (prop)

Blakemore, R E (Newport)
Born 1 September 1924
1 cap 1947 (prop)

Blyth, W R (Swansea)
Born 2 April 1950
6 caps 1974-80 (full-back)

Blythe, L G (Swansea)
Born 20 November 1920
2 caps 1952 (flanker)

Bowen, B
(S Wales Police, Swansea)
Born 16 July 1961
14 caps 1984-89
(centre, stand-off)

Brace, D O
(Llanelli, Oxford U)
Born 16 November 1932
9 caps 1956-61 (scrum-half)

Braddock, K J (Newbridge)
Born 28 August 1938
2 caps 1967 (flanker)

Bradshaw, K (Bridgend)
Born 7 April 1939
8 caps 1964-66 (centre)

Brewer, T J (Newport)
Born 16 August 1930
3 caps 1950-55 (wing)

Bridges, C J (Neath)
Born 31 August 1968
3 caps 1991 (scrum-half)

Britton, G R (Newport)
Born 10 September 1939
1 cap 1961 (centre)

Brown, M A (Pontypool)
Born 18 December 1958
2 caps 1986 (flanker)

Bryant, D J (Bridgend)
Born 21 February 1967
4 caps 1989 (flanker)

Buchanan, D A (Llanelli)
Born 30 June 1955
1 cap 1988 (prop)

Burcher, D H (Newport)
Born 26 October 1950
4 caps 1977 (centre)

Burgess, R C (Ebbw Vale)
Born 25 November 1950
9 caps 1977-82 (flanker)

Burnett, R (Newport)
Born 6 October 1926
1 cap 1953 (stand-off)

Butler, E T (Pontypool)
Born 8 May 1957
13 caps 1980-84 (No 8)

Cale, W R (Pontypool)
Born 18 July 1922
7 caps 1949-50 (flanker)

Carter, A J (Newport)
Born 13 December 1964
2 caps 1991 (flanker)

Cleaver, W B (Cardiff)
Born 15 September 1921
13 caps 1947-50
(centre, stand-off, full-back)

Clegg, B G (Swansea)
Born 30 October 1951
1 cap 1979 (lock)

Clement, A (Swansea)
Born 8 February 1967
10 caps 1988-93
(full-back, wing, stand-off)

Cobner, T J (Pontypool)
Born 10 January 1946
17 caps 1974-78 (flanker)

Coleman, E O (Newport)
Born 3 November 1917
3 caps 1949 (prop)

Coles, F G (Pontypool)
Born 14 September 1937
3 caps 1960 (wing)

Collins, J E (Aberavon)
Born 16 January 1931
9 caps 1958-61 (wing).

Collins, R G
(S Wales Police, Cardiff)
Born 2 March 1962
9 caps 1987-90 (flanker)

Cook, T (Cardiff)
Born 27 June 1927
2 caps 1949 (wing)

Copsey, A H (Llanelli)
Born 25 January 1965
7 caps 1992-93 (lock)

Coslett, T K (Aberavon)
Born 14 January 1942
3 caps 1962 (full-back)

Cresswell, B R (Newport)
Born 9 November 1934
4 caps 1960 (flanker)

Cunningham, L J (Aberavon)
Born 3 January 1931
12 caps 1960-64 (prop)

Dacey, M (Swansea)
Born 12 July 1960
9 caps 1983-87
(stand-off, full-back)

Daniel, L T D (Newport)
Born 5 March 1942
1 cap 1970 (wing)

Daniels, P C T (Cardiff)
Born 15 May 1957
1 cap 1982 (centre)

David, T
(Llanelli, Pontypridd)
Born 2 April 1948
3 caps 1973-76 (flanker)

Davidge, G D (Newport)
Born 31 December 1933
8 caps 1959-61

Davies, C (Cardiff)
Born 12 December 1919;
died 28 January 1967
15 caps 1947-51 (prop)

Davies, C (Llanelli)
Born 17 April 1964
3 caps 1989 (wing)

Davies, C A H
(Llanelli, Cardiff)
Born 21 November 1936
5 caps 1957-61 (centre)

Davies, C H
(Swansea, Llanelli)
Born 25 December 1916;
died 5 November 1987
4 caps 1947 (full-back)

Davies, C L (Cardiff)
Born 30 December 1929
3 caps 1956 (wing)

Davies, D B (Llanelli)
Born 7 July 1941
3 caps 1962-63 (centre)

Davies, D J (Neath)
Born 20 February 1941;
died 16 April 1969
1 cap 1962 (flanker)

Davies, D M
(Somerset Police)
Born 2 May 1925
15 caps 1950-54 (hooker)

Davies, E P (Aberavon)
Born 15 January 1922
1 cap 1948 (prop)

Davies, G
(Cambridge U, Pontypridd)
Born 24 August 1927;
died 7 November 1976
10 caps 1947-51 (stand-off)

Davies, H (Bridgend)
Born 6 June 1959
4 caps 1984 (full-back)

Davies, H J
(Cambridge U, Aberavon)
Born 21 November 1936
2 caps 1959 (centre)

Davies, J (Neath, Llanelli)
Born 24 October 1962
13 caps 1985-88 (stand-off)

Davies, J D (Neath)
Born 1 February 1969
3 caps 1991-93 (prop)

Davies, L (Bridgend)
Born 2 February 1940
3 caps 1966 (wing)

Davies, L M (Llanelli)
Born 29 December 1930;
died 23 September 1957
3 caps 1954-55 (flanker)

Davies, M (Swansea)
Born 9 July 1958
1 cap 1982 (flanker)

Davies, N G (London Welsh)
Born 29 November 1927
1 cap 1955 (flanker)

Davies, N G (Llanelli)
Born 29 March 1965
3 caps 1989-93 (centre)

Davies, P T (Llanelli)
Born 19 October 1963
18 caps 1985-93
(No 8, lock, flanker)

Davies, R H
(Oxford U, London Welsh)
Born 12 January 1934
5 caps 1957-62 (flanker)

Davies, S (Swansea)

Born 2 September 1965
7 caps 1992-93 (No 8)

Davies, T G R
(Cardiff, London Welsh)
Born 7 February 1945
38 caps 1967-78
(centre, wing)

Davies, T J (Devonport Services, Swansea, Llanelli)
Born 24 September 1933
19 caps 1953-61 (full-back)

Davies, T M
(London Welsh, Swansea)
Born 9 December 1946
31 caps 1969-76 (No 8)

Davies, W G (Cardiff)
Born 29 September 1955
16 caps 1979-85 (stand-off)

Davis, C E (Newbridge)
Born 17 September 1949
2 caps 1981 (lock)

Dawes, S J (London Welsh)
Born 29 June 1940
17 caps 1964-71 (centre)

Delaney, L (Llanelli)
Born 8 May 1956
7 caps 1989-92 (prop)

Devereux, D B (Neath)
Born 18 October 1932
2 caps 1958 (prop)

Devereux, J A (S Glamorgan Inst, Bridgend)
Born 30 March 1966
10 caps 1986-89 (centre)

Donovan, A J (Swansea)
Born 5 October 1955
3 caps 1981-82 (centre)

Donovan, R E
(S Wales Police)
Born 20 January 1963
1 cap 1983 (wing)

Douglas, M H J (Llanelli)
Born 10 December 1960
3 caps 1984 (scrum-half)

Edmunds, D A (Neath)
Born 8 October 1961
1 cap 1990 (wing)

Edwards, A B
(London Welsh, Army)
Born 7 October 1927;
died 10 September 1984
2 caps 1955 (full-back)

Edwards, B O (Newport)
Born 29 May 1923;
died 2 September 1978
1 cap 1951 (lock)

Edwards, G O (Cardiff, Cardiff Coll of Ed)
Born 12 July 1947
45 caps 1967-78 (scrum-half)

Eidman, I H (Cardiff)
Born 31 October 1956
10 caps 1983-86 (prop)

Emyr, A (see Jones, A E)

Evans, C (Pontypool)
Born 20 November 1936;
died 23 November 1992
1 cap 1960 (scrum-half)

Evans, D W
(Oxford U, Cardiff)
Born 1 November 1965
6 caps 1989-90
(centre, stand-off)

Evans, G (Cardiff)
Born 17 August 1918
11 caps 1947-49 (flanker)

Evans, G (Maesteg)
Born 6 September 1957
8 caps 1981-83
(wing, full-back, centre)

Evans, G L (Newport)
Born 2 November 1952
2 caps 1977-78 (wing)

Evans, I C (Llanelli)
Born 21 March 1964
23 caps 1987-93 (wing)

Evans, J D (Cardiff)
Born 30 June 1926;
died 25 March 1989
2 caps 1958 (prop)

Evans, P D (Llanelli)
Born 20 June 1928
2 caps 1951 (flanker)

Evans, R (Bridgend)
Born 6 November 1941
3 caps 1963 (centre)

Evans, R L (Llanelli)
Born 23 June 1960
4 caps 1993 (prop)

Evans, R T (Newport)
Born 16 February 1921
10 caps 1947-51 (flanker)

Evans, S (Swansea, Neath)
Born 14 June 1963
4 caps 1985-87 (prop)

Evans, T G (London Welsh)
Born 1 May 1942
6 caps 1970-72 (lock)

Evans, T P (Swansea)
Born 26 November 1947
9 caps 1975-77 (flanker)

Evans, V (Neath)
Born 14 July 1919
3 caps 1954 (full-back)

Evans, W J (Pontypool)
Born 12 May 1914
1 cap 1947 (prop)

Evans, W R (Bridgend)
Born 19 December 1934
11 caps 1958-62 (lock)

Faulkner, A G (Pontypool)
Born 27 February 1941
15 caps 1975-79 (prop)

Faull, J (Swansea)
Born 30 June 1933
11 caps 1957-60 (No 8, lock)

Fenwick, S P (Bridgend)
Born 23 July 1951
25 caps 1975-81 (centre)

Finlayson, A A J (Cardiff)
Born 18 March 1948
3 caps 1974 (centre)

Ford, I R (Newport)
Born 6 June 1929
2 caps 1959 (lock)

Ford, S P (Cardiff)
Born 15 August 1965
4 caps 1990-91 (wing)

Forward, A
(Pontypool, Mon Police)
Born 4 June 1921
5 caps 1951-52 (flanker)

Francis, P W (Maesteg)
Born 9 July 1957
1 cap 1987 (prop)

Gale, N R (Swansea, Llanelli)
Born 24 July 1939
18 caps 1960-1968 (hooker)

Gallacher, I S (Llanelli)
Born 22 May 1946
1 cap 1970 (lock)

George, G M (Newport)
30 September 1964
2 caps 1991 (flanker)

Gibbs, I S (Neath, Swansea)
Born 23 January 1971
12 caps 1991-93 (centre)

Gore, W (Newbridge)
Born 19 November 1919
3 caps 1947 (hooker)

Gravell, R W R (Llanelli)
Born 12 September 1951
19 caps 1975-82 (centre)

Gray, A J (London Welsh)
Born 14 June 1942
2 caps 1968 (flanker)

Greenslade, D (Newport)
Born 11 January 1933
1 cap 1962 (prop)

Griffiths, C R (Llanelli)
Born 2 April 1954
1 cap 1979 (full-back)

Griffiths, G M (Cardiff)
Born 27 November 1931
11 caps 1953-57
(wing, centre)

Griffiths, J L (Llanelli)
Born 23 August 1964
1 cap 1989 (scrum-half)

Griffiths, M
(Bridgend, Cardiff)
Born 18 March 1962
12 caps 1989-92 (prop)

Gwilliam, J A
(Cambridge U, Newport)
Born 28 February 1923
20 caps 1948-54 (lock, No 8)

Hadley, A M (Cardiff)
Born 1 March 1963
16 caps 1984-88 (wing)

Hall, I (Aberavon)
Born 4 November 1946
6 caps 1970-74 (wing, centre)

Hall, M R (Cambridge U, Bridgend, Cardiff)
Born 13 October 1965
14 caps 1989-93
(wing, centre)

Harris, D J E
(Pontypridd, Cardiff)
Born 27 May 1937
7 caps 1959-61 (lock)

Hayward, D J (Newbridge)
Born 30 June 1925
14 caps 1949-52 (lock, prop)

Hayward, D J (Cardiff)
Born 1 March 1934
4 caps 1963-64 (flanker)

Hodgson, G T R (Neath)
Born 1 December 1936
13 caps 1962-67 (full-back)

Holmes, T D (Cardiff)
Born 10 March 1957
20 caps 1979-85 (scrum-half)

Hopkins, K
(Cardiff, Swansea)
Born 29 September 1961
4 caps 1985-87 (centre)

Hopkins, R (Maesteg)
Born 8 July 1946
1 cap 1970 (scrum-half)

Howells, W G (Llanelli)
Born 29 October 1929
4 caps 1957 (wing)

Hughes, D (Newbridge)
Born 3 July 1941
3 caps 1970 (flanker)

Hughes, K (Cambridge U, London Welsh)
Born 15 December 1949
2 caps 1970-74 (wing, centre)

Hullin, W G (Cardiff)
Born 2 January 1942
1 cap 1967 (scrum-half)

Hurrell, R J (Newport)
Born 17 August 1933
1 cap 1959 (centre)

James, C R (Llanelli)
Born 2 November 1929;
died 10 January 1983
1 cap 1958 (centre)

James, D M (Cardiff)
Born 28 June 1913
4 caps 1948 (hooker)

James, J B (Bridgend)
Born 4 September 1938
1 cap 1968 (prop)

James, W J (Aberavon)
Born 18 July 1956
16 caps 1983-87 (hooker)

Jarrett, K S (Newport)
Born 18 May 1948
7 caps 1967-69
(full-back, centre)

Jenkins, G R (Swansea)
Born 18 August 1966
4 caps 1992 (hooker)

Jenkins, L H
(Monmouth TC, Newport)
Born 1 July 1931
5 caps 1954-56 (No 8, lock)

Jenkins, N R (Pontypridd)
Born 8 July 1971
12 caps 1991-93
(stand-off, centre)

John, B (Llanelli, Cardiff)
Born 6 January 1945

19 caps 1967-72 (stand-off)

John, E R (Neath)
Born 3 December 1925;
died 30 September 1981
17 caps 1950-54
(lock, flanker)

John, G
(St Luke's College, Exeter)
Born 22 February 1932;
died 7 June 1983
2 caps 1954
(centre, stand-off)

Johnson, W D (Swansea)
Born 5 December 1923
1 cap 1953 (flanker)

Jones, A E (known as Emyr, A) (Swansea)
Born 27 July 1962
6 caps 1989-91 (wing)

Jones, B J (Newport)
Born 10 May 1935
2 caps 1960 (centre)

Jones, B L
(Devonport Services, Llanelli)
Born 11 April 1931
9 caps 1950-52
(full-back, centre, wing)

Jones, D C J (Swansea)
Born 30 April 1916
7 caps 1947-49 (prop)

Jones, D K (Llanelli, Cardiff)
Born 7 August 1941
12 caps 1962-66 (centre)

Jones, G (Ebbw Vale)
Born 24 November 1933
3 caps 1963 (flanker)

Jones, G (Llanelli)
Born 17 July 1960
3 caps 1989-90 (flanker)

Jones, I C (London Welsh)
Born 2 March 1940
1 cap 1968 (lock)

Jones, K D (Cardiff)
Born 5 August 1935
8 caps 1961-63 (prop)

Jones, K J (Newport)
Born 30 December 1921
41 caps 1947-56 (wing)

Jones, M A (Neath)
Born 22 June 1965
9 caps 1987-90 (No 8)

Jones, R E (Coventry)
Born 24 February 1943
5 caps 1967-68
(flanker, No 8)

Jones, R N (Swansea)
Born 10 November 1965
28 caps 1986-93 (scrum-half)

Jones, S T (Pontypool)
Born 4 January 1959
7 caps 1983-88 (prop)

Jones, W D (Llanelli)
Born 25 October 1925;
died 15 August 1987
1 cap 1948 (lock)

Jones, W K (Cardiff)
Born 13 January 1945

4 caps 1968 (wing)

Judd, S (Cardiff)
Born 14 August 1928;
died 24 February 1959
9 caps 1953-55
(flanker, No 8)

Keen, L (Aberavon)
Born 13 November 1954

4 caps 1980 (wing)

Knight, P (Pontypridd)
Born 30 April 1959
2 caps 1991 (prop)

Knill, F M D (Cardiff)
Born 22 December 1941
1 cap 1976 (prop)

Lamerton, A E H (Llanelli)
Born 28 May 1970
1 cap 1993 (hooker)

Lane, S M (Cardiff)
Born 12 November 1952
3 caps 1979-80 (flanker)

Leleu, J
(London Welsh, Swansea)

The last Wales team to win the Grand Slam: Wales v France 1978. Back: MJ Wat TJ Cobner, TP Evans (replacement). Front: DB Williams (replacement), RWR Gra GL Evans.

Born 13 March 1935
3 caps 1959-60 (flanker)

Lewis, A J L (Ebbw Vale)
Born 26 September 1941
11 caps 1970-73 (centre)

Lewis, E W (Llanelli)
Born 29 August 1968
9 caps 1991-3 (flanker, No 8)

Lewis, G W (Richmond)
Born 7 April 1936
2 caps 1960 (centre)

Lewis, J R
(S Glam Inst, Cardiff)
Born 25 February 1959
7 caps 1981-82 (flanker)

Lewis, P I (Llanelli)
Born 6 January 1961
7 caps 1985-86 (wing)

Lewis, R A (Abertillery)
Born 7 October 1942
5 caps 1966-67 (scrum-half)

Llewellyn, G D (Neath)
Born 9 August 1965
4 caps 1991 (lock)

Llewellyn, G O (Neath)
Born 27 February 1969
13 caps 1990-93 (lock)

Llewellyn, P D (Swansea)
Born 12 May 1947
4 caps 1973-74 (prop)

Llewelyn, D B
(Newport, Llanelli)
Born 6 January 1948
11 caps 1970-72 (prop)

Lloyd, D J (Bridgend)
Born 29 March 1943
21 caps 1966-73 (prop)

Lloyd, T (Maesteg)
Born 5 September 1924
2 caps 1953 (scrum-half)

Maddocks, K (Neath)
Born 16 June 1927
1 cap 1957 (wing)

Main, D R (London Welsh)
Born 29 November 1931
4 caps 1959 (prop)

Mainwaring, G T (Aberavon)
Born 24 January 1941
5 caps 1967-68 (lock)

Mainwaring, H J (Swansea)
Born 10 June 1933
1 cap 1961 (centre)

Major, W C (Maesteg)
Born 15 June 1929
2 caps 1949-50 (wing)

Manfield, L
(Mountain Ash, Cardiff)
Born 10 November 1915
4 caps 1948 (No 8)

Mantle, J (Loughborough Colleges, Newport)
Born 13 March 1942
1 cap 1964 (flanker)

Martin, A J (Aberavon)
Born 11 December 1948
28 caps 1974-81 (lock)

Mathias, R (Llanelli)
Born 2 September 1949
1 cap 1970 (wing)

Matthews, J (Cardiff)
Born 21 June 1920
16 caps 1947-51 (centre, wing)

May, P S (Llanelli)
Born 1 July 1956
4 caps 1988 (lock)

Meek, N N (Pontypool)
Born 20 October 1963
3 caps 1993 (hooker)

Meredith, A
(Devonport Services)
Born 1919
3 caps 1949 (lock)

Meredith, B V
(St Luke's College, London Welsh, Newport)
Born 21 November 1930
32 caps 1954-62 (hooker)

Meredith, C C (Neath)
Born 23 September 1926
13 caps 1953-57 (prop)

placement), G Price, J Squire, DL Quinnell, AJ Martin, GAD Wheel, AG Faulkner,
Fenwick, JPR Williams, RW Windsor, P Bennett (captain), GO Edwards, JJ Williams,

Michaelson, R C B
(Aberavon, Cambridge U)
Born 31 March 1941
1 cap 1963 (No 8)

Moon, R H StJ B (Llanelli)
Born 1 February 1968
1 cap 1993 (scrum-half)

Morgan, C H (Llanelli)
Born 22 December 1932
2 caps 1957 (prop)

Morgan, C I
(Cardiif, Bective Rangers)
Born 7 April 1930
27 caps 1951-58 (stand-off)

Morgan, D R R (Llanelli)
Born 29 August 1941
8 caps 1962-63 (wing)

Morgan, G R (Newport)
Born 9 June 1954
1 cap 1984 (prop)

Morgan, H J (Abertillery)
Born 30 July 1936
26 caps 1958-1966 (flanker)

Morgan, H P (Newport)
Born 16 June 1930
4 caps 1956 (centre)

Morgan, N H (Newport)
Born 26 March 1935
3 caps 1960 (full-back)

Morgan, P E J (Aberavon)
Born 21 December 1937
3 caps 1961 (prop)

Morgan, P J (Llanelli)
Born 1 January 1959
3 caps 1980-81
(stand-off, centre)

Moriarty, R D (Swansea)
Born 1 May 1957
12 caps 1982-85
(lock, flanker, No 8)

Moriarty, W P (Swansea)
Born 16 July 1964
10 caps 1986-88
(flanker, No 8)

Morris, H T (Cardiff)
Born 14 July 1928
3 caps 1951-55 (wing)

Morris, M S
(S Wales Police, Neath)
Born 23 August 1962
7 caps 1985-92 (flanker)

Morris, W D (Neath)
Born 11 November 1941
28 caps 1967-74
(No 8, flanker)

Morris, W J (Newport)
Born 16 June 1941
2 caps 1965-66 (lock)

Morris, W J B (Pontypool)
Born 21 May 1940
2 caps 1963 (wing)

Moseley, K
(Pontypool, Newport)
Born 2 July 1963
3 caps 1989-90 (lock)

Nash, D (Ebbw Vale)
Born 15 July 1939
5 caps 1961-62 (No 8, lock)

Nicholas, D L (Llanelli)
Born 3 March 1955
4 caps 1981 (wing)

Nicholls, H C W (Cardiff)
Born 2 June 1931
1 cap 1958 (wing)

Norris, C H (Cardiff)
Born 11 June 1934
2 caps 1963-66 (prop)

Norster, R L (Cardiff)
Born 23 June 1957
23 caps 1982-89 (lock)

O'Connor, A (Aberavon)
Born 24 April 1934
4 caps 1961-62 (scrum-half)

O'Connor, R (Aberavon)
Born 14 September 1932;
died 7 March 1986
1 cap 1957 (flanker)

O'Shea, J P (Cardiff)
Born 2 June 1940
5 caps 1967-68 (prop)

Owen, G D (Newport)
Born 20 March 1932
6 caps 1955-56 (full-back)

Parsons, G (Newport)
Born 21 April 1926
1 cap 1947 (lock)

Pask, A E I (Abertillery)
Born 10 September 1937
23 caps 1961-67
(flanker, No 8)

Payne, G W
(Army, Pontypridd)
Born 8 September 1935
3 caps 1960 (lock)

Pearce, P G (Bridgend)
Born 11 November 1960
3 caps 1981-82 (stand-off)

Perego, M A (Llanelli)
Born 8 February 1964
2 caps 1990-93 (flanker)

Perkins, S J (Pontypool)
Born 27 February 1954
15 caps 1983-86 (lock)

Perrins, V C (Newport)
Born 3 September 1944
1 cap 1970 (hooker)

Phillips, A J (Cardiff)
Born 21 August 1954
13 caps 1979-82 (hooker)

Phillips, D H (Swansea)
Born 24 August 1928
1 cap 1952 (wing)

Phillips, K H (Neath)
Born 15 June 1961
10 caps 1987-91 (hooker)

Phillips, R D (Neath)
Born 28 July 1965
6 caps 1988-89 (flanker)

Pickering, D F (Llanelli)
Born 16 December 1960
19 caps 1983-87 (flanker)

Powell, G (Ebbw Vale)
Born 17 November 1932
2 caps 1957 (centre)

Price, B (Newport)
Born 30 October 1937
26 caps 1961-69 (lock)

Price, G (Pontypool)
Born 24 November 1951
35 caps 1975-83 (prop)

Price, M J (Pontypool, RAF)
Born 8 December 1937
9 caps 1959-62 (centre)

Price, T G (Llanelli, London Welsh, Hendy)
Born 16 July 1945;
died 7 April 1993
7 caps 1965-67 (full-back)

Priday, A J (Cardiff)
Born 23 January 1933
2 caps 1958-61 (full-back)

Proctor, W T (Llanelli)
Born 12 June 1972
2 caps 1993 (wing)

Prosser, T R (Pontypool)
Born 2 March 1927
20 caps 1956-61 (prop)

Prothero, G J (Bridgend)
Born 7 December 1941
11 caps 1964-66 (flanker)

Pugh, J D (Neath)
Born 4 March 1960
2 caps 1988-90 (prop)

Quinnell, D L (Llanelli)
Born 22 May 1949
18 caps 1972-79 (No 8, lock)

Raybould, W H
(London Welsh, Cambridge U, Newport)
Born 6 March 1944
9 caps 1967-70 (centre)

Rayer, M A (Cardiff)
Born 21 July 1965
4 caps 1992-93 (full-back)

Rees, A (Maesteg)
Born 17 February 1938
3 caps 1962 (stand-off)

Rees, B I (London Welsh)
Born 28 August 1942
3 caps 1967 (hooker)

Rees, C F W (London Welsh)
Born 6 October 1951
10 caps 1974-83 (wing)

Rees, D (Swansea)
Born 15 January 1944
3 caps 1968 (full-back)

Rees, H E (Neath)
Born 5 January 1954
12 caps 1979-83 (wing)

Rees, P (Llanelli)
Born 8 February 1925
2 caps 1947 (wing)

Rees, P M (Newport)
Born 14 October 1937
4 caps 1961-64 (wing)

Richards, D S (Swansea)
Born 23 May 1954
15 caps 1979-83
(centre, wing)

Richards, K H L (Bridgend)
Born 29 January 1934;
died 8 January 1972
4 caps 1961 (stand-off)

Richards, M C R (Cardiff)
Born 2 February 1945
6 caps 1968-69 (wing)

Richards, R C (Cross Keys)
Born 4 February 1934;
died 6 March 1989
1 cap 1956 (prop)

Richards, T B (Swansea)
Born 23 November 1932
1 cap 1960 (stand-off)

Richardson, S J (Aberavon)
Born 1 April 1947
1 cap 1979 (prop)

Ring, M G
(Cardiff, Pontypool)
Born 15 October 1962
17 caps 1983-91 (centre)

Ringer, P
(Ebbw Vale, Llanelli)
Born 28 January 1948
6 caps 1979-80 (flanker)

Roberts, C R (Neath)
Born 19 December 1930
2 caps 1958 (wlng)

Roberts, G J (Cardiff)
Born 15 January 1959
2 caps 1985 (flanker)

Roberts, H M (Cardlff)
Born 11 September 1934
7 caps 1961-63 (centre)

Roberts, M G
(London Welsh)
Born 20 February 1946
8 caps 1971-79 (lock)

Robins, J D
(Birkenhead Park)
Born 17 May 1926
11 caps 1950-53 (prop)

Robins, R J (Pontypridd)
Born 21 February 1932
13 caps 1953-57
(No 8, lock, flanker)

Robinson, I R (Cardiff)
Born 21 February 1944
2 caps 1974 (lock)

Rowlands, D C T (Pontypool)
Born 14 May 1938
12 caps 1963-65 (scrum-half)

Rowlands, G (RAF, Cardiff)
Born 19 December 1928
3 caps 1954-56 (wing)

Rowlands, K A (Cardiff)
Born 7 February 1936
5 caps 1962-65 (lock)

Shanklin, J L
(London Welsh)
Born 11 December 1948
3 caps 1970-73 (wing)

Shaw, G (Neath)
Born 11 April 1951
10 caps 1973-77 (prop)

Sparks, B A (Neath)
Born 23 June 1931

7 caps 1954-57 (flanker)

Squire, J
(Newport, Pontypool)
Born 23 September 1951
25 caps 1977-83
(No 8, flanker)

Stephens, C J (Llanelli)
Born 29 November 1969
3 caps 1992 (stand-off)

Stephens, I (Bridgend)
Born 22 May 1952
11 caps 1981-84 (prop)

Stephens, J R G (Neath)
Born 16 April 1922
30 caps 1947-57 (No 8, lock)

Stone, P (Llanelli)
Born 20 June 1924;
died 10 July 1971
1 cap 1949 (flanker)

Sutton, S (Pontypool, S Wales Police)
Born 17 February 1958
6 caps 1982-87 (lock)

Tamplin, W E (Cardiff)
Born 10 May 1917;
died 20 October 1989
6 caps 1947-48 (lock~

Tanner, H (Swansea, Cardiff)
Born 9 January 1917
12 caps 1947-49 (scrum-half)

Taylor, J (London Welsh)
Born 21 July 1945
22 caps 1967-73 (flanker)

Thomas, A G
(Swansea, Cardiff)
Born 3 February 1926;
died 8 May 1991
13 caps 1952-55
(centre, wing, stand-off)

Thomas, A R F (Newport)
Born 16 April 1940
1 cap 1964 (flanker)

Thomas, B (Neath)
Born 18 May 1940
16 caps 1963-69 (lock)

Thomas, D L (Aberavon)
Born 29 April 1941
1 cap 1961 (centre)

Thomas, J D (Llanelli)
Born 21 April 1929
1 cap 1954 (centre)

Thomas, M C (Newport, Devonport Services)
Born 25 April 1929
26 caps 1949-59
(centre, wing, stand-off)

Thomas, R C C (Swansea)
Born 28 January 1929
24 caps 1949-59 (flanker)

Thomas, W D (Llanelli)
Born 12 September 1942
20 caps 1968-74 (lock)

Thomas, W J (Cardiff)
Born 1 September 1933
2 caps 1961-63 (hooker)

Thorburn, P H (Neath)
Born 24 November 1962
22 caps 1985-91 (full-back)

Titley, M H
(Bridgend, Swansea)
Born 3 May 1959
9 caps 1984-90 (wing)

Travers, W (Newport)
Born 2 December 1913
4 caps 1949 (hooker)

Trott, R F (Cardiff)
Born 14 March 1915;
died 28 March 1987
8 caps 1948-49 (full-back)

Turner, P (Newbridge)
Born 13 February 1959
3 caps 1989 (stand-off)

Uzzell, J (Newport)
Born 28 March 1942
4 caps 1965 (centre)

Waldron, R G (Neath)
Born 14 December 1933
4 caps 1965 (prop)

Walker, N (Cardiff)
Born 15 June 1963
2 caps 1993 (wing)

Wanbon, R (Aberavon)
Born 16 November 1943
1 cap 1968 (No 8)

Warlow, D J (Llanelli)
Born 13 February 1939
1 cap 1962 (prop)

Waters, D R (Newport)
Born 4 June 1955
4 caps 1986 (lock)

Watkins, D (Newport)
Born 5 March 1942
19 caps 1963-67 (stand-off)

Watkins, I J (Ebbw Vale)

Delme Thomas.

Born 10 March 1963
8 caps 1988-1989 (hooker)

Watkins, M J (Newport)
Born 9 January 1952
3 caps 1984 (hooker)

Watkins, S J
(Newport, Cardiff)
Born 5 June 1941
23 caps 1964-70 (wing)

Watkins, W R (Newport)
Born 22 March 1933
1 cap 1959 (scrum-half)

Weaver, D S (Swansea)
Born 8 January 1942
1 cap 1964 (wing)

Webbe, G M C (Bridgend)
Born 21 January 1962
4 caps 1987-88 (wing)

Webster, R E (Swansea)
Born 9 July 1967
8 caps 1992-93 (flanker)

Wells, G T (Cardiff)
Born 25 October 1928
6 caps 1955-58 (centre, wing)

Wheel, G A D (Swansea)
Born 30 June 1951
27 caps 1974-82 (lock)

Wheeler, P J (Aberavon)
Born 5 February 1947
1 cap 1968 (full-back)

Whitefoot, J (Cardiff)
Born 18 April 1956
12 caps 1985-87 (prop)

Whitson, G K (Newport)
Born 4 December 1930;
died 18 May 1984
3 caps 1956-60 (flanker)

Williams, B (Cardiff)
Born 22 February 1923
19 caps 1947-55
(stand-off, centre)

Williams, B R (Neath)
Born 9 July 1960
4 caps 1990-91 (prop)

Williams, C
(Aberavon, Swansea)
Born 2 November 1948
7 caps 1977-83 (prop)

Williams, C D
(Cardiff, Neath)
Born 28 November 1924
2 caps 1955-56 (flanker)

Williams, D (Ebbw Vale)
Born 17 October 1938
29 caps 1963-71 (prop)

Williams, D B
(Newport, Swansea)
Born 29 October 1951
2 caps 1981 (scrum-half)

Williams, G (London Welsh)
Born 22 April 1924
11 caps 1950-54 (full-back)

Williams, G (Bridgend)
21 October 1954
4 caps 1981-82 (scrum-half)

Williams, G P (Bridgend)
Born 6 November 1954
3 caps 1981-82
(No 8, flanker)

Williams, H R (Llanelli)
Born 13 November 1927
2 caps 1954-57 (wing)

Williams, J J (Llanelli)
Born 1 April 1948
25 caps 1973-79 (wing)

Williams, J P R
(London Welsh, Bridgend)
Born 2 March 1949
44 caps 1969-81 (full-back)

Williams, L H (Cardiff)
Born 19 October 1933
13 caps 1957-62 (scrum-half)

Williams, O (Llanelli)
Born 12 April 1921;
died 23 March 1988
6 caps 1947-48 (flanker)

Williams, R H (Llanelli)
Born 14 July 1930;
died 27 January 1993
22 caps 1954-60 (lock)

Williams, S (Llanelli)
Born 4 November 1914;
died 21 November 1967
6 caps 1947-48 (lock)

Williams, W A (Newport)
Born 9 September 1921
3 caps 1952-53 (scrum-half)

Williams, W J (Neath)
Born 14 December 1943;
died 10 March 1985
2 caps 1974 (prop)

Williams, W L T
(Llanelli, Cardiff)
Born 10 May 1922
6 caps 1947-49 (wing, centre)

Williams, W O G (Swansea, Devonport Services)
Born 19 November 1929
20 caps 1951-56 (prop)

Williams-Jones, H
(S Wales Police)
Born 10 January 1963
8 caps 1989-93 (prop)

Willis, W R (Cardiff)
Born 25 October 1924
19 caps 1950-55 (scrum-half)

Wiltshire, M L (Aberavon)
Born 16 July 1938
3 caps 1968 (lock)

Windsor, R W (Pontypool)
Born 31 January 1946
23 caps 1974-79 (hooker)

Wyatt, M A (Swansea)
Born 12 February 1957
9 caps 1983-87 (full-back)

Young, D (Swansea, Cardiff)
Born 27 June 1967
6 caps 1988-90 (prop)

Young, J (Harrogate, RAF, London Welsh)
Born 16 September 1942
21 caps 1968-73 (hooker)

FRANCE

Abadie, A (Pau)
Born 31 January 1932
1 cap 1964 (hooker)

Abadie, A (Graulhet)
Born 27 July 1934
2 caps 1968 (prop)

Aguerre, R (Biarritz Ol)
Born 13 March 1957
1 cap 1979 (stand-off)

Aguirre, J-M (Bagnères)
Born 2 November 1951
21 caps 1972-80
(scrum-half, full-back)

Albaladejo, P (Dax)
Born 14 December 1933
18 caps 1954-64
(full-back, stand-off)

Alvarez, A-J (Tyrosse)
Born 26 May 1923
14 caps 1947-51
(full-back, stand-off)

Amestoy, J-B
(Mont-de-Marsan)
Born 28 August 1935
1 cap 1964 (prop)

Andrieu, M (Nîmes)
Born 19 September 1959
11 caps 1988-90 (wing, centre)

Arcalis, R (Brive)
Born 1 June 1927;
died 27 April 1987
5 caps 1950-51 (full-back)

Aristouy, P (Pau)
Born 18 October 1920;
died 20 April 1974
5 caps 1948-50 (prop, lock)

Armary, L (Lourdes)
Born 24 July 1963
15 caps 1988- 93 (prop)

Arnaudet, M (Lourdes)
Born 11 March 1943
2 caps 1964-67 (centre, wing)

Arrieta, J (Stade Francais)
Born 11 September 1924
2 caps 1953 (hooker)

Astre, R (Béziers)
Born 28 August 1948
5 caps 1972-75 (scrum-half)

Averous, J-L (La Voulte)
Born 22 October 1954
14 caps 1975-80 (wing)

Azarete, J-L
(Dax, St-Jean-de-Luz Ol)
Born 8 May 1945
13 caps 1969-75 (prop)

Badin, C (Châlon)
Born 11 September 1949
2 caps 1973 (centre)

Barrau, M
(Beaumont, Toulouse)
Born 26 November 1950
10 caps 1971-74 (scrum-half)

Barthe, J (Lourdes)
Born 22 July 1932
15 caps 1955-59
(lock, No 8, flanker)

Basquet, G (Agen)
Born 13 July 1921
24 caps 1947-52 (No 8)

Bastiat, J-P (Dax)
Born 11 April 1949
20 caps 1970-78 (lock, No 8)

Baudry, N (Montferrand)
Born 1 April 1914
3 caps 1949 (full-back)

Baulon, R (Vienne, Bayonne)
Born 21 October 1930
12 caps 1954-57
(lock, No 8, flanker)

Bayardon, J (Châlon)
Born 25 January 1934
2 caps 1964 (prop)

Bégu, J (Dax)
Born 22 April 1957
2 caps 1984 (wing)

Belascain, C (Bayonne)
Born 1 November 1953
16 caps 1978-83 (centre)

Belletante, G (Nantes)
Born 13 March 1927
3 caps 1951 (centre)

Benazzi, A (Agen)
Born 20 August 1968
5 caps 1991-93 (No 8, lock)

Bénésis, R (Narbonne)
Born 29 August 1944
20 caps 1969-74 (hooker)

Benetton, P (Agen)
Born 17 May 1968
4 caps 1993 (flanker)

Berbizier, P (Lourdes, Agen)
Born 17 June 1958
30 caps 1981-91 (scrum-half)

Berejnoi, J-C (Tulle)
Born 20 April 1939
15 caps 1964-67 (prop)

Berges-Cau, R (Lourdes)
Born 28 October 1949;
died 22 May 1983
1 cap 1976 (full-back)

Bergougnan, Y (Toulouse)
Born 8 May 1924
9 caps 1947-49 (scrum-half)

Bernard, R (Bergerac)
Born 11 May 1925
4 caps 1951 (prop)

Bérot, J-L (Toulouse)
Born 28 July 1947
12 caps 1969-74
(scrum-half, stand-off)

Bérot, P (Agen)
Born 29 January 1965
8 caps 1987-89 (wing)

Bertrand, P (Bourg)
Born 27 October 1927
7 caps 1951-53 (prop)

Bertranne, R (Bagnères)
Born 6 December 1949
37 caps 1971-81 (centre, wing)

Besson, P (Brive)
Born 11 April 1940
3 caps 1963 (wing)

Bidart, L (La Rochelle)
Born 11 January 1930
1 cap 1953 (stand-off)

Biemouret, P (Agen)
Born 11 April 1943
12 caps 1969-73 (flanker)

Bienes, R (Cognac)
Born 2 August 1923
23 caps 1950-56
(flanker, prop, No 8)

Bilbao, L (St-Jean-de-Luz Ol)
Born 14 September 1956
2 caps 1978-79 (wing)

Blanco, S (Biarritz Ol)
Born 31 August 1958
42 caps 1981-91
(wing, full-back)

Blond, X (RCF)
Born 28 August 1967
4 caps 1991 (flanker)

Boffelli, V (Aurillac)
Born 20 March 1947
9 caps 1972-75
(flanker, No 8)

Bonal, J-M (Toulouse)
Born 31 May 1943
7 caps 1968-70 (wing)

Boniface, A
(Mont-de-Marsan)
Born 14 August 1934
29 caps 1954-66 (wing, centre)

Boniface, G
(Mont-de-Marsan)
Born 6 March 1937;
died 1 January 1968
19 caps 1960-66 (centre)

Bonneval, E (Toulouse)
Born 19 November 1963
8 caps 1985-88 (wing)

Bonnus, F (Toulon)
Born 25 August 1924;
died 26 April 1970
4 caps 1950 (lock)

Bordenave, L (Toulon)
Born 11 May 1920
4 caps 1948-49 (stand-off)

Bouguyon, G (Grenoble)
Born 24 November 1935
3 caps 1961 (lock)

Bouquet, J
(Bourgoin, Vienne)
Born 3 June 1933
26 caps 1954-62
(centre, stand-off)

Bourdeu, J-R (Lourdes)
Born 6 January 1927
7 caps 1952-53 (flanker, wing)

Bourgarel, R (Toulouse)
Born 21 April 1947
5 caps 1970-73 (wing)

Bourguignon, G (Narbonne)
Born 31 January 1964
2 caps 1989 (lock)

Brejassou, R (Tarbes)
Born 12 August 1929
12 caps 1952-55 (prop, lock)

Brun, G (Vienne)
Born 23 December 1922
11 caps 1950-53
(full-back, centre, wing)

Buchet, E (Nice)
Born 28 November 1957
1 cap 1982 (flanker)

Buonomo, Y (Béziers)
Born 19 September 1946
1 cap 1972 (No 8)

Bustaffa, D (Carcassonne)
Born 11 January 1956
4 caps 1978-80 (wing)

Buzy, C-E (Lourdes)
Born 13 February 1917
12 caps 1947-49 (prop)

Cabanier, J-M (Montauban)
Born 13 May 1936
14 caps 1964-68 (hooker)

Cabannes, L (RCF)
Born 6 February 1964
12 caps 1991-93 (flanker)

Cadieu, J-M (Toulouse)
Born 16 October 1963
2 caps 1992 (lock)

Camberabero, D
(La Voulte, Béziers)
Born 9 January 1961
13 caps 1983-93 (stand-off)

Camberabero, G (La Voulte)
Born 17 May 1936
6 caps 1967-68 (stand-off)

Camberabero, L (La Voulte)
Born 15 July 1937
10 caps 1965-68 (scrum-half)

Campaes, A (Lourdes)
Born 30 March 1944
7 caps 1965-69 (wing)

Cantoni, J (Béziers)
Born 11 May 1948
11 caps 1970-75
(wing, full-back)

Capdouze, J (Pau)
Born 31 August 1942
3 caps 1965 (stand-off)

Carabignac, G (Agen)
Born 10 October 1929;
died 21 February 1973
6 caps 1951-53 (stand-off)

Carminati, A (Béziers)
Born 17 August 1966
6 caps 1988-90
(flanker, No 8)

Caron, L (Lyon Ol, Castres)
Born 13 December 1916;
died 7 December 1984
8 caps 1947-49 (prop)

Carpentier, M (Lourdes)
Born 15 October 1959
5 caps 1980-82 (No 8, lock)

Carrère, C (Toulon)
Born 27 July 1943
16 caps 1967-71 (flanker)

Carrère, J (Vichy, Toulon)
Born 5 April 1930
5 caps 1956-59 (flanker)

Carrère, R (Mont-de-Marsan)
Born 13 March 1921
1 cap 1953 (prop)

Casaux, L (Tarbes)
Born 15 July 1938
2 caps 1959-62
(centre, full-back)

Caussade, A (Lourdes)
Born 27 July 1952
8 caps 1979-81
(stand-off, wing)

Cazenave, F (RCF)
Born 26 November 1924
5 caps 1950-54 (wing)

Cecillon, M (Bourgoin)
Born 30 January 1959
15 caps 1988-93
(flanker, No 8, lock)

Celaya, M
(Biarritz Ol, SBUC)
Born 4 July 1930
29 caps 1953-61
(No 8, flanker, lock)

Cester, E (TOEC, Valence)
Born 27 July 1942
23 caps 1966-74 (lock)

Chadebech, P (Brive)
Born 3 May 1959
2 caps 1986 (centre)

Champ, E (Toulon)
Born 8 June 1962
13 caps 1986-90 (flanker)

Charvet, D (Toulouse)
Born 12 May 1962
11 caps 1986-91
(centre, wing)

Chevallier, B (Montferrand)
Born 7 December 1925
18 caps 1952-57 (lock)

Cholley, G (Castres)
Born 6 June 1945
17 caps 1975-79 (prop)

Claverie, H (Lourdes)
Born 21 January 1925
1 cap 1954 (full-back)

Clemente, M (Oloron)
Born 3 November 1955
2 caps 1980 (No 8)

Codorniou, D (Narbonne)
Born 13 February 1958
19 caps 1980-85 (centre)

Colombier, J (St Junien)
Born 23 September 1928
2 caps 1952 (wing)

Condom, J
(Boucau, Biarritz Ol)
Born 15 August 1960
28 caps 1983-90 (lock)

Costes, F (Montferrand)
Born 27 June 1957
4 caps 1979-80 (wing)

Crancee, R (Lourdes)
Born 24 September 1932
1 cap 1961 (No 8)

Crauste, M (RCF, Lourdes)
Born 6 July 1934
35 caps 1958-66
(flanker, No 8)

Cremaschi, M (Lourdes)
Born 26 April 1956
4 caps 1982-84 (prop)

Danos, P (Toulon, Béziers)
Born 4 June 1929
10 caps 1958-60
(scrum-half)

Darrieussecq, A
(Biarritz Ol)
Born 4 June 1947
1 cap 1973 (prop)

Darrouy, C
(Mont-de-Marsan)
Born 13 January 1937
22 caps 1957-67 (wing)

Dauga, B
(Mont-de-Marsan)
Born 8 May 1942
32 caps 1964-72
(lock, No 8)

Dauger, J (Bayonne)
Born 12 November 1919
1 cap 1953 (centre)

Dedieu, P (Béziers)
Born 8 May 1933
7 caps 1963-65 (full back)

De Gregorio, J (Grenoble)
Born 9 December 1935
14 caps 1960-64 (hooker)

Delage, C (Agen)
Born 16 January 1954
2 caps 1983 (stand-off)

Deslandes, C (RCF)
Born 2 January 1965
1 cap 1991 (No 8)

Devergie, T (Nimes)
Born 27 July 1966
4 caps 1990 (lock)

Dintrans, P (Tarbes)
Born 29 January 1957
24 caps 1980-89 (hooker)

Dizabo, P (Tyrosse)
Born 4 October 1929
8 caps 1948-50 (centre)

Domec, H (Lourdes)
Born 9 August 1932
14 caps 1953-58 (flanker)

Domenech, A (Vichy, Brive)
Born 3 May 1933
29 caps 1954-63 (prop)

Dospital, P (Bayonne)
Born 15 May 1950
16 caps 1980-85 (prop)

Dourthe, C (Dax)
Born 20 November 1948
13 caps 1967-75 (centre)

Droitecourt, M (Montferrand)
Born 30 October 1949
6 caps 1973-76 (full-back)

Dubertrand, A (Montferrand)
Born 25 April 1950
4 caps 1974-76 (wing)

Dubois, D (Bègles)
Born 17 June 1944
1 cap 1971 (flanker)

Dubroca, D (Agen)
Born 25 April 1954
17 caps 1982-88
(prop, hooker)

Dufau, G (RCF)
Born 27 August 1924
30 caps 1948-57 (scrum-half)

Duhard, Y (Bagnères)
Born 11 July 1955
1 cap 1980 (lock)

Dupont, J-L (Agen)
Born 17 March 1956
1 cap 1983 (hooker)

Duprat, B (Bayonne)
Born 17 July 1943
8 caps 1966-72 (wing)

Dupuy, J-V (Tarbes)
Born 25 May 1934
24 caps 1956-64 (wing)

Dutrain, H (Toulouse)
Born 3 July 1922
4 caps 1947-49 (wing, centre)

Echavé, L (Agen)
Born 18 June 1934
1 cap 1961 (lock)

Erbani, D (Agen)
Born 16 August 1956
23 caps 1983-90 (flanker)

Esponda, J-M (RCF)
Born 24 April 1943
3 caps 1969 (prop)

Estève, A (Béziers)
Born 15 September 1946
12 caps 1972-75 (lock)

Estève, P
(Narbonne, Lavelanet)
Born 14 February 1959
14 caps 1983-86 (wing)

Etchenique, J-M (Biarritz Ol)
Born 17 January 1954
1 cap 1975 (centre)

Etcheverry, M (Pau)
Born 23 August 1942
2 caps 1971 (prop)

Fabre, J (Toulouse)
Born 7 November 1935
6 caps 1963-64 (No 8)

Fabre, M (Béziers)
Born 11 September 1956
1 cap 1982 (wing)

Ferrien, R (Tarbes)
Born 9 November 1924
4 caps 1950 (prop)

Fite, R (Brive)
Born 13 October 1938
1 cap 1963 (lock)

Fort, J (Agen)
Born 16 January 1938
2 caps 1967 (lock)

Foures, H (Toulouse)
Born 29 August 1925
4 caps 1951 (lock)

Fournet, F (Montferrand)
Born 26 November 1922;
died 3 July 1982
1 cap 1950 (stand-off)

Fouroux, J (La Voulte)
Born 24 July 1947
11 caps 1974-77 (scrum-half)

Furcade, R (Perpignan)
Born 22 January 1928
1 cap 1952 (stand-off)

Gabernet, S (Toulouse)
Born 6 February 1955
7 caps 1980-82 (full-back)

Gachassin, J (Lourdes)
Born 23 December 1941
21 caps 1961-69 (wing, stand-off, full-back, centre)

Gallart, P (Béziers)
Born 18 December 1962
2 caps 1992 (prop)

Gallion, J (Toulon)
Born 4 April 1955
20 caps 1978-85 (scrum-half)

Galthié, F (Colomiers)
Born 20 March 1969
3 caps 1992
(scrum-half)

Galy, J (Perpignan)
Born 22 December 1929
1 cap 1953 (centre)

Garuet-Lempirou, J-P
(Lourdes)
Born 15 June 1953
19 caps 1984-90 (prop)

Genet, J-P (RCF)
Born 15 October 1962
2 caps 1992 (hooker)

Gensane, R (Béziers)
Born 4 February 1934
5 caps 1962-63 (flanker)

Gimbert, P (Bègles)
Born 20 March 1966
2 caps 1992 (prop)

Gourdon, J-F
(RCF, Bagnères)
Born 28 September 1954
15 caps 1974-80 (wing)

Gourragne, J-F (Béziers)
Born 20 November 1963
1 cap 1991 (lock)

Gratton, J (Agen)
Born 29 November 1957
5 caps 1985-86 (flanker)

Greffe, M (Grenoble)
Born 27 October 1940
1 cap 1968 (No 8)

Gruarin, A (Toulon)
Born 5 February 1938
16 caps 1964-68 (prop)

Guilbert, A (Toulon)
Born 28 September 1950
6 caps 1975-79 (lock, No 8)

Haget, A (PUC)
Born 26 April 1931;
died 31 January 1989
7 caps 1953-57 (stand-off)

Haget, F (Agen, Biarritz Ol)
Born 1 October 1949
21 caps 1976-87 (lock)

Harize, D (Cahors, Toulouse)
Born 26 February 1956
4 caps 1977 (wing)

Hauser, M (Lourdes)
Born 10 July 1945
1 cap 1969 (flanker)

Herice, D (Bègles)
Born 7 September 1921
1 cap 1950 (flanker)

Herrero, A (Toulon)
Born 28 January 1938
11 caps 1964-67
(flanker, lock, No 8)

Herrero, B (Nice)
Born 19 September 1957
1 cap 1983 (hooker)

Hiquet, J-C (Agen)
Born 4 November 1939
1 cap 1964 (stand-off)

Hoche, M (PUC)
Born 20 September 1932
3 caps 1957 (lock)

Hontas, P (Biarritz Ol)
Born 19 July 1966
6 caps 1990-93 (wing)

Hueber, A (Lourdes, Toulon)
Born 5 April 1967
5 caps 1992-93 (scrum-half)

Imbernon, J-F (Perpignan)
Born 17 October 1951
16 caps 1976-83 (lock)

Iraçabal, J (Bayonne)
Born 6 July 1941
18 caps 1969-74 (prop)

Jeanjean, P (Toulon)
Born 3 February 1924
1 cap 1948 (wing)

Joinel, J-L (Brive)
Born 21 September 1953
30 caps 1979-86
(flanker, No 8)

Jol, M (Biarritz Ol)
Born 16 March 1923;
died 22 June 1981
8 caps 1947-49 (hooker)

Junquas, L (Tyrosse)
Born 11 September 1920
6 caps 1947-48 (centre)

Kaczorowski, D (Le Creusot)
Born 31 October 1952
1 cap 1974 (flanker)

Labadie, P (Bayonne)
Born 27 April 1928
16 caps 1952-57 (hooker)

Labarthète, R (Pau)
Born 5 October 1924
1 cap 1952 (full-back)

Labazuy, A (Lourdes)
Born 9 February 1929
9 caps 1952-59 (stand-off)

Laborde, C (RCF)
Born 25 August 1940
1 cap 1965 (scrum-half)

Lacans, P (Béziers)
Born 23 April 1957;
died 30 September 1985
3 caps 1981-82 (flanker)

Lacaussade, R (Bègles)
Born 30 January 1922
1 cap 1948 (wing)

Lacaze, C
(Lourdes, Angoulême)
Born 5 March 1940
16 caps 1962-69
(full-back, stand-off)

Lacaze, P (Lourdes)
Born 4 May 1934
4 caps 1959 (full-back)

Lacroix, P
(Mont-de-Marsan, Agen)
Born 23 January 1935
14 caps 1960-63 (scrum-half)

Lacroix, T (Dax)
Born 2 March 1967
5 caps 1991-93 (centre)

Lafarge, Y (Montferrand)
Born 16 January 1953
1 cap 1981 (centre)

Lafond, J-B (RCF, Bègles)
Born 29 December 1961
22 caps 1986-93
(wing, full-back)

Lagisquet, P (Bayonne)
Born 4 September 1962
15 caps 1984-91 (wing)

Laporte, G (Graulhet)
Born 15 December 1952
7 caps 1981-86 (stand-off)

Larrue, H (Carmaux)
Born 5 July 1935
2 caps 1960 (lock)

Lasaosa, P (Dax)
Born 13 July 1927;
died 3 July 1988
4 caps 1950-52 (scrum-half)

Lascubé, G (Agen)
Born 3 April 1962
6 caps 1991-92 (prop)

Lassegue, J-B (Toulouse)
Born 15 February 1924
7 caps 1947-49 (wing)

Lasserre, J-C (Dax)
Born 12 May 1938
6 caps 1964-67 (scrum-half)

Lasserre, M (Agen)
Born 21 January 1940
8 caps 1968-71 (prop, lock)

Laudouar, J
(Soustons, SBUC)
Born 3 January 1934
1 cap 1962 (hooker)

Lauga, P (Vichy)
Born 17 January 1922;
died 8 July 1984
4 caps 1950
(stand-off, centre)

Lavergne, P (Limoges)
Born 18 March 1922
1 cap 1950 (prop)

Lavigne, B (Agen)
Born 23 August 1954
1 cap 1985 (wing)

Lazies, H (Auch)
Born 1 November 1929
2 caps 1956-57 (No 8, prop)

Le Droff, J (Auch)
Born 22 June 1939
5 caps 1964-71 (lock)

Lepatey, J (Mazamet)
Born 25 September 1929
4 caps 1955 (wing)

Lescarboura, J-P (Dax)
Born 19 January 1961
14 caps 1982-88 (stand-off)

Lhermet, J-M (Montferrand)
Born 14 August 1967
2 caps 1990 (flanker)

Lira, M (La Voulte)
Born 30 April 1931;
died 25 January 1986
7 caps 1963-65
(flanker, lock, No 8)

Lorieux, A (Grenoble, Aix)
Born 26 March 1956
10 caps 1982-89 (lock)

Lubrano, A (Béziers)
Born 19 September 1946
1 cap 1973 (hooker)

Lux, J-P (Tyrosse, Dax)
Born 9 January 1946
27 caps 1967-75
(centre, wing)

Maleig, A (Oloron)
Born 10 July 1952
4 caps 1979-80 (lock, No 8)

Malquier, Y (Narbonne)
Born 7 May 1956
1 cap 1979 (No 8)

Mantoulan, C (Pau)
Born 5 March 1936;
died 9 September 1983
1 cap 1959 (stand-off)

Marchal, J-F (Lourdes)
Born 16 December 1949
4 caps 1979-80 (lock)

Marocco, P (Montferrand)
Born 14 June 1960
10 caps 1986-91
(prop, hooker)

Marot, A (Brive)
Born 11 March 1948
3 caps 1970 (centre)

Marquesuzaa, A (RCF)
Born 14 July 1934
5 caps 1959-60 (centre)

France's team which
D Erbani, J Condom, A Lo

Martin, J-L (Béziers)
Born 17 July 1948
2 caps 1972 (prop)

Martin, L (Pau)
Born 28 September 1920
5 caps 1948-50 (hooker)

Martine, R (Lourdes)
Born 3 January 1930
14 caps 1952-61
(centre, stand-off, full-back)

Martinez, G (Toulouse)
Born 30 March 1955
5 caps 1982-83 (scrum-half)

Mas, F (Béziers)
Born 8 November 1936
4 caps 1963 (prop)

Maso, J
(Perpignan, Narbonne)
Born 27 December 1944
10 caps 1967-73
(centre, stand-off)

Matheu-Cambas, J (Agen)
Born 23 June 1920;
died 26 May 1989
16 caps 1947-51 (flanker)

Mauduy, G (Périgueux)
Born 10 December 1937

…s in Paris in 1987: the fourth French side to take the Grand Slam. Back: J-P Garuet, P Ondarts, L Rodriguez, …mp. Front: P Bérot, P Sella, F Mesnel, P Berbizier, D Dubroca (captain), S Blanco, D Charvet, E Bonneval.

3 caps 1958-61 (wing)

Mauran, J (Castres)
Born 1 May 1929
4 caps 1952-53 (centre)

Melville, E (Toulon)
Born 27 June 1961
1 cap 1990 (flanker)

Menthiller, Y (Romans)
Born 7 December 1941
2 caps 1964-65 (hooker)

Mericq, S (Agen)
Born 16 June 1937
5 caps 1959-61 (wing)

Merquey, J (Toulon)
Born 26 September 1929
4 caps 1950 (centre)

Mesnel, F (RCF)
Born 30 June 1961
22 caps 1987-93
(stand-off, centre)

Mesny, P (RCF, Grenoble)
Born 19 August 1954
3 caps 1981-82 (centre)

Meyer, G-S (Périgueux)
Born 1 June 1934
2 caps 1960 (flanker)

Mias, L (Mazamet)
Born 28 September 1930
20 caps 1951-59 (lock)

Mir, J-H (Lourdes)
Born 21 February 1945
1 cap 1968 ((stand-off)

Moga, A-M-A (Bègles)
Born 1 May 1923;
died 5 April 1983
12 caps 1947-49 (lock)

Mommejat, B (Cahors, Albi)
Born 18 May 1934
15 caps 1958-63 (lock)

Moncla, F (RCF, Pau)
Born 1 April 1932
15 caps 1957-61 (flanker)

Monié, R (Perpignan)
Born 2 January 1934
1 cap 1957 (centre)

Montlaur, P (Agen)
Born 7 February 1963
1 cap 1992 (centre)

Moraitis, B (Toulon)
Born 2 January 1946
2 caps 1969 (wing)

Moscato, V (Bègles)
Born 28 July 1965
2 caps 1992 (hooker)

Mougeot, C (Bègles)
Born 22 November 1963
2 caps 1992 (lock)

Noble, J-C (La Voulte)
Born 29 December 1944
2 caps 1968 (prop)

Novès, G (Toulouse)
Born 5 February 1954
3 caps 1978-79 (wing)

Olive, D (Montferrand)
Born 12 July 1924
2 caps 1951-52 (wing)

Ondarts, P (Biarritz Ol)
Born 1 April 1956
18 caps 1987-91
(prop, hooker)

Orso, J-C (Nice, Toulon)
Born 6 January 1958
7 caps 1983-88 (lock, No 8)

Ougier, S (Toulouse)
Born 5 October 1967
1 cap 1993 (wing)

Paco, A (Béziers)
Born 1 May 1952
19 caps 1975-80 (hooker)

Palmié, M (Béziers)
Born 1 December 1951
12 caps 1976-78 (lock)

Paparemborde, R (Pau)
Born 5 July 1948
29 caps 1976-83 (prop)

Pardo, L (Bayonne)
Born 19 February 1958
9 caps 1981-85 (wing)

Paries, L (Biarritz Ol)
Born 4 August 1947
6 caps 1970-75 (stand-off)

Pascalin, P
(Mont-de-Marsan)
Born 21 September 1926
7 caps 1950-51 (hooker)

Pauthe, G (Graulhet)
Born 24 October 1932
1 cap 1956 (scrum-half)

Pebeyre, E-J (Fumel, Brive)
Born 27 January 1923
4 caps 1947 (wing)

Pebeyre, M
(Vichy, Montferrand)
Born 21 June 1948
3 caps 1970-73 (scrum-half)

Pecune, J (Tarbes)
Born 3 March 1951
6 caps 1974-76 (centre)

Pedeutour, P (Bègles)
Born 30 March 1955
1 cap 1980 (stand-off)

Penaud, A (Brive)
Born 19 July 1969
4 caps 1992 (stand-off)

Perrier, P (Bayonne)
Born 20 January 1957
4 caps 1982 (centre)

Phliponeau, J-F (Montferrand)
Born 23 November 1950; died 9 May 1976
2 caps 1973 (wing)

Pilon, J (Périgueux)
Born 14 October 1925
2 caps 1949-50 (stand-off)

Piqué, J (Pau)
Born 17 September 1935
8 caps 1962-65 (centre, wing)

Plantefol, A (RCF)
Born 26 December 1942
4 caps 1968-69 (lock)

Pomathios, M (Agen, Lyon U, Bourg)
Born 18 March 1924
21 caps 1948-54

Porthault, A (RCF)
Born 15 July 1929
6 caps 1951-53 (wing)

Portolan, C (Toulouse)
Born 16 December 1960
2 caps 1989 (prop)

Prat, J (Lourdes)
Born 1 August 1923
35 caps 1947-55 (flanker)

Prat, M (Lourdes)
Born 17 November 1928
22 caps 1951-58 (centre)

Prin-Clary, J (Cavaillon, Brive)
Born 15 July 1912
3 caps 1947 (prop)

Puget, M (Toulouse)
Born 28 September 1940
4 caps 1966-70 (scrum-half)

Pujolle, M (Nice)
Born 18 September 1962
2 caps 1990 (prop)

Quaglio, A (Mazamet)
Born 17 February 1932
8 caps 1958-59 (prop)

Quilis, A (Narbonne)
Born 28 October 1941
1 cap 1971 (flanker)

Rancoule, H (Lourdes, Toulon, Tarbes)
Born 6 February 1933
13 caps 1955-62 (wing)

Razat, P (Agen)
Born 15 October 1940
2 caps 1963 (full-back)

Rebujent, R (RCF)
Born 27 September 1942
1 cap 1963 (hooker)

Revailler, D (Graulhet)
Born 20 August 1948
7 caps 1981-82 (lock)

Rives, J-P (Toulouse, RCF)
Born 31 December 1952
39 caps 1975-84 (flanker)

Rodriguez, L (Mont-de-Marsan, Montferrand, Dax)
Born 25 June 1960
26 caps 1982-90
(No 8, lock, flanker)

Rogé, L (Béziers)
Born 19 October 1932
10 caps 1953-60
(wing, centre)

Rollet, J (Bayonne)
Born 18 August 1934
1 cap 1963 (hooker)

Romero, H (Montauban)
Born 21 September 1935
5 caps 1962-63 (No 8)

Romeu, J-P (Montferrand)
Born 15 April 1948
16 caps 1973-77 (stand-off)

Roques, A (Cahors)
Born 17 February 1925
19 caps 1958-63 (prop)

Roques, J-C (Brive)
Born 19 March 1943
2 caps 1966 (stand-off)

Rouan, J-C (Narbonne)
Born 30 October 1933
2 caps 1953 (full-back)

Roucaries, G (Perpignan)
Born 13 August 1932
1 cap 1956 (lock)

Rouffia, L (Narbonne)
Born 6 January 1924; died 8 March 1980
1 cap 1948 (full-back)

Roumat, O (Dax)
Born 16 June 1966
16 caps 1990-93 (lock)

Rupert, J-J (Tyrosse)
Born 7 March 1938
8 caps 1964-68 (flanker)

Sadourny, J-L (Colomiers)
Born 26 August 1966
3 caps 1992
(centre, full-back)

Saint-André, P (Montferrand)
Born 19 April 1967
11 caps 1991-93 (wing)

Saisset, O (Béziers)
Born 7 June 1949
8 caps 1972-75
(flanker, No 8)

Salas, P (Narbonne)
Born 3 March 1954
2 caps 1980 (prop)

Sallefranque, M (Dax)
Born 6 April 1960
3 caps 1982 (full-back)

Salut, J (TOEC)
Born 14 April 1943
4 caps 1967-69 (flanker)

Sanac, A (Perpignan)
Born 4 August 1929
7 caps 1953-57 (prop, lock)

Sangalli, F (Narbonne)
Born 8 September 1952
6 caps 1975-77 (centre)

Sanz, H (Narbonne)
Born 17 January 1963
2 caps 1990 (scrum-half)

Saux, J-P (Pau)
Born 13 November 1928
11 caps 1960-63 (lock)

Seigne, L (Merignac)
Born 12 August 1960
4 caps 1993 (prop)

Sella, P (Agen)
Born 14 February 1962
42 caps 1983-93
(wing, centre)

Senal, G (Béziers)
Born 21 April 1947
1 cap 1975 (lock)

Serrière, P (RCF)
Born 7 July 1960
1 cap 1988 (lock)

Sillières, J (Tarbes)
Born 15 November 1946
7 caps 1970-72 (wing)

Siman, M (Montferrand)
Born 12 July 1924
6 caps 1948-50 (wing)

Sitjar, M (Agen)
Born 13 September 1942
5 caps 1964-67 (flanker)

Skrela, J-C (Toulouse)
Born 1 October 1949
23 caps 1972-78 (flanker)

Soro, R (Lourdes, Romans)
Born 28 November 1922
12 caps 1947-49 (lock)

Sorondo, M (Montauban)
Born 16 July 1919; died 24 July 1976
5 caps 1947-48 (centre)

Spanghero, C (Narbonne)
Born 16 June 1948
12 caps 1971-75 (lock, No 8)

Spanghero, W (Narbonne)
Born 21 December 1943
24 caps 1965-73
(lock, No 8, flanker)

Stener, G (PUC)
Born 11 February 1931; died 12 December 1967
3 caps 1956 (centre)

Sutra, G (Narbonne)
Born 21 March 1936
3 caps 1969-70 (scrum-half)

Swierczinski, C (Bègles)
Born 28 July 1947
1 cap 1969 (hooker)

Tachdjian, M (RCF)
Born 6 June 1962
3 caps 1991 (lock)

Taffary, M (RCF)
Born 25 April 1950
4 caps 1975 (full-back)

Tarricq, P (Lourdes)
Born 18 May 1929
2 caps 1958 (wing)

Terreau, M-M (Bourg)
Born 30 January 1923
9 caps 1947-51
(stand-off, centre)

Tignol, P (Toulouse)
Born 26 May 1933
2 caps 1953 (lock, No 8)

Tordo, J-F (Nice)
Born 1 August 1964
8 caps 1992-93
(flanker, hooker)

Torreilles, S (Perpignan)
Born 31 December 1931
1 cap 1956 (wing)

Trillo, J (Bègles)
Born 27 October 1944
11 caps 1968-73 (centre)

Ugartemendia, J-L (St-Jean-de-Luz Ol)
Born 10 July 1943
2 caps 1975 (hooker)

van Heerden, A (Tarbes)
Born 6 October 1961
2 caps 1992 (No 8)

Vannier, M (RCF, Châlon)
Born 21 July 1931
26 caps 1953-61 (full-back)

Vaquerin, A (Béziers)
Born 21 February 1951; died 10 July 1993
14 caps 1972-80 (prop)

Varenne, F (RCF)
Born 26 July 1926
1 cap 1952 (lock)

Viard, G (Narbonne)
Born 19 May 1945
4 caps 1969-71 (flanker)

Viars, S (Brive)
Born 24 June 1971
3 caps 1992 (wing)

Vigier, R (Montferrand)
Born 5 December 1926; died 1 September 1986
14 caps 1956-59 (hooker)

Vignes, C (RCF)
Born 5 June 1934
2 caps 1958 (stand-off, centre)

Villepreux, P (Toulouse)
Born 5 July 1943
18 caps 1967-72 (full-back)

Viviès, B (Agen)
Born 3 September 1953
5 caps 1978-81 (stand-off)

Wolf, J-P (Béziers)
Born 7 November 1960
1 cap 1982 (prop)

Yachvili, M (Tulle, Brive)
Born 25 July 1946
5 caps 1968-71 (hooker, lock)

Zago, F (Montauban)
Born 27 February 1942
2 caps 1963 (prop)

APPENDIX

GRAND SLAM WINNERS 1947-93

England : 1957, 1980, 1991, 1992.
Scotland : 1984, 1990.
Ireland : 1948.
Wales : 1950, 1952, 1971, 1976, 1978.
France : 1968, 1977, 1981, 1987.

FIVE NATIONS WINNERS 1947-93

1947 Wales & England
1948 Ireland
1949 Ireland
1950 Wales
1951 Ireland
1952 Wales
1953 England
1954 England, Wales & France
1955 Wales & France
1956 Wales
1957 England
1958 England
1959 France
1960 France & England
1961 France
1962 France
1963 England
1964 Scotland & Wales
1965 Wales
1966 Wales
1967 France
1968 France
1969 Wales
1970 Wales & France
1971 Wales
1972 Championship not completed
1973 Quintuple tie
1974 Ireland
1975 Wales
1976 Wales
1977 France
1978 Wales
1979 Wales
1980 England
1981 France
1982 Ireland
1983 France & Ireland
1984 Scotland
1985 Ireland
1986 France & Scotland
1987 France
1988 Wales & France
1989 France
1990 Scotland
1991 England
1992 England
1993 France

Brian Moore - double Grand Slam winner, 1991 and 1992.

FIVE NATIONS RECORDS 1947-1993

ENGLAND v SCOTLAND

1947 Twickenham **England 24 Scotland 5**
1948 Murrayfield **Scotland 6 England 3**
1949 Twickenham **England 19 Scotland 3**
1950 Murrayfield **Scotland 13 England 11**
1951 Twickenham **England 5 Scotland 3**
1952 Murrayfield **England 19 Scotland 3**
1953 Twickenham **England 26 Scotland 8**
1954 Murrayfield **England 13 Scotland 3**
1955 Twickenham **England 9 Scotland 6**
1956 Murrayfield **England 11 Scotland 6**
1957 Twickenham **England 16 Scotland 3**
1958 Murrayfield **Scotland 3 England 3**
1959 Twickenham **England 3 Scotland 3**
1960 Murrayfield **England 21 Scotland 12**
1961 Twickenham **England 6 Scotland 0**
1962 Murrayfield **Scotland 3 England 3**
1963 Twickenham **England 10 Scotland 8**
1964 Murrayfield **Scotland 15 England 6**
1965 Twickenham **England 3 Scotland 3**
1966 Murrayfield **Scotland 6 England 3**
1967 Twickenham **England 27 Scotland 14**
1968 Murrayfield **England 8 Scotland 6**
1969 Twickenham **England 8 Scotland 3**
1970 Murrayfield **Scotland 14 England 5**
1971 Twickenham **Scotland 16 England 15**
1972 Murrayfield **Scotland 23 England 9**
1973 Twickenham **England 20 Scotland 13**
1974 Murrayfield **Scotland 16 England 14**
1975 Twickenham **England 7 Scotland 6**
1976 Murrayfield **Scotland 22 England 12**
1977 Twickenham **England 26 Scotland 6**
1978 Murrayfield **England 15 Scotland 0**
1979 Twickenham **England 7 Scotland 7**
1980 Murrayfield **England 30 Scotland 18**
1981 Twickenham **England 23 Scotland 17**
1982 Murrayfield **Scotland 9 England 9**
1983 Twickenham **Scotland 22 England 12**
1984 Murrayfield **Scotland 18 England 6**
1985 Twickenham **England 10 Scotland 7**
1986 Murrayfield **Scotland 33 England 6**
1987 Twickenham **England 21 Scotland 12**
1988 Murrayfield **England 9 Scotland 6**
1989 Twickenham **England 12 Scotland 12**
1990 Murrayfield **Scotland 13 England 7**
1991 Twickenham **England 21 Scotland 12**
1992 Murrayfield **England 25 Scotland 7**
1993 Twickenham **England 26 Scotland 12**

ENGLAND v IRELAND

1947 Dublin **Ireland 22 England 0**
1948 Twickenham **Ireland 11 England 10**
1949 Dublin **Ireland 14 England 5**
1950 Twickenham **England 3 Ireland 0**
1951 Dublin **Ireland 3 England 0**
1952 Twickenham **England 3 Ireland 0**
1953 Dublin **Ireland 9 England 9**
1954 Twickenham **England 14 Ireland 3**
1955 Dublin **Ireland 6 England 6**
1956 Twickenham **England 20 Ireland 0**
1957 Dublin **England 6 Ireland 0**
1958 Twickenham **England 6 Ireland 0**
1959 Dublin **England 3 Ireland 0**
1960 Twickenham **England 8 Ireland 5**
1961 Dublin **Ireland 11 England 8**
1962 Twickenham **England 16 Ireland 0**
1963 Dublin **Ireland 0 England 0**
1964 Twickenham **Ireland 18 England 5**
1965 Dublin **Ireland 5 England 0**
1966 Twickenham **England 6 Ireland 6**
1967 Twickenham **England 8 Ireland 3**
1968 Twickenham **England 9 Ireland 9**
1969 Dublin **Ireland 17 England 15**
1970 Twickenham **England 9 Ireland 3**
1971 Dublin **England 9 Ireland 6**
1972 Twickenham **Ireland 16 England 12**
1973 Dublin **Ireland 18 England 9**
1974 Twickenham **Ireland 26 England 21**
1975 Dublin **Ireland 12 England 9**
1976 Twickenham **Ireland 13 England 12**
1977 Dublin **England 4 Ireland 0**
1978 Twickenham **England 15 Ireland 9**
1979 Dublin **Ireland 12 England 7**
1980 Twickenham **England 24 Ireland 9**
1981 Dublin **England 10 Ireland 6**
1982 Twickenham **Ireland 16 England 15**
1983 Dublin **Ireland 25 England 15**
1984 Twickenham **England 12 Ireland 9**
1985 Dublin **Ireland 13 England 10**
1986 Twickenham **England 25 Ireland 20**
1987 Dublin **Ireland 17 England 0**
1988 Twickenham **England 35 Ireland 3**
1989 Dublin **England 16 Ireland 3**
1990 Twickenham **England 23 Ireland 0**
1991 Dublin **England 16 Ireland 7**
1992 Twickenham **England 38 Ireland 9**
1993 Dublin **Ireland 17 England 3**

ENGLAND v WALES

1947 Cardiff **England 9 Wales 6**
1948 Twickenham **England 3 Wales 3**
1949 Cardiff **Wales 9 England 3**
1950 Twickenham **Wales 11 England 5**
1951 Swansea **Wales 23 England 5**
1952 Twickenham **Wales 8 England 6**
1953 Cardiff **England 8 Wales 3**
1954 Twickenham **England 9 Wales 6**
1955 Cardiff **Wales 3 England 0**
1956 Twickenham **Wales 8 England 3**
1957 Cardiff **England 3 Wales 0**
1958 Twickenham **England 3 Wales 3**
1959 Cardiff **Wales 5 England 0**
1960 Twickenham **England 14 Wales 6**
1961 Cardiff **Wales 6 England 3**
1962 Twickenham **England 0 Wales 0**
1963 Cardiff **England 13 Wales 6**
1964 Twickenham **England 6 Wales 6**
1965 Cardiff **Wales 14 England 3**
1966 Twickenham **Wales 11 England 6**
1967 Cardiff **Wales 34 England 21**
1968 Twickenham **England 11 Wales 11**
1969 Cardiff **Wales 30 England 9**
1970 Twickenham **Wales 17 England 13**
1971 Cardiff **Wales 22 England 6**
1972 Twickenham **Wales 12 England 3**
1973 Cardiff **Wales 25 England 9**
1974 Twickenham **England 16 Wales 12**
1975 Cardiff **Wales 20 England 4**
1976 Twickenham **Wales 21 England 9**
1977 Cardiff **Wales 14 England 9**
1978 Twickenham **Wales 9 England 6**
1979 Cardiff **Wales 27 England 3**
1980 Twickenham **England 9 Wales 8**
1981 Cardiff **Wales 21 England 19**
1982 Twickenham **England 17 Wales 7**
1983 Cardiff **Wales 13 England 13**
1984 Twickenham **Wales 24 England 15**
1985 Cardiff **Wales 24 England 15**
1986 Twickenham **England 21 Wales 18**
1987 Cardiff **Wales 19 England 12**
1988 Twickenham **Wales 11 England 3**
1989 Cardiff **Wales 12 England 9**
1990 Twickenham **England 34 Wales 6**
1991 Cardiff **England 25 Wales 6**
1992 Twickenham **England 24 Wales 0**
1993 Cardiff **Wales 10 England 9**

ENGLAND v FRANCE

1947 Twickenham **England 6 France 3**
1948 Paris **France 15 England 0**
1949 Twickenham **England 8 France 3**
1950 Paris **France 6 England 3**
1951 Twickenham **France 11 England 3**
1952 Paris **England 6 France 3**
1953 Twickenham **England 11 France 0**
1954 Paris **France 11 England 3**
1955 Twickenham **France 16 England 9**
1956 Paris **France 14 England 9**
1957 Twickenham **England 9 France 5**
1958 Paris **England 14 France 0**
1959 Twickenham **England 3 France 3**
1960 Paris **France 3 England 3**
1961 Twickenham **England 5 France 5**
1962 Paris **France 13 England 0**
1963 Twickenham **England 6 France 5**
1964 Paris **England 6 France 3**
1965 Twickenham **England 9 France 6**
1966 Paris **France 13 England 0**
1967 Twickenham **France 16 England 12**
1968 Paris **France 14 England 9**
1969 Twickenham **England 22 France 8**
1970 Paris **France 35 England 13**
1971 Twickenham **England 14 France 14**
1972 Paris **France 37 England 12**
1973 Twickenham **England 14 France 6**
1974 Paris **France 12 England 12**
1975 Twickenham **France 27 England 20**
1976 Paris **France 30 England 9**
1977 Twickenham **France 4 England 3**
1978 Paris **France 15 England 6**
1979 Twickenham **England 7 France 6**
1980 Paris **England 17 France 13**
1981 Twickenham **France 16 England 12**
1982 Paris **England 27 France 15**
1983 Twickenham **France 19 England 15**
1984 Paris **France 32 England 18**

1985	Twickenham	**England 9 France 9**
1986	Paris	**France 29 England 10**
1987	Twickenham	**France 19 England 15**
1988	Paris	**France 10 England 9**
1989	Twickenham	**England 11 France 0**
1990	Paris	**England 26 France 7**
1991	Twickenham	**England 21 France 19**
1992	Paris	**England 31 France 13**
1993	Twickenham	**England 16 France 15**

SCOTLAND v IRELAND

1947	Murrayfield	**Ireland 3 Scotland 0**
1948	Dublin	**Ireland 6 Scotland 0**
1949	Murrayfield	**Ireland 13 Scotland 3**
1950	Dublin	**Ireland 21 Scotland 0**
1951	Murrayfield	**Ireland 6 Scotland 5**
1952	Dublin	**Ireland 12 Scotland 8**
1953	Murrayfield	**Ireland 26 Scotland 8**
1954	Belfast	**Ireland 6 Scotland 0**
1955	Murrayfield	**Scotland 12 Ireland 3**
1956	Dublin	**Ireland 14 Scotland 10**
1957	Murrayfield	**Ireland 5 Scotland 3**
1958	Dublin	**Ireland 12 Scotland 6**
1959	Murrayfield	**Ireland 8 Scotland 3**
1960	Dublin	**Scotland 6 Ireland 5**
1961	Murrayfield	**Scotland 16 Ireland 8**
1962	Dublin	**Scotland 20 Ireland 6**
1963	Murrayfield	**Scotland 3 Ireland 0**
1964	Dublin	**Scotland 6 Ireland 3**
1965	Murrayfield	**Ireland 16 Scotland 6**
1966	Dublin	**Scotland 11 Ireland 3**
1967	Murrayfield	**Ireland 5 Scotland 3**
1968	Dublin	**Ireland 14 Scotland 6**
1969	Murrayfield	**Ireland 16 Scotland 0**
1970	Dublin	**Ireland 16 Scotland 11**
1971	Murrayfield	**Ireland 17 Scotland 5**
1972	**No Match**	
1973	Murrayfield	**Scotland 19 Ireland 14**
1974	Dublin	**Ireland 9 Scotland 6**
1975	Murrayfield	**Scotland 20 Ireland 13**
1976	Dublin	**Scotland 15 Ireland 6**
1977	Murrayfield	**Scotland 21 Ireland 18**
1978	Dublin	**Ireland 12 Scotland 9**
1979	Murrayfield	**Scotland 11 Ireland 11**
1980	Dublin	**Ireland 22 Scotland 15**
1981	Murrayfield	**Scotland 10 Ireland 9**
1982	Dublin	**Ireland 21 Scotland 12**
1983	Murrayfield	**Ireland 15 Scotland 13**
1984	Dublin	**Scotland 32 Ireland 9**
1985	Murrayfield	**Ireland 18 Scotland 15**
1986	Dublin	**Scotland 10 Ireland 9**
1987	Murrayfield	**Scotland 16 Ireland 12**
1988	Dublin	**Ireland 22 Scotland 18**
1989	Murrayfield	**Scotland 37 Ireland 21**
1990	Dublin	**Scotland 13 Ireland 10**
1991	Murrayfield	**Scotland 28 Ireland 25**
1992	Dublin	**Scotland 18 Ireland 10**
1993	Murrayfield	**Scotland 15 Ireland 3**

SCOTLAND v WALES

1947	Murrayfield	**Wales 22 Scotland 8**
1948	Cardiff	**Wales 14 Scotland 0**
1949	Murrayfield	**Scotland 6 Wales 5**
1950	Swansea	**Wales 12 Scotland 0**
1951	Murrayfield	**Scotland 19 Wales 0**
1952	Cardiff	**Wales 11 Scotland 0**
1953	Murrayfield	**Wales 12 Scotland 0**
1954	Swansea	**Wales 15 Scotland 3**
1955	Murrayfield	**Scotland 14 Wales 8**
1956	Cardiff	**Wales 9 Scotland 3**
1957	Murrayfield	**Scotland 9 Wales 6**
1958	Cardiff	**Wales 8 Scotland 3**
1959	Murrayfield	**Scotland 6 Wales 5**
1960	Cardiff	**Wales 8 Scotland 0**
1961	Murrayfield	**Scotland 3 Wales 0**
1962	Cardiff	**Scotland 8 Wales 3**
1963	Murrayfield	**Wales 6 Scotland 0**
1964	Cardiff	**Wales 11 Scotland 3**
1965	Murrayfield	**Wales 14 Scotland 12**
1966	Cardiff	**Wales 8 Scotland 3**
1967	Murrayfield	**Scotland 11 Wales 5**
1968	Cardiff	**Wales 5 Scotland 0**
1969	Murrayfield	**Wales 17 Scotland 3**
1970	Cardiff	**Wales 18 Scotland 9**
1971	Murrayfield	**Wales 19 Scotland 18**
1972	Cardiff	**Wales 35 Scotland 12**
1973	Murrayfield	**Scotland 10 Wales 9**
1974	Cardiff	**Wales 6 Scotland 0**
1975	Murrayfield	**Scotland 12 Wales 10**
1976	Cardiff	**Wales 28 Scotland 6**
1977	Murrayfield	**Wales 18 Scotland 9**
1978	Cardiff	**Wales 22 Scotland 14**
1979	Murrayfield	**Wales 19 Scotland 13**
1980	Cardiff	**Wales 17 Scotland 6**
1981	Murrayfield	**Scotland 15 Wales 6**
1982	Cardiff	**Scotland 34 Wales 18**
1983	Murrayfield	**Wales 19 Scotland 15**
1984	Cardiff	**Scotland 15 Wales 9**
1985	Murrayfield	**Wales 25 Scotland 21**
1986	Cardiff	**Wales 22 Scotland 15**
1987	Murrayfield	**Scotland 21 Wales 15**
1988	Cardiff	**Wales 25 Scotland 20**
1989	Murrayfield	**Scotland 23 Wales 7**
1990	Cardiff	**Scotland 13 Wales 9**
1991	Murrayfield	**Scotland 32 Wales 12**
1992	Cardiff	**Wales 15 Scotland 12**
1993	Murrayfield	**Scotland 20 Wales 0**

SCOTLAND v FRANCE

1947	Paris	**France 8 Scotland 3**
1948	Murrayfield	**Scotland 9 France 8**
1949	Paris	**Scotland 8 France 0**
1950	Murrayfield	**Scotland 8 France 5**
1951	Paris	**France 14 Scotland 12**
1952	Murrayfield	**France 13 Scotland 11**
1953	Paris	**France 11 Scotland 5**
1954	Murrayfield	**France 3 Scotland 0**
1955	Paris	**France 15 Scotland 0**
1956	Murrayfield	**Scotland 12 France 0**
1957	Paris	**Scotland 6 France 0**
1958	Murrayfield	**Scotland 11 France 9**
1959	Paris	**France 9 Scotland 0**
1960	Murrayfield	**France 13 Scotland 11**
1961	Paris	**France 11 Scotland 0**
1962	Murrayfield	**France 11 Scotland 3**
1963	Paris	**Scotland 11 France 6**
1964	Murrayfield	**Scotland 10 France 0**
1965	Paris	**France 16 Scotland 8**
1966	Murrayfield	**Scotland 3 France 3**
1967	Paris	**Scotland 9 France 8**
1968	Murrayfield	**France 8 Scotland 6**
1969	Paris	**Scotland 6 France 3**
1970	Murrayfield	**France 11 Scotland 9**
1971	Paris	**France 13 Scotland 8**
1972	Murrayfield	**Scotland 20 France 9**
1973	Paris	**France 16 Scotland 13**
1974	Murrayfield	**Scotland 19 France 6**
1975	Paris	**France 10 Scotland 9**
1976	Murrayfield	**France 13 Scotland 6**
1977	Paris	**France 23 Scotland 3**
1978	Murrayfield	**France 19 Scotland 16**
1979	Paris	**France 21 Scotland 17**
1980	Murrayfield	**Scotland 22 France 14**
1981	Paris	**France 16 Scotland 9**
1982	Murrayfield	**Scotland 16 France 7**
1983	Paris	**France 19 Scotland 15**
1984	Murrayfield	**Scotland 21 France 12**
1985	Paris	**France 11 Scotland 3**
1986	Murrayfield	**Scotland 18 France 17**
1987	Paris	**France 28 Scotland 22**
1988	Murrayfield	**Scotland 23 France 12**
1989	Paris	**France 19 Scotland 3**
1990	Murrayfield	**Scotland 21 France 0**
1991	Paris	**France 15 Scotland 9**
1992	Murrayfield	**Scotland 10 France 6**
1993	Paris	**France 11 Scotland 3**

IRELAND v WALES

1947	Swansea	**Wales 6 Ireland 0**
1948	Belfast	**Ireland 6 Wales 3**
1949	Swansea	**Ireland 5 Wales 0**
1950	Belfast	**Wales 6 Ireland 3**
1951	Cardiff	**Wales 3 Ireland 3**
1952	Dublin	**Wales 14 Ireland 3**
1953	Swansea	**Wales 5 Ireland 3**
1954	Dublin	**Wales 12 Ireland 9**
1955	Cardiff	**Wales 21 Ireland 3**
1956	Dublin	**Ireland 11 Wales 3**
1957	Cardiff	**Wales 6 Ireland 5**
1958	Dublin	**Wales 9 Ireland 6**
1959	Cardiff	**Wales 8 Ireland 6**
1960	Dublin	**Wales 10 Ireland 9**
1961	Cardiff	**Wales 9 Ireland 0**
1962	Dublin	**Ireland 3 Wales 3**
1963	Cardiff	**Ireland 14 Wales 6**
1964	Dublin	**Wales 15 Ireland 6**
1965	Cardiff	**Wales 14 Ireland 8**
1966	Dublin	**Ireland 9 Wales 6**
1967	Cardiff	**Ireland 3 Wales 0**
1968	Dublin	**Ireland 9 Wales 6**
1969	Cardiff	**Wales 24 Ireland 11**
1970	Dublin	**Ireland 14 Wales 0**
1971	Cardiff	**Wales 23 Ireland 9**
1972	**No Match**	
1973	Cardiff	**Wales 16 Ireland 12**
1974	Dublin	**Ireland 9 Wales 9**
1975	Cardiff	**Wales 32 Ireland 4**
1976	Dublin	**Wales 34 Ireland 9**
1977	Cardiff	**Wales 25 Ireland 9**
1978	Dublin	**Wales 20 Ireland 16**
1979	Cardiff	**Wales 24 Ireland 21**
1980	Dublin	**Ireland 21 Wales 7**
1981	Cardiff	**Wales 9 Ireland 8**
1982	Dublin	**Ireland 20 Wales 12**
1983	Cardiff	**Wales 23 Ireland 9**
1984	Dublin	**Wales 18 Ireland 9**
1985	Cardiff	**Ireland 21 Wales 9**
1986	Dublin	**Wales 19 Ireland 12**
1987	Cardiff	**Ireland 15 Wales 11**
1988	Dublin	**Wales 12 Ireland 9**
1989	Cardiff	**Ireland 19 Wales 13**
1990	Dublin	**Ireland 14 Wales 8**
1991	Cardiff	**Wales 21 Ireland 21**
1992	Dublin	**Wales 16 Ireland 15**
1993	Cardiff	**Ireland 19 Wales 14**

IRELAND v FRANCE

1947 Dublin	**France 12 Ireland 8**
1948 Paris	**Ireland 13 France 6**
1949 Dublin	**France 16 Ireland 9**
1950 Paris	**France 3 Ireland 3**
1951 Dublin	**Ireland 9 France 8**
1952 Paris	**Ireland 11 France 8**
1953 Belfast	**Ireland 16 France 3**
1954 Paris	**France 8 Ireland 0**
1955 Dublin	**France 5 Ireland 3**
1956 Paris	**France 14 Ireland 8**
1957 Dublin	**Ireland 11 France 6**
1958 Paris	**France 11 Ireland 6**
1959 Dublin	**Ireland 9 France 5**
1960 Paris	**France 23 Ireland 6**
1961 Dublin	**France 15 Ireland 3**
1962 Paris	**France 11 Ireland 0**
1963 Dublin	**France 24 Ireland 5**
1964 Paris	**France 27 Ireland 6**
1965 Dublin	**Ireland 3 France 3**
1966 Paris	**France 11 Ireland 6**
1967 Dublin	**France 11 Ireland 6**
1968 Paris	**France 16 Ireland 6**
1969 Dublin	**Ireland 17 France 9**
1970 Paris	**France 8 Ireland 0**
1971 Dublin	**Ireland 9 France 9**
1972 Paris	**Ireland 14 France 9**
1973 Dublin	**Ireland 6 France 4**
1974 Paris	**France 9 Ireland 6**
1975 Dublin	**Ireland 25 France 6**
1976 Paris	**France 26 Ireland 3**
1977 Dublin	**France 15 Ireland 6**
1978 Paris	**France 10 Ireland 9**
1979 Dublin	**Ireland 9 France 9**
1980 Paris	**France 19 Ireland 18**
1981 Dublin	**France 19 Ireland 13**
1982 Paris	**France 22 Ireland 9**
1983 Dublin	**Ireland 22 France 16**
1984 Paris	**France 25 Ireland 12**
1985 Dublin	**Ireland 15 France 15**
1986 Paris	**France 29 Ireland 9**
1987 Dublin	**France 19 Ireland 13**
1988 Paris	**France 25 Ireland 6**
1989 Dublin	**France 26 Ireland 21**
1990 Paris	**France 31 Ireland 12**
1991 Dublin	**France 21 Ireland 13**
1992 Paris	**France 44 Ireland 12**
1993 Dublin	**France 21 Ireland 6**

WALES v FRANCE

1947 Paris	**Wales 3 France 0**
1948 Swansea	**France 11 Wales 3**
1949 Paris	**France 5 Wales 3**
1950 Cardiff	**Wales 21 France 0**
1951 Paris	**France 8 Wales 3**
1952 Swansea	**Wales 9 France 5**
1953 Paris	**Wales 6 France 3**
1954 Cardiff	**Wales 19 France 13**
1955 Paris	**Wales 16 France 11**
1956 Cardiff	**Wales 5 France 3**
1957 Paris	**Wales 19 France 13**
1958 Cardiff	**France 16 Wales 6**
1959 Paris	**France 11 Wales 3**
1960 Cardiff	**France 16 Wales 8**
1961 Paris	**France 8 Wales 6**
1962 Cardiff	**Wales 3 France 0**
1963 Paris	**France 5 Wales 3**
1964 Cardiff	**Wales 11 France 11**
1965 Paris	**France 22 Wales 13**
1966 Cardiff	**Wales 9 France 8**
1967 Paris	**France 20 Wales 14**
1968 Cardiff	**France 14 Wales 9**
1969 Paris	**France 8 Wales 8**
1970 Cardiff	**Wales 11 France 6**
1971 Paris	**Wales 9 France 5**
1972 Cardiff	**Wales 20 France 6**
1973 Paris	**France 12 Wales 3**
1974 Cardiff	**Wales 16 France 16**
1975 Paris	**Wales 25 France 10**
1976 Cardiff	**Wales 19 France 13**
1977 Paris	**France 16 Wales 9**
1978 Cardiff	**Wales 16 France 7**
1979 Paris	**France 14 Wales 13**
1980 Cardiff	**Wales 18 France 9**
1981 Paris	**France 19 Wales 15**
1982 Cardiff	**Wales 22 France 12**
1983 Paris	**France 16 Wales 9**
1984 Cardiff	**France 21 Wales 16**
1985 Paris	**France 14 Wales 3**
1986 Cardiff	**France 23 Wales 15**
1987 Paris	**France 16 Wales 9**
1988 Cardiff	**France 10 Wales 9**
1989 Paris	**France 31 Wales 12**
1990 Cardiff	**France 29 Wales 19**
1991 Paris	**France 36 Wales 3**
1992 Cardiff	**France 12 Wales 9**
1993 Paris	**France 26 Wales 10**